JUSTIFYING OUR
AN ESSAY IN AP!

MW01519206

In his magnum opus *Being and Time* (1927), Martin Heidegger (1889–1976) argued that individuals have assumed that their existence is 'a given,' when in fact they simply have the ability to be. *Justifying Our Existence* examines the ways in which human beings attempt to create meaning in their lives, often by magnifying and proving their existence through phenomena such as self-righteousness, carecrism, nationalism, and religion.

In this remarkably accessible and concise study, Graeme Nicholson analyses Heidegger's methods to indicate how his work has a practical application for existential concerns. Nicholson shows how phenomenology, as defined by Heidegger, can be used to explore fundamental questions of human existence, while shedding new light on important aspects of human behaviour and the motivation behind many of our social systems. Scholarly yet eminently readable, *Justifying Our Existence* is an original and thoroughly engaging work that touches on many realms of everyday human experience – both political and personal – while offering fresh insights on one of the twentieth century's most important philosophers.

GRAEME NICHOLSON is a professor emeritus in the Department of Philosophy at the University of Toronto.

New Studies in Phenomenology and Hermeneutics

Kenneth Maly, General Editor

New Studies in Phenomenology and Hermeneutics aims to open up new approaches to classical issues in phenomenology and hermeneutics. Thus its intentions are the following: to further the work of Edmund Husserl, Maurice Merleau-Ponty, and Martin Heidegger – as well as that of Paul Ricoeur, Hans-Georg Gadamer, and Emmanuel Lévinas; to enhance phenomenological thinking today by means of insightful interpretations of texts in phenomenology as they inform current issues in philosophical study; to inquire into the role of interpretation in phenomenological thinking; to take seriously Husserl's term *phenomenology* as 'a science which is intended to supply the basic instrument for a rigorously scientific philosophy and, in its consequent application, to make possible a methodical reform of all the sciences'; to take up Heidegger's claim that 'what is own to phenomenology, as a philosophical "direction," does not rest in being *real*. Higher than reality stands *possibility*. Understanding phenomenology consists solely in grasping it as possibility'; to practise *phenomenology* as 'underway,' as 'the *praxis* of the self-showing of the matter for thinking,' as 'entering into the movement of enactment-thinking.'

The commitment of this book series is also to provide English translations of significant works from other languages. In summary, **New Studies in Phenomenology and Hermeneutics** intends to provide a forum for a full and fresh thinking and rethinking of the way of phenomenology and interpretive phenomenology, that is, hermeneutics.

GRAEME NICHOLSON

Justifying Our Existence

An Essay in Applied Phenomenology

UNIVERSITY OF TORONTO PRESS
Toronto Buffalo London

© University of Toronto Press Incorporated 2009
Toronto Buffalo London
www.utppublishing.com
Printed in Canada

ISBN 978-0-8020-9929-7 (cloth)
ISBN 978-0-8020-9620-3 (paper)

Printed on acid-free paper

Library and Archives Canada Cataloguing in Publication

Nicholson, Graeme
Justifying our existence : an essay in applied phenomenology / Graeme
Nicholson.

(New studies in phenomenology and hermeneutics)
ISBN 978-0-8020-9929-7 (bound).   ISBN 978-0-8020-9620-3 (pbk.)

1. Ontology.   2. Phenomenology.   3. Heidegger, Martin, 1889–1976.
I. Title.   II. Series: New studies in phenomenology and hermeneutics
(Toronto, Ont.)

B3279.H49N533 2009   111   C2008-905673-6

University of Toronto Press acknowledges the financial assistance to its
publishing program of the Canada Council for the Arts and the Ontario
Arts Council.

University of Toronto Press acknowledges the financial support for its
publishing activities of the Government of Canada through the Book
Publishing Industry Development Program (BPIDP).

This book has been published with the help of a grant from the Canadian
Federation for the Humanities and Social Sciences, through the Aid
to Scholarly Publications Program, using funds provided by the Social
Sciences and Humanities Research Council of Canada.

Contents

Acknowledgments   vii

1 INTRODUCTION   3

    Life, Existence, Being   4
    Phenomenology   8
    How Our Being Concerns Us   12

2 THE ABILITY TO BE   19

    Existence   20
    Die Sorge: Care, Concern   24
    The Phenomenology of *Da-sein*: the Self   28
    The Phenomenology of Existence: Ecstasis   35
    Being as the Ability to Be   39
    The 'Letter on Humanism'   44
    Excursus: 'Exist' in the Philosophical Tradition   45
    Transition: Formalism and Application   47

3 MAGNIFYING THE SELF   50

    Phenomenology and Hermeneutics   53
    The Meaning of Success   54
    Failure   61
    Achievement   67
    Magnifying the Self and Magnifying its Being   73

4 JUSTIFYING THE SELF   75

    Morality   76

The Concept of Justification   78
Inauthenticity   80
The Phenomenology of Inauthenticity   84
Shame and Remorse   92
Conscience and Guilt   95
Ascetic Autonomy   104

5 MAGNIFYING THE COMMUNITY   111

Existence and Community   112
Magnifying the *Polis*   116
The Nation: Magnitude through Justification   118
Militant Religion   123

6 JUSTIFYING THE COMMUNITY   125

Caring for the *Polis*   126
Existence and History   130
Nation and Civilization   133

7 A SPIRITUAL EXISTENCE   141

What Is Spirit?   143
The Existing Spirit   150
The Phenomenology of Spirit: Intensity   154
The Problem of Grounding   156
God and the Self   159
Forgiveness and Justification   163
A Spiritual Community   166

8 CONCLUSION   169

Heidegger's Question Concerning the Meaning of Being   169
Summary of the Argument   170

Notes   173

Index   189

Acknowledgments

The text that is being published now owes a great deal to three commentators who reported on earlier versions to the University of Toronto Press. I am grateful to them and to Len Husband, who guided the manuscript through the different stages of publishing. Like the other authors in the New Studies in Phenomenology and Hermeneutics Series, I am indebted to Ken Maly for establishing the series and for accepting my manuscript.

Opposite the title page above, we see that the series has as one of its aims to further the work of Paul Ricoeur. It was Ricoeur who first introduced me to the thought of Heidegger and Kierkegaard when he came as a visiting professor from France to Union Theological Seminary in New York, where I was a student many years ago. And to our good fortune, some years later, Ricoeur spent several semesters here at the University of Toronto.

JUSTIFYING OUR EXISTENCE:
AN ESSAY IN APPLIED PHENOMENOLOGY

1 Introduction

Although we pursue many goals during our lifetime, life itself is not one of our goals. It is something that we care about, but not in the sense that we try to bring it about. It is because we already care about our lives that we make the plans and accomplish the goals that we do, and the plans and actions do not produce this care: they proceed from it. We need to recognize, then, that what we care about is not only that which we plan and accomplish. Another example: because we care about our health, we pay heed to our doctors and engage in exercise, but health itself is not something we decide upon or plan or choose. It is the prior care about health that leads us to act according to doctor's orders and take some exercise. This is one expression of our care about life. My point here is that, in the present day, our thinking tends to be so heavily oriented to practical choices and goals of action that, even in philosophy, we often overlook those deeper things that we care about but do not cause or produce. The point I am making is indebted to Heidegger's *Being and Time* (*SZ*), section 41,[1] where he is showing how deeply our being is marked by care, *die Sorge*, and stressing that the latter is not to be reduced to particular acts of willing or wishing, since it is their condition. Another example: though there are many changes that we would like to see in the world, we do not see the world itself. And yet, in all our activity and practice, the world is something that we care about: today, people are willing to reduce their consumption and try alternative technologies because they care about the environment, and that is one expression of a care about the world. There are other things I could mention that are matters of our care, that guide and direct our actions without being items of choice or goals of action themselves: our families and communities, for instance. It is because of this care that we try to help our children and cultivate our neighbours.

We can identify these items of our care because we have the words to name them, and the vocabulary also gives us the means to think about them: not only about the particular choices, actions, and goals that are motivated by our care, but also about these greater matters themselves – life, world, community – insofar as they themselves bear upon us. At this point, our thought might be diverted into traditional philosophical questions about language and knowledge. A philosopher could argue, I suppose, that we have no acquaintance with life in general, but only as abstracted from the empirical domain of these and those living things, and might argue something similar for the world and the community. This kind of diversion could be prompted by a nominalist linguistic theory, the sort of theory we find in Goodman, for instance, or an empiricist theory of knowledge, such as we might find in Ayer.[2] But if we were to explore this linguistic theory or this theory of knowledge, we would not learn from them how and why we care about life or the world, for they leave such matters aside; they are not devised to throw light on why we care about things. Their theoretical orientation to reference and knowledge circumvents the very thing that we are asking here: what life, world, and community mean to us, how they bear upon ourselves.

Life, Existence, Being

Even in its generality, and apart from all hypotheses about knowledge and language, the term 'life' has a wide diversity of meanings. Most commonly, it signifies something common to all living things, where tissues are organized in such a way as to permit movement, reproduction, nutrition, growth, the subjects of biology. This was signified by the ancient Greek word *zōē*. And this is a matter of intimate concern to all of us, for we do know about the *zōē* within us and its fragility – this undergirds our preoccupation with health.

We have a second word that is applied only to human beings who lead or have led a 'life.' This is a life-history, one that could be recorded in a biography. Even if someone's life is just remembered by his or her intimate friends, not written, it is still a life-history, and this is a different idea from the one we call *zōē*. It was this narrative sense that the ancient Greeks called a *bios*. It comes through in English not in the word 'biology' but in the word 'biography.' *Zōē* signifies what is common to all living things, but *bios* means what is significant in one person's life-history, though of course nobody could ever have a *bios* without possessing *zōē*. Since we all live with some internal remembered lifespan, and want to find some meaning in it, we are all concerned about our *bios* as well as our *zōē* – it doesn't just apply to other people.

We employ the term 'life' in a third sense that cannot be explicated on the basis of *bios* or *zōē*. Quite apart from any biography that might be written about us, distinct from our profile among our acquaintances, is that life which we have yet to live at any given moment, our remaining life. Here is a form of life that exceeds the usual categories of life: 'a remaining life,' an 'anticipated life.' You may decide to dedicate your life to a political or religious cause. Or you may undertake marriage with the intent of sharing your coming life with your spouse. The life that we have already led and are leading can be known to others in part, but this further part, our future life, is different. People can only guess or predict what our future life will be like. For you yourself, your future life is not mainly a matter for guesswork or prediction. It is you who must undertake it, undertake to live it. Our future life, i.e., what is still possible for us, is not merely something we imagine for ourselves, as if we were daydreaming. Instead, this remaining life is what we still have to carry out, and it is for us a matter of our care or concern. So too the death that belongs to our future is not just some possible event that we depict in our imagination – it is the death that we'll have to undergo. Death especially is a powerful component of the concern we all have, at each moment, with the leftover life we have yet to live. Doing what we can to avoid injury and death shows what care we take of ourselves. Our *existence* is that *future and as-yet-unlived life that concerns us even now*. It is this third sense that will loom largest in the present book, and we shall offer some reasons for giving it the name 'existence.' No doubt we too are living beings (*zōa*) and are so studied by biological and medical sciences, but our existence is not disclosed by those sciences. As existing beings, we are not merely 'alive.' And while everyone no doubt has a *bios*, even if not a famous one, we need to differentiate that from this further matter: existence. And although death has one kind of significance in relation to *zōē* (as a natural limit), and a different significance in relation to *bios* (as the completion of the whole), it has a completely different relation to existence: as a possibility for existence that awaits us.

The existential import of death is certainly a more dark and difficult theme than its biological and biographical sense, but that is owing to the general difficulty in the entire theme of existence. It creates the temptation among intellectuals to leave the matter to one side, given that there is so much positive knowledge to be accumulated in biology and history.

Heidegger's main idea in *SZ* was to undertake a description of life in the sense of existence, and this brought a reorientation of phenomenology. Modern philosophy had usually taken its start from the problem of knowledge, and especially investigated human experience, understood as the richest source of our stock of knowledge. Even Husserl's phenomenology retained this focus on experience, adding the proviso that every kind of experience, indeed every form of consciousness, was intentional, meaning to say that it outreached itself for an encounter with some object or other, real or otherwise. Heidegger reoriented phenomenology, not to dismiss questions of experience and knowledge, nor to deny the intentionality of consciousness, but rather to claim that all experience and all consciousness were expressions of existence, and derived their intentionality from the intentionality of existence itself, what he called 'transcendence.' For instance, Heidegger writes in the 1929 essay 'On the Essence of Ground'[3] that 'if one characterizes all comportment toward beings as intentional, then intentionality is possible only on the grounds of transcendence ' (*Pathmarks*, p. 106). And in context, he explains that by 'transcendence' he means a movement of surpassing that marks our existence as such: 'Transcendence, however, is that surpassing that makes possible such a thing as existence in general, thereby also making it possible to move "oneself" in space' (*Pathmarks*, p. 108). In fact, he had already clarified these points in lectures of a couple of years earlier. In the 1927 lectures *The Basic Problems of Phenomenology* (*BPP*),[4] Heidegger made the case that the intentionality of consciousness was an expression of our transcendence,[5] and later he added that this transcendence is the key element of our existence.[6] I shall devote chapter 2 to an exposition of Heidegger's account of our existence and our being, highlighting the movement that is at work in them, and highlighting as well the concern or care that human beings have about them. The study of existence in chapter 2 will show that it is more deeply bonded to care than to anything else – and especially to our care *about* our existence. And that is the reason why questions about empiricism and knowledge, and about the philosophy of language, have only a subordinate place in *SZ*.

One thing we can derive from the Continental philosophers of the twentieth century is to come to see life, or existence, as an adventure. An adventure begins with someone breaking free to venture far out into the unknown, often in a country far away. The adventure could be in pursuit of a prize, a prize one may have heard of only by repute and could imagine only vaguely. An adventure brings the risks of opposition and danger. Above all, what marks adventure is that something unexpected befalls you precisely because you have ventured out into unknown territory. The core of an adventure is what you had never planned on but must now assimilate and master – to confront and surmount this challenge you have to summon up all your powers. That is why an adventure changes you: you have had to strengthen yourself. One who returns home from an adventure may not bring home the prize (and perhaps it never existed), but the one who returns has changed, and it could even be said that this change of character was the real prize. All this makes adventure an illuminating model for understanding human life as a whole, and is well exhibited in the philosophy of *Being and Time*.

Consider the long first division that explains how we live essentially as 'being-in-the-world,' bringing an exposure to all kinds of things that we may or may not succeed in mastering. Though we are 'thrown' into this world, the very core of our existence is for us to project ourselves, i.e., project our being into possibilities. The looming presence of possibilities never goes away, so that we always experience our life as incomplete, and the possibilities are often dark and at least partially concealed, so that we are thrust into risks and dangers of many kinds, and unanticipated hopes as well. The risks derive not only from the surrounding things, known and unknown, but from ourselves, for the essential possibilities are those of our own being; Heidegger summarizes them as the possibilities to be ourselves or not to be ourselves, adding that in our existence we may lose ourselves or gain ourselves. What this is referring to is that in being stretched out towards our possibilities we are concerned above all to understand our own being. It is true that we already have a vague presentiment of our being, enough that it can be of concern to us – but any 'pre-understanding' of that sort is never more than the motivation for a quest for further understanding. Our being concerns us: what we can be, what we are capable of, and for how long. This concern is what puts us on the road. In the midst of the stretching-out, we are thrust together with our co-travellers, co-adventurers, for being-with-others is inscribed as a necessary element of our constitution. So, to conclude this brief sketch: our stretching-out into our possibilities is, for Heidegger, the core character of our being. Risk and wager pertain to our being, because the latter is conceived, not as a self-contained substance, but as the *ability* to be. In our case, ability is written right into the phenomenon, so that we experience our being always as something we are capable of. Chapter 2 will follow through in detail the sections of this book that I just surveyed in a bird's-eye view. But that exposition will also serve a wider purpose, introducing a more comprehensive study that points us beyond existence.

Chapter 2 will explain why existence has its special link with the human being or self, and offer an archaeology of the concept of existence to justify that link. But it will also show that there is more to *being* (*Sein*) than *existence*. We shall see this first of all within the singular self, whose existence proves to be only one component in its being, essentially modified by other components identified as facticity and ruination. In this way we learn that, while our being concerns us, this cannot be due entirely to our existence. And this limitation of existence proves to have a wider import. The existence of the self is in each case singular, it is 'in each case my own' (*SZ*, p. 44); existence itself is singularizing. And yet we discover that community also pertains to our being. Even the singular individual exists in such a way that 'being-with' others is inscribed in his or her constitution. We require some account of the human community that leads us beyond the existence of the individual. A further well-known point is that all the things that surround us in the environment have a mode of being (readiness-to-hand, and presence-at-hand, both comprehended under the category 'reality'; see *SZ*, sec. 43) that is different from our own existence – but I shall not be pursuing that point in the present book.

After the expository treatment in chapter 2 of our existence and our being, the remaining chapters will reflect the diverse levels at which being manifests itself. Chapters 3 and 4 will be devoted to studies of the singular self and its existence. But chapters 5 and 6 will proceed to studies of the community that reach beyond the singular self. This structure is intended to re-inforce the ontological truth that 'being is said in many ways'; here, for instance, being is disclosed first as existence and then as community. But I also hope that the treatment of the existing self in chapters 3 and 4 will have some resonance in the later treatments of community: common marks of being become manifest in both contexts. Chapters 3 and 4 will demonstrate how our being *concerns* us at the level of the singular individual, while chapters 5 and 6 will show how our collective being, our community, is likewise of *concern* to us.

Phenomenology

The kind of thinking that can encompass being or existence or life is phenomenology, which in Heidegger's view is the core discipline of philosophy.

In the course of the adventure that is our life, many and various things appear to us, including ourselves and a vast and immeasurable throng, all of which take on the status that Heideger calls 'phenomenon.' The human being has from the beginning been engaged in the disclosure of the things that are, has been a revealer all along, both throughout an individual life and in the long vista of history, and the things themselves had already been showing themselves all along, quite in advance of any explicit disclosures from philosophy. We have been engaged in letting the things show themselves. 'Disclosedness in general belongs essentially to the constitution of the being of *Da-sein*' (*SZ*, p. 221). Our power of disclosure is dependent upon several interlinked constituents, and we shall be treating them in chapter 2, for disclosure is a central operation of existence. We reveal ourselves and others, we bring to light, through perception and science, all the phenomena that the world contains.

We occupy the world in such a way as to disclose or reveal the things that are in the world, and not only 'things' but other living beings and ourselves as well, what Heidegger calls 'phenomena' in the ordinary sense of the term (*SZ*, p. 31). Since his study focuses on this very disclosure that is accomplished through existence, it is a phenomeno-logy. Disclosure itself is the theme of phenomenology. This point introduces several subtler shadings, to render which is the real point of phenomenology: we are to pay heed to the variations, levels, limits, biases, vistas of that which shows itself, and therefore varying types and levels of disclosure itself, variations that are the core issue of phenomenological philosophy. Some of these variations arise because it is the existing adventuring self who has taken on the role of experiencing and exposing them all. Some of the variations are due to the different character of the phenomena themselves. The theme of phenomenology is disclosure in all its forms, how being and beings come into appearance and also retreat from appearance; therefore its researches deal with everything that is imperfectly known: partly revealed and partly concealed. Phenomenology is not a science that investigates a particular segment of the world (what is physical, or living, or historical) with a view to new information; it is a thinking that attends to everything that both discloses itself and limits its own disclosure.

In an early section of *SZ*, section 7, devoted to expounding the phenomenological method, Heidegger offers his normative and basic concept of the phenomenon. The central element is that something or other, anything given that name, is *manifest, offenbar*. He understands *Phänomen* on the basis of the Greek word *phainomenon*, the participle of *phainesthai*, something that shows itself, is manifest and evident (p. 28). What shows itself is something that we can see or can discern in some way, which is to say that it is not hidden or concealed. This is not to say that we do see it, but that we can or could see it. The normative and basic concept of the *phainomenon* is that something or other, anything given that name, is manifest, *offenbar*, 'shows itself,' *sich zeigt*, is 'in its own right visible,' *an ihm selbst sichtbar*; it is 'the sum total of that which lies open to view,' *die Gesamtheit dessen, was am Tage liegt*, and 'can be brought to light,' *ans Licht gebracht werden kann* (p. 28). We note here the factor of possibility in most of these German expressions: the *Phänomen* is not what is seen, but what can be seen.

Phenomenological research discovers a range of *further* phenomena that account for this possibility of the 'self-showing' of the ordinary phenomena, and here we find many of the principal topics of *SZ*: being-in-the world, worldhood, significance, understanding and interpretation, discourse and language, truth, temporality. These further phenomena become manifest and intelligible only through philosophical research, but still they themselves *also* deserve the title 'phenomena' – they are 'the phenomena of phenomenology' (p. 35). The 'common' or ordinary phenomena in his sense of the term (p. 31) – tools and signification, being-with and society, death and conscience – are things that 'show themselves' to all who encounter them in everyday experience. In his treatment of them, Heidegger seeks to bring out into the light of day something that does not show itself so generally and promiscuously – our existence, our being, our concern. The study of the common phenomena is to demonstrate that they serve as vehicles for everyone's understanding of being, of existence, of care. That counts as a 'phenomenological' exploration, because it lets being, existence, and care show themselves, rather than remain in retreat, shrouded in the inarticulate, pre-philosophical understanding that guides our daily lives. Phenomenology as Heidegger defines it enables the philosophical study of that which hitherto was only pre-theoretically disclosed and understood: being, existence, care, and so on, matters to be made manifest *through* the ordinary phenomena of life that are already understood by us all (tools, vehicles, and the like). Being, existence, truth, and so on are called 'the phenomena of phenomenology' (p. 36) because they only come into their self-showing through a phenomenological treatment. But they *are* also phenomena, not abstractions; they too show themselves; phenomenology is the experience in which they appear.

It follows that while phenomenological philosophy accomplishes a manifesting, that cannot be the first manifesting – prior to that, we had already been engaged in revealing things. Yet that everyday disclosure has its limits, limits that prompt the initiative of philosophy. The philosophical practice of phenomenology does not concern itself primarily with living creatures, human beings, or material objects. Phenomenology aims to reveal or disclose that which mostly lies hidden in our experience: being, time, worldhood, etc., what Heidegger identifies as 'the phenomenological phenomena,' matters that only 'show themselves' to the gaze of phenomenology (pp. 31, 36):

> What is it that by its very essence becomes the *necessary* theme when we indicate something *explicitly*? ... [W]hat remains *concealed* in an exceptional sense, or what falls back and is *covered up* again, or shows itself only in a *distorted* way, is not this or that being but rather ... the *being* of beings. It can be covered up to such a degree that it is forgotten and the question about it and its meaning altogether omitted. (p. 35)

These phenomena are not abstractions; they are genuine forces operative in human life, even though initially and for the most part withdrawn from our understanding, self-concealing until phenomenology attempts to bring them too to 'show themselves,' an undertaking that only succeeds up to a point:

> something that does not show itself initially and for the most part, something that is concealed, in contrast to what initially and for the most part does show itself. But at the same time it is something that essentially belongs to what initially and for the most part shows itself, indeed in such a way that it constitutes its meaning and ground. (p. 35)

Phenomenology makes us acquainted with something that is 'there' but remains concealed to the mode of experience in which we live in the world. All this will take on more concrete form in chapter 2.

The self and its existence are *phainomena*, according to Heidegger (sec. 7, C). Withdrawal and concealment actually belong to the being of many phenomena, and here we can add that this is true of other people whom we seek to understand – for if we do not allow them their secrecy, we shall not understand them. And it is pre-eminently true that existence and being withdraw from appearance as well as entering into it, pre-eminently true of life or existence itself, for which there can be no final interpretation.

There are other kinds of philosophy, of course, that have not culti-vated phenomenology, with its awareness of the many forms of disclo-sure and the limitations of each, but it is to be hoped that this kind of thinking may come to penetrate them. That would encourage more ad-venture in our lives, and more attention to the ontological import of ad-venture within human life.

How Our Being Concerns Us

Many philosophical applications of Heidegger's philosophy have al-ready been attempted. His philosophy has been applied to ethics. Though it is well known (or notorious) that he did not develop an eth-ics himself,[7] several studies of Heidegger have developed his thought in this direction,[8] with considerable promise. An even more prominent movement has sought to show the application of Heidegger and phe-nomenology generally to epistemology and the philosophy of science.[9] Methodologically, this kind of work consists in taking a pre-existing tradition or discourse, such as the current state of epistemology or eth-ics, and then 'applying' thoughts of Heidegger there – the point is that new ideas are being introduced into an existing discourse.

There is another sense of 'application': a thinker or reader can apply a philosophy quite directly to his or her life, to try to lead the life that may be implicit in a philosophy such as phenomenology or critical the-ory or scholasticism. And when we seek to think along with a philoso-pher, we are always engaged in applying the thought – to our own world and thought. Whenever you begin to think about something in a rigorous and focused way, you need to consider all kinds of cases to which it might apply, and especially how it will find application in your own experience and practice. This is as true for those who are following an argument as it is for those who are developing an argument. Every philosophy needs to be applied to the phenomena. In 'applying' Heidegger's phenomenology here, I intend to offer a reading of his text that foregrounds one major idea, or rather one major phenomenon, and then proceed to a number of applications of this in distinct areas of human experience. The outline of the book is formed by that intention. Chapter 2 is expository, a reading of Heidegger that is centred on one crucial insight: the 'concern' or 'care' (*die Sorge*) over our being that we introduced above. The chapters that follow will be applying that insight, to economic life, national and international life, and our moral relationships. It is not some sort of compendium of practical philosophy that I intend here, nor do I aspire to treat 'the Good' or the 'human Good' or that to which all human beings aspire. The discussion is much more confined. It treats, not that which we want or aim for, or what gives meaning to our lives, but rather the manner in which we reflect upon our *own* being and appraise it. I intend to highlight the ways in which we give expression to our concern over our own being or our own existence.

Care is an expression of our existence, and as such it must be differentiated from choice, decision, or willing. These latter are aspects of our existence too, of course, and so are thinking and acting. But we shall need to bring out the difference. When we make a decision, we are making a selection from an array of alternative courses of action. We express our system of values by the ordering of our preferences. But the care we have for our being is never just one of these preferences. It is pervasive and constant; it embraces every field of preferences and accompanies every choice. In chapter 3, I'll contrast our theme of care in more detail with some of the well-known analyses philosophers have made of the topics of decision and preference. But as for care, one expression of it is the effort to *magnify* our being.

Magnifying

In the usual circumstances of our life, we may be highly aware of differences and feel ourselves at a disadvantage in comparison to certain other people – often this arises from differences in rank in an organization. Every professional success matters to us because it has the effect of magnifying us, magnifying that self of ours that is always of concern to us. Our self-magnifying is the claim to be significant, and success is one means for accomplishing that. Everybody has probably met the sort of person whose conversation consists largely of boasting – and while it can be about house or family, it is more often about success in business or in a profession. But the effect of difference in magnitude is not confined to the order of rank set out in a business organization. And this is not only a difference between individual persons. It seems as well that there are certain groups who count for more than other groups. Whether or not each of us is objectively correct in estimating that someone possesses greater magnitude than we do, we are inevitably led to seek to gain upon them – i.e., we seek to magnify ourselves, to gain some 'weight,' and often we rely on success.

Since we are discussing magnitude only with reference to our care for our existence, it is intended only subjectively. I am not interested in measuring human greatness in the various domains of achievement: Alexander the greatest general, Plato the greatest philosopher, and so on. Although 'magnify' means to make something great, I am not interested in any real state of greatness achieved, but only in a movement towards greatness, and only in the subjective sense of movement at that. Greatness enters into the argument only as a possibility that gives direction to our sense of movement. Seeking to make oneself seem to be great is all I mean. And it is clear that 'magnify' is a quantitative and comparative concept. It requires some scale or other on which you can become greater than you once were, or seem greater, or seem to be greater than somebody else according to the measure of that scale. You magnify yourself through attaining higher and higher office; your words are heeded more than they once were, more than the words of those you have surpassed; you are admired and flattered more than you used to be, more than other people you know.

One fruitful approach to understanding these phenomena is psychoanalysis. Much of the effort of our having-to-be is burdened with our weaknesses, detriments, and struggles with others that leave their mark on us: insecurity, vulnerability, an 'inferiority complex.' This concept was made famous by Alfred Adler, whose individual psychology offered a form of analysis and therapy that differed significantly from Freud's, with less emphasis on libido, more on our choices and plans. Everyone inherits a sense of inferiority from the traces of infantile weakness and vulnerability, the inferiority complex. In the narrow sense, this was made manifest in compulsive neurosis, striving for perfection, megalomania, and sadism. But in the broad sense, which is the point relevant to my present argument, Adler traced in normal people the psychic residues of the child's weakness, and his therapy helped them to confront these residues.[10] My point will be that many things fuse here. We seek to realize some stature in our lives, a matter of our concern. But this is also the territory of guilt. I feel puny, and then guilty for being puny. There is a collusion between being small and being wrong. This appears not only through psychology and psychoanalysis: similar results appear through a phenomenology of existence that does not make use of infant experience or the evidence of neurosis. Psychoanalysis has a therapeutic application, and so its focus is primarily on the self and its feelings; in Adler, for instance, the feeling of inferiority is to be channelled away from all its neurotic expressions. But phenomenology seeks only to understand, not to correct, and its primary focus is not on the self and its feelings but on the being or existence of the self, in which feelings are only one element. I shall try to show in chapter 2 how phenomenology is able to make existence itself a theme accessible to thought. Our hopes express the urgent question of the self in its singularity, a quest that may arise when existence has become unbearable to me. It arises just as surely where I am viewed with contempt by others, where I must assert myself before them. It arises in our self-examination. This quest also arises as the collective hope of justifying our community where it has received no respect, and our nation where it must make trouble for other nations. Phenomenology does not cure any of these afflictions, but, grasping them all as evident phenomena, undertakes to explore their conditions and their meaning. A therapy may well treat our feelings, and politics may well give direction to our protests. Phenomenology does not usurp their role. It claims to show how all these detriments appear to us in the light of our understanding of existence, our way of being, in the light of the self-magnifying and self-justifying that express our understanding of being. All the detriments make themselves known because the self has already projected itself as an existing being; feelings are a subordinate phenomenon, precipitated by the self-projection.

Because of the character of existence itself – the ability to be – there is more to self-magnifying than mere egocentricity. What is to become magnified is not merely the self, but the *being* or *existence* of the self. And in magnifying the community, it is likewise the *being* of the community that is intended, not merely the community itself.

Justification

Our existence is marked by another kind of burden. We may think of it as a sense of guilt, an anxiety over guilt, a sense that one is condemned, blamed, and in that way unworthy and unfit. To a greater or less extent this enters into our awareness, but even where the awareness is weak the burden weighs on us. The self that has cause to reproach itself morally, or that endures the reproaches of others, for wrongdoing or for a pattern of wrongdoing, is most intensely in need of justification – if it can be found. The domain of morality is the central one for an account of justification. Later we shall be discussing some odd and unwholesome applications of morality, whereby accusing others becomes a means of vindicating ourselves, and a justification of one of our deeds is intended to justify our person as a whole.

One might try to justify some particular deed, but also try to justify oneself as a whole. In fact, these fall into two quite different groups, and the difference is in part that reason is decisive in the first group but not in the second, as we shall see in chapter 4. Our interest in this book is confined to the second group.

While 'magnify' is a quantitative and comparative concept, this is not true of 'justify.' When we say that someone or something is justified, we mean that there has been a denial, and that the denial did not prevail. If you are justified in what you have said, that means that a rebuttal has been answered; if you are justified in what you did, that means that reproaches have been silenced. Unlike magnifying, therefore, justifying is a response to a negation.

This theme has not only a philosophical and a psychological dimension, but also a theological one, for some of the deepest explorations of it have derived from theologians' doctrines of sin and salvation. We shall bear in mind the theological concept of justification throughout the study, and mention it again in chapter 4, but it will come into focus only in chapter 7. Throughout the philosophical studies in chapters 3 to 6, I shall not pretend to show that one way of justifying the self or one's deeds or one's utterances or one's country is objectively effective and that others are not. The discussion remains resolutely subjective. My theme is the myriad of ways in which human beings undertake to justify themselves, and the logic of the discussion is to see what is implied by this or that way of justifying oneself. The intent of the study is to bring to the fore that stratum in human existence that is active whenever we seek to justify ourselves, whether through our supposed morality or through other means.

John Rawls, for example, studies self-respect (using the phrase 'self-esteem' interchangeably with it), postulating it as one of the primary social goods, along with liberty, opportunity, income, and wealth.[11] This obviously has a lot to do with what I've called self-magnifying and self-justifying. Rawls would accept the idea that I have been following here that our significance or magnitude is something we care about. Self-respect, according to Rawls, comprises two essential dimensions: (a) one's 'secure conviction that his conception of the good, his plan of life, is worth carrying out,' and (b) a 'confidence in one's ability, so far as it is in one's power, to fulfill one's intentions' (*Theory of Justice*, p. 440). As a stipulation in a theory of ethics, this is clear and to the point.

The questions I shall be pursuing, however, are ones that Rawls did not need to pursue for the purpose of a theory of justice. How do we form a 'plan of life'? What assures us that it is worth carrying out? On what does the 'security' of our conviction rest? Could our 'confidence' be misplaced? Why should anybody ever have self-esteem or self-respect? I do not pose these questions as an outsider, seeking to disturb the confidence of the moral agent. Rather, I hope to show that, in our existence, we never escape the doubts that such questions express. While it is appropriate for a theory of justice to emphasize the importance of self-respect or self-esteem, that theory does not explain the subjective conditions under which we can achieve it.

As was the case with magnifying, the impulse to justify arises with our very existence, and accordingly we shall be seeing that our being or our existence is also to become justified, and not merely the self and not merely the community.

The present argument seeks to give some articulation to the care we all have about our being: magnifying and justifying are to be understood as two of those articulated dimensions. They do not by any means exhaust the topic. There is one further dimension that will come to the fore in chapter 7, a concern for the *intensity* of our being, but for now we can postpone that topic to the later chapter.

Outline of the Book

Chapter 2 will elucidate what Heidegger says about existence and about being in *SZ*, taking special note of the place that care, *die Sorge*, holds in the constitution of our being. This phenomenological elucidation issues in the insight that *being* is one and the same as the *ability* to be. That lays the basis for the series of applications that appear in chapters 3 to 7. These studies too are phenomenological in that they sketch a series of adventures whose evident meaning is clear and familiar, but which prove to have a further and deeper meaning, indicating some aspects of our care that are generally hidden from us. Care itself appears as the impetus to self-magnifying and self-justifying – though these two are, of course, overlapping and connected concerns. Chapter 3, starting from a few sketches of our economic life, shows that our more obvious economic motives are intertwined with a concern to magnify our being. What is particularly subtle in this study is the relationship between the self and its being (or existence), for our concern for magnitude touches on both. The possibility that magnifying our being can serve also to justify our being emerges here as well. Chapter 4, starting from familiar territory in moral experience, shows how this experience, insofar as it is expressed in our existence, is entangled with the concern to justify ourselves. The lengthier phenomenology of moral existence shows how existence can appear as both justified and unjustified. The next two chapters follow a similar logic, though they are applied to our communal life. Chapter 5, 'Magnifying the Community,' uses familiar narratives from ancient and modern times to show that the countless efforts to magnify our communities have an ontological import. The self and the community are linked in their being – one indication of our unitary theme of our concern for our being. Chapter 6, 'Justifying the Community,' shows the communal dimension of the concern for justifying our existence.

The treatment of moral existence (and moral justification) in chapter 4 is left incomplete, in that there is a certain possibility developing out of moral existence that we do not follow up at that point. In chapter 7 we return to that possibility, describing it as a spiritual existence. This requires a phenomenological exposition of spirit, which will lead us to the contrast between a devout existence and an autonomous existence. Where there is a devout existence, we discover the possibility of a divine justification of the self and its being.

Throughout all these studies, there is a background question that has arisen out of some major controversies about Heidegger's philosophy. Do we all possess in some way an understanding of being or existence, what Heidegger called on occasion a 'pre-ontological understanding of being'? I hope to show, through these phenomenological investigations, that this question is to be answered in the affirmative.

2 The Ability to Be

Being and Time (*SZ*) is above all else an inquiry, the pursuit of a question.[1] The opening quotation from Plato and the eight-section Introduction lead the reader into the pursuit of the question: they awaken the spirit of inquiry, which is something more than the mere repetition of interrogative words. 'What do we mean by "being"?' This pursuit is a very long one, longer than *SZ* itself, and can only be begun by way of a lengthy preparation that is offered us by the text's first division, a fundamental analysis that is 'preparatory' to the posing and the treatment of the question concerning the meaning of being. In the Introduction, sections 1 and 2, we learn that it is only because we already have some understanding of being – vague and indeterminate – that we can engage in this lengthy inquiry, an understanding that is something more than the possession of certain words or concepts. The preparatory first division shows that while we tend to understand the being of external things as substance, extension, and objective presence, we have a less articulated understanding of our *own* being through caring about the crucial possibilities of our lives. And it is this treatment – not the broader scope of the whole question of being – that will concern us in the present chapter. The present exposition has selected just one theme, our concern about our existence, that is treated especially in sections 4 and 9.[2] We want to follow Heidegger's explanation of the strange word *Da-sein* that he uses for ourselves, and also of the core sense of his technical term *Existenz*.

SZ has generated many controversies,[3] but the one that is particularly relevant to the present exposition is the question whether the true theme of *SZ* really is human existence, an interpretation that is often called 'existentialist.' That seemed for many years to be the natural interpretation, promoted as it was by Sartre,[4] and accepted among both those who were favourable to Heidegger[5] and those who were not.[6] But when Heidegger published his 'Letter on "Humanism"'[7] in 1947, he reinterpreted the earlier text by marginalizing the human 'subject,' attacking existentialism especially in the Sartrean version, and insisting that his 'thinking' (not 'philosophy') had always been enroute to the unveiling of being itself through language. And many more publications followed with the same message.[8] The effect of this, especially in the French- and English-speaking worlds, was to divert attention away from *SZ* itself, which was now thought (in the extreme version) to be contaminated somehow by subjectivity and humanism.[9] Derrida also contributed to this overstatement (even if unwillingly) when he argued[10] that subjectivity and humanism had combined with metaphysics itself in overpowering Heidegger's thought in *SZ*. The very topic of *being* was now taken to be the relic of metaphysics!

It cannot be my purpose here to explore this history any further. Instead, I offer an exposition of key passages of *SZ*, to see how they treat the relation of existence and being, and how they are understood by the self, that is known here as *Da-sein*. None of the later history can impugn the stature of *SZ* as an inquiry, as a pathway of questioning. We shall look first at existence, understood as our mode of being, and then at care, *die Sorge*, which also constitutes our being, though in a different way. We shall look at the term *Da-sein* in connection with an account of phenomenology, to prepare us for the rigorous phenomenological elucidation that links existence to ecstasis. Thereupon, we see what emerges from this phenomenology: the disclosure of being as the *ability* to be. At the end of the exposition, we return to the 'Letter on "Humanism,"' and a few of the interpretative questions it raises.

Existence

In *SZ*, section 4, Heidegger is saying that our being is not merely something of which we take note and cognizance, not just something studied in human science or ontology. It concerns us. It matters to us. We read of *Da-sein* (and that means us): 'It is ontically distinguished by the fact that, in its being, it is concerned *about* its very being' (p. 12).[11] Heidegger does not say here what kind of concern this might be, but his point will be grounded in the entire theme of care, *die Sorge*, treated in *SZ*, section 41. In all the following chapters, I'll show in more detail the ways in which our concern for our being is expressed: taking ideas that are expressed formally in *SZ* – i.e., being, care, concern (*die Sorge*) – and making a deformalizing of them; taking what is stated abstractly and seeking to make it concrete and expressed in detail.

This theme of being will bring Heidegger to a discussion of our being in the world, and to a discussion of community: our 'being-with.' The topic of being leads very naturally into both. As for our care about the world, I shall say that the German term *Sein* carries the very implication so central to Heidegger: that our being is *in-der-Welt-sein*, being in the world. And the principle of community is likewise implicit in the idea of being – *Sein* also implicates *Mit-sein*, being with others. By our discussion of these further reaches, we shall recognize more concretely what it is to have a concern about our very being.

Why is it then that our being concerns us? We might consider some psychological explanations, or a word from moral philosophy or sociology, but in fact the explanation is derived from Heidegger's phenomenology. It is on account of our being, i.e., our way of being, that our being is of concern to us. We can cite here the point made early in *SZ* that I quoted in part above: human beings do not merely occur in the midst of all the other surrounding beings. Rather, we are differentiated by the fact that, by virtue of our way of being, our own being is of concern to us. *SZ* studies the human way of being, showing that we do not merely 'occur' in the present moment but are extended into the future and the past. What concerns us is not merely that which is here and now, but even more that which is to come, what is moving in upon us from the future. Because of our way of being, we have concern for the future, and project our being into the future. And it is on the basis of such concern that we have an understanding of what is to come. We understand that much of what is to come is our own responsibility, for instance: we have already projected our being into the future and must now assume responsibility. And this always leads us to re-examine our past as well, recalling the circumstances that prompted our current concerns. What is apprehended in the present proves to be the convergence of the future and the past. And because of the perpetual agitation of our being, we are impelled to seek to justify our lives, our being.

Heidegger continues his text by identifying what the sense of 'being' is that we are concerned with and relate ourselves to: 'We shall call the very being to which *Da-sein* [the self] can relate in one way or another, and somehow always does relate, existence' (p. 12).[12] And his definitive statement on existence follows in this prominent sentence: '*Da-sein* [the self] always understands itself in terms of its existence, in terms of its possibility to be itself or not to be itself' (p. 12).[13] So what is it that concerns the self, by virtue of its very being? It is its ability to be itself, which also contains within it a further negative ability, not to be itself. And he has emphasized that we understand both these possibilities: being ourselves and not being ourselves.

We are always out in advance of our current state, anticipating what is foreseen and even what is unforeseen, constantly exiting from the present state of things to be concerned with this possibility or that. But most central is this alternative of existence. Thus it is possible for us not to remain true to our promises, and moreover we are always aware of that possibility. By virtue of the very formula of our being, our opening to the future is slippery and sliding. There is in human being no firm nature binding us in our behaviour, but at best an undertaking or promise to which we have the possibility of being faithful. That is one meaning of the claim that even 'being itself' is only one possibility for the self, never an ontological given. This can never be the firmness or truth of a natural substance, for the self cannot forget or become free of the present alternative that is open to it through existence. Any ability to be itself must always have reckoned with the double possibility of existence that is given in advance.

Though an everyday decision may confront alternatives (to work or to rest?), the alternative lying in existence itself is *formal* – not one choice among others, but an open alternative present in every concrete choice. And it is ontological, not merely practical, for it is the choice to be this way or that way, and, deepest of all, our being is not given prior to the choice nor is our self or identity given prior to it, for the choice is between being oneself or not being oneself. Being is a possibility. Selfhood is a possibility. They never lose that status.

Why does this form of being, peculiar to ourselves, deserve the name 'existence'? I shall say more about the history of this term in an excursus at the end of the present chapter, but provisionally we can trace this use of the term back to Kierkegaard. What Kierkegaard called 'existence' is the orientation we have to our remaining life, an orientation to that which at any given time is possible. The salient feature is that existence is an openness to the future that is never closed up, never finished, a perpetual becoming. Let me document this with a couple of quotations, and then see where they lead.

One who is existing is continually in the process of becoming; the actually existing subjective thinker, thinking, continually reproduces this in his existence and invests all his thinking in becoming ... To be continually in the process of becoming in this way is the elusiveness of the infinite in existence.[14]

See also p. 121:

> The question is what existing beings have to be satisfied with insofar as they are existing – then the continued striving will be unique in not involving illusion ... The continued striving is the expression of the existing subject's ethical life-view ... the continued striving is the consciousness of being an existing individual.

What I pick out from both quotations is the self-surpassing into a future, a striving forth into an undefined openness, as the movement and agitation expressed by the term 'exist.' Heidegger will give expression to the same point, but with a clarity of expression that I think improves on the diffuse style of Johannes Climacus.

We need to recognize that it is only the human being who is under discussion in Climacus's account of existence. He is not referring to animals whose life cycle will continue into the future, nor does the 'existence' of atoms and quasars concern him. Because it is only ourselves who are under discussion, Climacus invariably qualifies existence as subjective. I am thinking of remarks like these:

> The subjective thinker is an existing person, and yet he is a thinking person. He does not abstract from existence and from the contradiction, but he is in them, and yet he is supposed to think. In all his thinking, then, he has to include the thought that he himself is an existing person. (p. 351)

So frequently does the *Postscript* link existence to being an individual and being subjective that it could seem that they give the very definition of existence, so there is the danger in reading the *Postscript* of confusing the issue of existence with the issue of singularity or subjectivity. But if we regard the very first quotations above as capturing the heart of the matter, it follows that individuality and subjectivity are only the consequence of the fundamental conception of existence. Thus, in summary: existence is the moving entry into an open future, though, as it happens, Kierkegaard (or Climacus) insisted that only the subject, only the individual, was capable of making this movement, and that the movement was inaccessible to systematic thought (see p. 118).

It is clear that Kierkegaard's treatment of existence exercised influence on Heidegger.[15] This shows up not only over the theme of existence itself (see *SZ*, footnote p. 235), but also on closely related matters such as anxiety (footnote p. 190) and the moment (footnote p. 338). In these and other cases Heidegger shows some anxiety of his own in acknowledging the influence of Kierkegaard, and later, in the 1930s, he came to distance himself from 'existence-philosophy' and Kierkegaard.[16] Though the Kierkegaard-influence diminished in Heidegger's work, it had nonetheless gone into the making of *SZ*, and in his earlier lectures[17] he was ready to acknowledge it frankly. Near the opening of the 1923 lectures (pp. 16, 19), Heidegger indicates that his topic is *Existenz*, and the concluding section (pp. 101–104) reinterprets that as *Sorge*. Indeed, this is already the first draft of *SZ*. We shall certainly respect Heidegger's later scruples about Kierkegaard and existentialism, but we cannot ignore this context for *SZ* itself. Careful readers have always seen the hand of Kierkegaard in Heidegger's account of the 'existentials,' the major structures of our existence such as guilt and repetition, readers like Gadamer, who commented on the idea of existence.[18] The central role of possibility in existence is a point for which Heidegger was indebted to Kierkegaard by the time he completed *SZ*. In Heidegger, that implies that we are always out in advance of our current state, anticipating what is foreseen and even what is unforeseen, constantly exiting from the present state of things to be concerned with this possibility or that. In section 31, Heidegger will describe this forward thrust as our self-projection, *Sichentwerfen*, that maps out possibilities for ourselves, for those others with whom we interact, and for all the things that preoccupy us. This can be comprehended as a concern for our ability to be, *Seinkönnen*. Our coming life, that we partly understand, is something that is possible for us: in view of it, we have an ability to be, to go on living, to exist.

Die Sorge: Care, Concern

The self has a care about its being, and that care is first and foremost for existence as its possible ability to be. But this concern about our own existence is generated by the perpetual agitation of our being that makes our entire life volatile.

We can extract two points from our opening quotations from p. 12 that will guide us deeper into the constitution of the human way of being; they involve the complex relationship between existence and care.

> (1) We are concerned about our being (*uns geht es um das Sein*), that is, about our existence.

Heidegger construes this more closely: the concern is about our ability to be ourselves or not to be ourselves, as we mentioned above. The second point was also communicated in the same paragraph:

> (2) Not only does our being concern us – it is also by virtue of our being, that is, our way of being (*in seinem Sein*), that we have this concern.

In order to clarify how these are connected, we need to see a qualification that Heidegger has recognized. Heidegger is beginning to introduce us, through his double point, to the complex convolution that is proper to being. First, our being concerns us, and that is especially our existence. Secondly, it is on account of our being that we are imbued with this concern. But we need to ask whether this 'being' that is mentioned in the second proposition also means 'existence.' I shall try to show that it refers rather to the fusion of existence with facticity that he calls 'care,' *die Sorge*.

Existence is one component in our being or our life, and essentially modified by facticity, as Heidegger calls it. In practice, while we all move into the future with concern, we are still imbued with a culture, a history, our personal past, a nation, a family, a language, and a situation, what Heidegger calls *Faktizität*. Choices that we make are never without encumbrance and guidance. But this qualification must never obscure the primacy of existence in the constitution of our being. Even as the self projects possibilities for itself and for the things in the world, it has already found itself in one locale, adopting some posture, already exposed to the effects of an environment and registering them. Sections 39 and 41 introduce facticity as the aspect of our being that becomes revealed through our attunement to our environment. Thus Heidegger can say: '*Da-sein* exists factically. We are asking about the ontological unity of existentiality and facticity, namely whether facticity belongs essentially to existentiality' (p. 181). It should be clear that two powers of disclosure, understanding and attunement, are coincident with these two expressions of our being, existence and facticity. 'An understanding of being belongs to the ontological structure of *Da-sein*. In existing, it is disclosed to itself in its being. Attunement and understanding constitute the kind of being of this disclosedness. Is there an understanding attunement in *Da-sein* in which it is disclosed to itself in a distinctive way?' (p. 182).

Existence is inwardly penetrated by facticity. It is in the structure of care that these two 'existentials' enter into their relation. If we refer again to the two propositions we introduced above, based on the page 12 quotation, we see that, while it is its own existence that concerns the self, this concern itself is motivated not only by existence but by care, which incorporates facticity as well. While our being concerns us, and while it is on account of our being that our being concerns us, the first mention of 'being' here means existence, while the second one means care, the composite of existence and facticity. (Indeed, the structure of care incorporates a third factor that Heidegger calls 'falling,' *Verfallen*, by which the self is led away from its self-understanding to become preoccupied with whatever things and temptations the surrounding world offers to view. We won't be paying much heed to this factor in the present chapter, but it will recur in chapter 4, where we'll retitle it 'ruin-ation,' after Heidegger's earlier term *Ruinanz*. Here we merely note that, through this third factor, the full structure of care is filled in: being-ahead-of-oneself-already-in-the-world-as-being-with-innerworldly-beings-encountered.)

Quoting from the same paragraph we have cited from p. 12: 'It is constitutive of the being of *Da-sein* to have, in its very being, a relation of being to this being.'[19] *And that relation is care.*

Being in the sense of existence is not available as a body of information that we could share with others. And mere guesses and predictions about your future never encompass your existence. Still, if your existence concerns you, it must be accessible to you in some way and not merely have the status of the Great Unknown. How, then, is it 'there' for you? What relationship do you have to existence? What understanding do you have of it? According to Heidegger, the care or the concern that we have about our existence is the very grounding for the understanding that we have of it. Quoting further from the same paragraph we have cited from p. 12: '[As we quoted already: It is constitutive of the being of *Da-sein* to have, in its very being, a relation of being to this being.] And this in turn means that *Da-sein* understands itself in its being in some way and with some explicitness.'[20] Our concerns determine our relationship to being, and therefore our understanding of it.

They constitute the yoke that binds us to our possible being. What understanding discloses to us is our existence, our being as the ability to be. '*Da-sein* is in such a way as to understand (or in certain cases not understand) how to be, whether in this way or in that. This understanding lets it "know" what is at issue for it, that is, what it is able to be' (p. 144).[21] 'What is contained in understanding existentially is that mode of being that is our ability to be' (p. 143).[22] The difficult idea of *Verstehen* in Heidegger links it intimately to existence and self-surpassing, and it is not pre-eminently a cognitive power.

We care about our being in the same thrust whereby we care about the world, and life and community, and we care about it not merely on account of all the things and phenomena that have being. But there is a difference that pertains to being in particular. Our being is disclosed to us in and through the care that we have concerning it, but that is not because it is something at hand or available for us to think about or worry about. What concerns us is our own *ability* to be, *Seinkönnen*. Heidegger shows in section 31 that in our existence we are not just capable of particular deeds and acts: we are capable of being in the sense of existing. Here indeed appears our very manner of being: the ability to be. We are not just some object that has as an attribute some capability or another: our very being lies in that possibility, which is our ability to be (p. 143).[23] And that is how we care about our being: our care is directed to that ability, by taking on the form of projection (*Entwerfen*). We *have* to be, and so we *can* be (in either of the two ways, being ourselves or not). The reader may wonder about an 'ability to be' that is not reducible to a series of further pragmatic abilities: to walk, to swim, and so on. The point that comes much later in Heidegger's text offers one route to understanding this: our relation to death. Death is that possibility that awaits us all: of no longer being able to be (we take up this point later). Heidegger, however, does not begin from that point, believing that his leading idea, the ability to be, is intelligible in its own right, not needing this contrast, for it constitutes what we care about most of all.

The duality that we noted in Heidegger's expression 'being' is not an equivocation but a complex formal structure. We are concerned about our being *qua* existence, but this concern is due to our being *qua* care. To avoid terminological confusion, we can note how Heidegger introduced both these factors in relation to *Da-sein* (i.e., in relation to the self). He says on p. 42, and often repeats it, that 'the "essence" of *Da-sein* lies in its existence.' Then he later says (title of Division 1, chapter 6, and often repeated) that the being of *Da-sein* is care. Formally then, the relation of existence to care is that of the 'essence of –' to the 'being of –'. Here 'essence' means what concerns us, what matters to us, what we understand, whereas the 'being of –' is what constitutes us so that we are able to have that understanding and that concern. Though we care about our existence, we do not care about care. This idea of 'essence' is all-important for philosophy, for it turns our attention, rightly, away from the social or animal or physical constitution of the human being, and directs it instead to that which concerns us, what drives us, or obsesses us: without attending to that essence, the philosopher will not understand the human being.

Our own being, i.e., existence, is for us all a special subject of our care or concern: we do not live merely in the Here and Now, and can be comprehended as a concern for our ability to be (*Seinkönnen*). The point that our being is *Seinkönnen* is repeated often in section 31, and in many, many later contexts (e.g., section 40, p. 184). This ability to be is reinterpreted in section 41, where Heidegger shows that, by virtue of our being, we are always ahead of ourselves, *sich vorweg* or *sich voraus*. It is because our being is the ability to be that care defines our being. All this means too that the self can only have a finite ability to be, always conditioned by its facticity. The ability to be brings continual agitation into the self, because of the double location of the ability to be, first of all as our projected existence, second because of our care that always includes existence. There is an unfixity proper to any self whose being is the ability to be – its being is by no means an inlaid program that the individual or the species follows. Human beings reinvent themselves throughout history and throughout a single lifetime. We should not think that the drive of self-surpassing is an instinct, for that would appropriate it wrongly to *zōē*. In fact, it pertains to our care about existence. Human life has always been more truly seen as an adventure or a pilgrimage than as a mere phenomenon of the species. It is care that keeps us going. What connects the self to its future, the yoke that connects us to possible being, is care.

The Phenomenology of *Da-sein*: The Self

Though we are confining this study to the theme of existence and care, we cannot overlook the general program of phenomenology in which they find their place. As we know, Heidegger is aiming to discuss the theme of being quite generally, and argues that such an ontology is possible only as phenomenology (*SZ*, p. 35). We recall from chapter 1 above that while a phenomenon in the ordinary sense is anything that shows itself to our everyday experience, the 'phenomena of phenomenology,' such as being, truth, and existence, only become self-showing phenomena in the course of phenomenological research. This is tied up with the circumstance that, for the most part, being is not truly manifest to us: it is either quite hidden or it is distorted and disguised in our ordinary experience (pp. 35–6). Heidegger initiates his inquiry into being with a study of the mode of being that is specific to us, *Existenz*, and the project was to proceed from an 'analytic of existence' to a broader ontological study, exploring 'the meaning of being' quite universally – all this in the mode of phenomenology. For the sake of brevity, we can be guided by comments on phenomenology from the commentator Friedrich-Wilhelm von Herrmann.

(*A*) The very possibility of phenomenology, Heidegger style, is tied up with his conception of ourselves, human beings, as *Da-sein*. As von Herrmann explains the term, it conceptualizes the human self, the one who exists, as the very revealer or discloser:

> The term '*Da-sein*' has a double meaning. First, it is the ontological title for that being whose ontological constitution is existence. But the second and decisive meaning emerges when we ask why it is that the being that exists is called '*Da-sein*.' Answer: because this being, by virtue of its being *qua* existence ('*–sein*'), holds open the fundamental domain of disclosedness ('*Da–*') as a whole. This totality of disclosure is certainly more than the disclosure of existence. Accompanying the ecstatic disclosure of self that arises in existence, this *Da-sein* is open for the disclosure of the being – i. e., the kinds of being – of every being, not just that which exists, and thus is open for the disclosure of what-is as a whole.[24]

Da-sein means, then, 'discloser, revealer.' Because of the universal function of disclosure, the theme of *Da-sein* is tightly interwoven with all the phenomena of truth, concealment, and unconcealment, and therefore with the whole program of phenomenology in Heidegger.[25] Not only is the term embedded in Heidegger's whole program – more than that, it has never had a satisfactory translation into English. That is why, later on, I shall propose a substitute term in place of it.

The universality of *Da-sein*'s disclosive role is manifest in many places in *SZ*. 'Truth in the most primordial sense is the disclosedness of *Da-sein*, to which belongs the discoveredness of innerworldly beings' (p. 223):

> Being true as discovering is a manner of being of *Da-sein* ... Discovering is a way of being of being-in-the-world. Taking care of things, whether in circumspection or in looking in a leisurely way, discovers innerworldly beings. The latter become what is discovered. They are 'true' in a secondary sense. Primarily 'true,' that is, discovering, is *Da-sein*. (p. 220)

In our quotidian experience we all engage perpetually in disclosure, bringing to light, through perception and science, all the phenomena that the world contains. We do it initially through our daily practice or dealings (*Umgang*) with things, notably through our practical glance (*umsichtiges Besorgen*). So it is that we differentiate the flowers that we want to grow from the weeds that threaten them, as we probe the soil with a spade. This is one kind of disclosure, and it has a share in unconcealment and truth. This kind of practical disclosure is characteristic of our being in the world: the things we disclose belong in a whole environment, the garden, which for its part belongs in a whole interconnected world: this is where and how flowers and weeds show themselves. Heidegger has little difficulty in showing, in sections 12 and 13, that our *knowledge* of the world and its denizens is not the basis for our *being* in the world, but that it is the other way around. And this is in accord with a fundamental point: that all the disclosures accomplished in quotidian experience are to be traced, *ultimately*, not to our conscious intentions but to our being or existence.

But, of course, Heidegger treats other modes of disclosure besides the practical glance. The theme of phenomenology, after all, is disclosure itself, all its modes and varieties, with the limits that pertain to each mode and its specific biases and concealments. Our practical glance is not able to encompass all the sources and powers of the seeds and the growth of the flowers – there is a blank or concealment here that will only be surmounted by a biological science, making us aware of the limitations of the disclosures of ordinary practical life. The deeper powers and structures of plant life are phenomena that are only made manifest to scientific disclosure (see especially *SZ*, section 69, and the later lecture course, *What Is a Thing?*)[26]

So *Da-sein* means 'discloser, revealer,' but this status of *Da-sein* – *indeed, the entire theme of Da-sein!* – is accessible only through a phenomcnological method: the entire theme of *Da-sein* is unintelligible to ordinary experience and discourse. This above all is a 'phenomenon of phenomenology.' For example, an ambiguity marks the term *Da-sein*, for it sometimes bears a sense (ontic) by which it signifies a subject such as the self or a human being, and sometimes bears a sense (ontological) by which it signifies being or existence themselves. Thus at p. 7 we read that *Da-sein* is 'the entity that we ourselves are,' but on p. 12 we read 'the term *Da-sein* [is] a pure expression of being.' This is not a mere equivocation. The ambiguous reference of the term is owing to the very constitution we are exploring here: that we cannot exist except by being overshadowed by care for our being, for existence and disclosure themselves; they accompany us; we never 'occur' without them. Thus our very being is in that way fused together with us, an ontic-ontological duality, a truth not easily encompassed in quotidian discourse.

A further reason why *Da-sein* can only be thematized within phenomenology appears through its resistance to the quantification implicit in ordinary language, subject to the categories. All its characters are 'existentials' rather than 'categories' (pp. 44–5). On the one hand, Heidegger stresses its individuality (it is 'in every case my own,' pp. 41–2).[27] Yet the term is also used collectively, not in the sense of a 'class' of similar beings but rather historically, signifying our whole history on the earth. This is evident in many places, none more so than section 44(C), where Heidegger is showing how truth is relative to *Da-sein*:

> *'There is' truth only insofar as Da-sein is and as long as it is*. Beings are discovered only *when Da-sein is*, and only *as long as Da-sein is* are they disclosed. Newton's laws, the law of contradiction, and any truth whatsoever, are true only as long as *Da-sein is*. Before there was any *Da-sein*, there was no truth; nor will here be any after *Da-sein* is no more. (p. 226)

None of that could be said of a singular self.

Incorporated in the word *Da-sein* is the theme that we occupy the world in such a way as to disclose or reveal what is in the world, and not only 'things' but other living beings and ourselves as well, 'phenomena' in the ordinary sense of the term (p. 31). The disclosure accomplished through our being, or existence, is something accomplished in advance of the explicit discovery of an item through perception or consciousness. That is why we can also express the point by saying that the things themselves had already been showing themselves all along. We had been engaged – unthematically, unconsciously – in letting the things show themselves. While calling attention to the role of the existing self in making the phenomena manifest, Heidegger also attributes to the phenomena themselves a certain power to show themselves: the *phainomenon* is 'that which shows itself, the manifest' (p. 28). The phenomenon does not derive its manifestness from somebody's current act of seeing, but rather precedes any such seeing, constituting one of the conditions for the possibility of seeing: 'Disclosedness in general belongs essentially to the constitution of the *being* [my emphasis] of *Da-sein*' (p. 221). This is not due to our intentions or consciousness – it is an expression of our *being*. Though disclosure is an attribute of existence, along with many others – still, Heidegger can also attribute to the phenomena themselves a certain power to show themselves, a kind of relative autonomy. As we made plain in chapter 1, Heidegger understands *Phänomen* on the basis of the Greek word *phainomenon*, the participle of *phainesthai*, something that shows itself, is manifest and evident (p. 28). What shows itself is something that we can see or can discern in some way, which is to say that it is not hidden or concealed. We noted the factor of possibility in most of these German expressions: the *Phänomen* is not what is seen, but what can be seen. That issue pertains to phenomenology in the narrow sense: the theory of appearance and reality. How can something be a phenomenon if nobody is looking? The task of explaining *why* there are phenomena in this sense is quite beyond our everyday awareness and is a philosophical undertaking, a task of phenomenology. By virtue of our being *qua* existence, we already belong to the world in advance of our conscious, perceptual activity, and therefore in our quotidian life we all engage perpetually in disclosure.

Given the contrast between the way we all reveal the world in everyday life, and what phenomenological philosophy undertakes, it follows that there is a double level of disclosure or revelation implicit in the phenomenological method: '[P]henomenology means *apophainesthai ta phainomena* – to let what shows itself be seen from itself, just as it shows itself from itself' (p. 34). Thus while phenomenology does accomplish a manifesting, prior to it there had been a different self-showing, that which *Da-sein* accomplishes in ordinary experience. But this is not forgotten by the phenomenologist, who continues to disclose the ordinary phenomena along with all the special themes, the phenomena of phenomenology: being, existence, truth, time, which had been partially or wholly hidden from the everyday understanding. Moreover, the phenomenologist does not merely abolish their earlier self-concealment. Phenomenology keeps its focus upon the original self-concealment even as it also proceeds to thematize the two classes of phenomena. The concealment of the phenomenological phenomena is no less central to phenomenology than their unconcealment. That is owing to the finitude of *Da-sein* as it lived in its everyday mode. In existence as we know it, there is always a pervasive non-disclosure, and Heidegger shows that this is not only polarized against the manifestness of the phenomena – there is a continuity between them. There are *limits* of disclosure, i.e., some partial concealment even along with unconcealment.

Moreover, the *phainomenon* is also capable of showing itself not as it really is – there are manifold variations on this in Heidegger's text: semblances (*Schein*), mere appearances (*Erscheinung*), and so on. Mere semblances and mere appearances are only deviant cases of *phainomena*, by contrast with 'the things themselves' (pp. 29–31). All the pseudo-disclosures of phenomena remain a permanent theme of phenomenology, while the *phainomenon* in the proper sense is not that which is shown by another or in another, but that which shows itself by itself and in itself, *das Sich-an-ihm-selbst-zeigende*.[28]

Existence is *the* phenomenon *par excellence*, that whereby we live, and this too is a domain of *Schein* und *Erscheinung*. That is, human existence does show itself and is a genuine phenomenon, but it does not always show itself just as it is, and from itself and in itself. There is semblance, distortion, and concealment in this domain too, especially because of inauthentic *Existenz*. Here too existence does not present itself just as it really and truly is. Indeed to the phenomenologist, the inauthentic and untrue are the foreground of the whole phenomenon.

So the phenomenology of Heidegger does not merely replicate the contents of our everyday consciousness: it studies them in the light of being, truth, and the other phenomena of phenomenology. In modern American psychology and cognitive science (Dennett[29] for example), phenomenology is merely the recounting of subjective experience. If an experimental subject is stimulated thus-and-so, the 'phenomenology' is what the subject feels, thinks, imagines, while the neurobiologist and other scientists record what actually happened – electrodes inserted *here*, graph-output recorded *there*, etc. The scientist then gets the subject to report on his or her 'phenomenology,' thus imagining the 'inner world' of a subject and, as in a planetarium, whatever show is displayed on the inside surface of the subject's mind counts as his or her 'phenomenology,' a mere preliminary to theory. Dennett's phenomenology is ultra-subjective. But for Heidegger, phenomenology is a disciplined form of research that corrects everyday awareness and substitutes a demonstrated truth in its place. The actual phenomena of phenomenology are for the most part hidden or occluded in everyday awareness.

(B) My wager is that we can discuss the existence of the one who exists without having to remind ourselves perpetually of every last possible phenomenological implication of *Da-sein*. For our interest is existence, not the manifold forms of disclosure that appear in the practical glance, in scientific practice, and in all the modes of truth – themes of phenomenology in the strict sense. The present study is consciously an exercise in applied phenomenology, not the fundamental phenomenology found in *SZ* itself. Therefore, I have sought out another term to replace the term *Da-sein* in philosophical discussion. Here, in referring to the one who exists, I'll speak of the 'self' instead. This is a substitution, not a translation. It permits the content of Heidegger's thought to be expressed in English as attributed to the self. It also permits an intelligible exposition in our language, an intelligibility admittedly gained by a simplification of Heidegger's argument. In speaking of the self, I am avoiding the ontic-ontological ambiguity contained in the term *Da-sein*. But this substitute is not inappropriate. Heidegger frequently speaks of *Da-sein* as a self (*das Selbst*), e.g., p. 114; he speaks of *Da-sein*'s *being* a self (*Selbstsein*), e.g., in the title of the first division, chapter 4; he explores the conditions for Da-sein's *ability* to be a self (*Selbstseinkönnen*), e.g., p. 267. Heidegger never refers to *Da-sein* where there is no selfhood. Our interpretative wager (making the self the pivot of our analysis of existence, rather than *Da-sein*) should pose no danger, for just as Heidegger frequently says that *Da-sein* is a self, we can always counter by recalling that, in *SZ*, the self is conceived as *Da-sein*, and thereby we open the door again to a fundamental phenomenological inquiry.[30]

For us, 'self' is a merely formal term whose instances would be expressed by personal pronouns, 'I,' 'you,' and so on. Not a predicate-term, it is a subject-term that is substituted grammatically for personal pronouns. To decide whether a statement about the self is true ('the self exists temporally,' for instance), the reader *de*-formalizes the statement, thus: '*I* exist temporally.' 'Self' is a formal term because the reader is not told what constitutes a self: essential concepts like 'spirit,' 'soul,' and 'mind' are kept at a distance. It is merely a grammatical function, or, to use an expression of the early Heidegger, it is a formal *indication*. What that means, among other things, is that the reader is only pointed towards a meaning that he or she must produce, by saying 'I exist temporally.'[31] Often in the present book, I shall say 'we' or 'you' in place of the noun 'the self.' We can now clarify that, like 'self,' existence too (and being and care) are understood to be formal structures in *SZ*. To summarize this paragraph, then: a formal expression like 'self' permits phenomenology to recognize the indexical reference of each personal pronoun while still speaking generally. This is not just a question of method: it is central to the account of *Da-sein*. A central feature of existence itself is that it is realized case by case: 'the being of *Da-sein* is in each case my own' (*SZ*, pp. 41–2).

The Phenomenology of Existence: Ecstasis

Though the term 'life' has many senses, and though all of them apply to ourselves, the one that discloses the most about ourselves is 'existence.' With this designation the human relation to time is seen most fully, for it shows that even our present existence is intertwined with the future. What is yet to come is moving in upon us even now, so much so as to constitute our way of being. That is perhaps the most important single thesis of Heidegger's *SZ*. For a full account of time itself we shall have to refer in footnotes to some of Heidegger's texts and some of the commentaries on it.[32] We do not capture Heidegger's point merely by acknowledging that human beings are open to the future or oriented to it, that our life is full of expectation and intention. Though that is true, what is salient is the further point that, if existence constitutes our mode of being, the future itself belongs to our being.

There is a strong yoke between the life that is yet to be lived and the present anticipation of it, and that yoke is existence. We possess the understanding of a possibility, and so the life yet to be lived is yoked together with the current anticipation of it. With the kind of being that Kierkegaard and Heidegger call existence, we undertake to be, and indeed we have to undertake to be. Creatures that do not project themselves into the future in this way do not have the same sort of being that we do, and so, philosophically, we can say they do not exist. Let us think of just one expression of existence: that the human being is the one who makes promises. The wedding vow 'I take thee ... for richer, for poorer, in sickness and in health' may be pronounced by persons who are thirty years old, but the life that still remains to each of them, though it is not now realized, is comprehended in that vow as a part of their present being. We are constituted by futurity. It is true that what the onlookers hear in a promise is only the persons' understanding of their future, their orientation to it, not the future itself. The future is dark, hidden and inaccessible. More than that, it *is* not, i.e., it is not actual, not real, not present. Their possible sickness and their possible health seem to be removed from all present knowledge, and even to be removed from being. But they are not removed from our human mode of being, existence, which differs in precisely this way from traditional concepts of being that are focused on what is real and actual.

Nothing is more out of accord with our mode of being than to suppose that we have a present self – occurrent at this moment – and that there is then some future self that will be occurrent at some future moment, whose relation with the present self must be clarified, whether through a 'principle of identity' or through some other means. Indeed, these matters must be clarified, but the solution will escape anyone who begins with the postulate of the 'present self.' In our scheme of things, indebted to Heidegger, the 'present self' is not a phenomenon but a mere construct, and the same holds for the 'future self.'[33]

In part 3 of Derek Parfit's main book,[34] he undertakes to show weaknesses in our common view, and its philosophical ancestors, that each of us is an identical person throughout the extent of his or her life. Speaking of our 'experiences' (pp. 214–17), Parfit says that the usual view is that they have been enjoyed by you or by me, the person or self who has them, but whose identity as a person is something over and above them all, having unity through time. But he has arguments intended to show that it can be indeterminate whether someone at time t is the same person as was known to us at $t - 1$. What he proposes instead is reductionism: the claim that the entire truth about someone's life could be stated through a complete description of each of the discrete units of experience. There is no other 'separate fact' that is You or the being of You. What matters is not You, but only the experiences themselves, as long as they are arrayed in the right kind of relation, relation R, which is a combination of 'psychological connectedness' (for instance, my memory of yesterday's events) and 'psychological continuity' (by which I can now remember many of last year's events, and the person I was a year ago could remember many of the previous year's events, and so on, back through my history). Such reductionism could cope well with the indeterminacies of identity, for each of the two successors of my dividing, or my brain-hemisphere transplants, could have a relation R to myself. Now if we *are* nothing more than an array of experiences governed by relation R, the question I want to pursue is the character of these 'units' called experiences. For Parfit, each of them seems to be constituted in principle on its own, capable of being without its particular and necessary place within your life, for they are the 'atoms' which, in entering into relation R, constitute a life. I see this as the empiricist part of his heritage.

The empiricist idea of experience conceives it as some sort of mental event, and the outline of Parfit that I have made recalls a critique that Heidegger made of the concept of experience (*Erlebnis*) in Wilhelm Dilthey (see *SZ*, pp. 46–8) and perhaps other empiricists (see pp. 372–7). It was just the idea that our life consists in a sequence of *Erlebnisse*, the 'cellular' components of a life, which, following in a certain order, added up to a total continuity of life (*Lebenszusammenhang*, pp. 46, 373). The point that tells against Dilthey and Parfit is that they work with a purely immanent concept of experience, conceived ontologically as something merely objectively present (*vorhanden*) in its own right, then to be brought into connectedness and continuity with other experiences. The sum total, the connectedness and continuity, thus becomes itself a *vorhanden* total of *vorhanden* units.

The idea that we are leading up to, and that must now be presented more fully, is that there are two connected elements in existence. The two belong together: you cannot have the one without the other.

First, existence is the life that is still possible for us.

Second, it is our present orientation towards that possible life.

Existence has, as its first component, something that is not present and not real, something that is not a being, a future that is still outstanding, still approaching us, an unreality that is united with our present projection of it. (It is perhaps possible to grant that existence itself is not a thing or a reality. In view of that alone, it must have some non-being in its constitution. By virtue of the second component, however, it has one foot in the present. Existence combines something that is present with something that is future, something that is with something that is not.) This yoke between the non-actual future and the present understanding is called 'ecstasis,' because it is what permits the understanding to outreach the present, to 'stand out.' Heidegger treats the ecstatic constitution of understanding in section 68(a), pp. 336–9. In the first place, those who are making their ceremonial wedding promises are fulfilling promises that they *already* made to one another, and indeed prior promises they already made to the whole community, which brought everyone here as witnesses. Now they commit themselves for the future with the vows they are undertaking. In the second place, the vows will continue to govern them in the future. We say that the faithful couple will 'remember' their vows, but that does not mean their mere retention of past history. It means being true to the vow. And the vow continues to govern them even if only in the deficient mode of breaking the vows, for these vows are what constitute desertion and divorce as such. Thirdly, this later 'remembering' of the vows is itself a futural intention, because their being true to the vow in the future means the further honouring of it in the still *more* removed future, 'till death us do part.'

So instead of speaking of *Erlebnisse*, experiences, in the way that Dilthey and Parfit did, we should understand our life as a whole, and each moment of it, in terms of *Existenz*, especially through the first component of existence, the life that is still possible for us. Of course, Heidegger does not want to abolish continuity in a life, but 'the self-hood [*Selbigkeit*, sameness] of an authentically existing self is ontologically divided by a great chasm from the identity of an "I" that holds through in a manifold of experiences' (p. 130). The chasm is between existence and objective presence or *Vorhandenheit*.

Earlier we correlated existence, as the 'essence' of *Da-sein* (the possibility of the self either to be itself or not to be itself), with care, *die Sorge*, as the being of *Da-sein* (the unity of existence with facticity and ruination). Our being, care, is what ordains our concern for our existence. Our most central concern is not for our facticity (or ruination), but for our possibility, our ability to be: that we renew our ability to be ourselves or not ourselves, for instance, to persevere in our promises. But this existence, about which we care primordially, is already a constituent in our care, and indeed not just one constituent, but in every way primary. A unity of ecstasis is achieved between the existence about which we care and the existence that is at work within our care. Because of this ecstatic unity, our facticity and our ruination are also pulled into the ecstatic unity of care, the synthetic unity of care. This primacy of existence among the three elements composing care is recognized throughout *SZ*, especially when Heidegger characterizes the structures of *Da-sein* as 'existential' – we have the 'existential' account of science in section 69, the 'existential' account of death in section 53, and, in general, existential accounts of conscience, of discourse, language, history, and so on.

This is the very heart of the matter that, in later chapters of this book, I shall seek to apply in accounts of our everyday life. What Heidegger has presented in fundamental ontology is care, and my rendering of it will interpret care itself as magnifying and justifying. It is existence that we shall be seeing magnified and justified, even as existence is the mainspring of the movement of care itself, the movement to magnify and justify. It is not particularly our facticity that we seek to magnify and justify. And while there is no doubt at all that people seek to magnify themselves and justify themselves, our phenomenological study will be looking somewhat deeper into these motivations, seeking to show that, behind the magnifying of the self and the justifying of the self, there is a deeper factor – the magnifying and justifying of the being of the self: existence.

Being as the Ability to Be

This study is showing us that existence and care are not ultimately left isolated from each other, but united – namely, in the ability to be. And the grasp of being as the ability to be is also the upshot of the preceding phenomenology. The point that our being is *Seinkönnen* is repeated often. Here is a quotation from section 63: 'The being of *Da-sein* is essentially ability to be [*Seinkönnen*] and being free for its own possibilities' (p. 312).[35] And *Seinkönnen* is so central to Heidegger's second division that we find the term on virtually every page from 231 to 237 and 250 to 267 (where the subject is being-towards-death) and from 267 to 323 (dealing with conscience and selfhood). To qualify *Sein* with *Können* means that being can contain the turbulence of temporality, and the darkness of our attunement and facticity. It also means that being contains the ecstasis, the stretching, that we spoke of in describing existence.

According to the Oxford English Dictionary, an ability is 'the quality in an agent which makes an action possible,' which could be further understood as 'a suitable or sufficient power' for something, 'a faculty or capacity.' So the possibility in question arises from something in the agent. Regarding 'ability' the dictionary continues, 'having the qualifications for, and means of, doing anything ... having sufficient power ... so that the thing is possible' for me. An ability, then, is that kind of possibility that arises from an agent's own form and constitution. This can be contrasted with another sense of possibility that is not rooted in one's own ability, e.g., the case of a possible thunderstorm tomorrow. If we have the ability to read, we might speak of this as the active sense of 'possible' – it's possible for me or for you to read. This is not the same as saying that 'it is possible that he will read [a book] tomorrow.' That phrase assumes that the subject has the ability to read, but it is not asserting that – it asserts rather that a certain event will occur tomorrow, perhaps somebody reading, perhaps a thunderstorm.

The ability to be is an active possibility like the ability to read, and is true only of beings who exist in the sense we are treating. An inert object or living creature that does not confront and anticipate the zone of life yet to be lived does not have an ability to be. Being is not a matter of ability for them. They just *are*. We could use the term 'continuants'[36] for beings like them whose future comes to them merely through the flow of time, contrasting them with ourselves who, in existing, also take on the ability to be.

One sense of 'possible' must be discriminated from our existential sense of 'ability': the modal sense. Heidegger takes the trouble to underline this distinction on p. 143 of *SZ*. In traditional logic and metaphysics, the possible is contrasted with the other modalities, the actual and the necessary, 'modes' initially, of judgment – the logical doctrine of modality – with the question also debated whether modality is objectively inscribed in things, or not. But even if there were thing-like (*de re*) modality, this would be a completely different matter from the ability to be that pertains to human existence. To paraphrase von Herrmann: the term 'can' does not just mean that something is 'possible.' It means being-able, being capable. But what *we* are capable of is being, our own being in the sense of existing. Being in our case means ability to be.[37] With real modality, on the other hand, some entities would be necessary beings, some actual, some only possible, an array holding for anything we'd be able to make judgments about. But the ability to be is not one such mode, not a logical or metaphysical possibility. As von Herrmann points out,[38] unlike a modal possibility, an existential possibility is not to be brought to a realization; rather, it is something that we either seize or do not seize. Ability is the sense of possibility that is relevant to a discussion of human existence. It is not the neutral state in which rain is possible and not-raining is also possible.

Neither should the ability to be that is constitutive of existence be confused with ancient and medieval ideas of potentiality (*dynamis, potentia*). The existential possibility that we call ability is not en route to an actualization, nor is it composed of some inner structure that would belong to a substance, like the germinative character, the potency, of the seed of a tree. So it is unfortunate that both current English translations of *SZ*[39] render *Seinkönnen* as 'potentiality of being.' If Heidegger had wanted to suggest anything of that sort, he did have at his disposal German words that would have evoked it, such as *Potenz, Anlage, Dynamis*. The ability to be is not a potentiality we have in advance of being, as if it were something that pertained to a non-being. Existential ability to be qualifies a being that already exists. Existence is co-constituted by the (continuing) ability to exist, ability to be. Possible being continues to qualify the existing self, and this is not in keeping with the traditional categories of potentiality and actuality.

The existential ability to be, *Seinkönnen*, is so fundamental to existence that many other phenomena become qualified by it. And we see in them all that facticity and existence together are motivating us. If the text were saying merely that we *had* to be, for instance, had to be a whole, it might not be offering any guidance as to how that was possible. But in speaking of the ability to be, e.g., the ability to be a whole, the text is not referring exclusively or principally to the future and our projection of it, but also to the past. Our ability or capability draws upon a power or movement of being – in carrying us forward, it reveals that the constitution of ability requires something that is already in place that permits us to advance. The constitution of ability is a forward projection that includes a backward openness, a receptiveness or facticity. We see here the operation of a past within the self's anticipation, past and future together in an ecstatic unity. We are perpetually stretched out of ourselves towards our ability to be, driven and prompted by our attunement, for because of it there is a rushing ingress of our being *qua* facticity and falling. This care-structure will afford us the terminology, in later chapters, for discussing the many forms of our magnifying our existence and justifying it. Our being is inherently agitated, a temporal truth that was hidden from the ancient philosophy that interpreted being as substance.

Because the ability to be constitutes our being, it is the primary subject of our concern. Thus, in the section on care or concern (section 41), Heidegger says that we have a concern about our being, or a relation to it, that is in fact a concern about the ability to be, a 'being-towards our own ability to be,' *Sein zum Seinkönnen* (p. 192). This is precisely the kind of care or concern that we shall be treating at length: the concern to magnify oneself and to justify oneself; the aspiration to being a success, to being morally in the right, to belong to a great and justified community, to be spiritually awakened. And he qualifies this further in the same passage, citing our 'being towards our own most intimate ability to be,' *Sein zum eigensten Seinkönnen* (p. 191), characterizing in this way the projection that constitutes what we are. What becomes revealed in anxiety is our *Sein zum eigensten Seinkönnen* (p. 188). That serves here as an index of our freedom to choose our being, and this point is repeated often.

We also have a concern, of course, about our being towards death. And Heidegger speaks of death itself in a related phrase, 'the possibility of no-more-being-able-to be,' *die Möglichkeit des Nicht-mehr-da-sein-könnens* (p. 250). And because of the intimate connection of ability to be with inability to be, Heidegger understands our relation to death as our self-projection upon 'this most intimate ability to be' (pp. 250, 262).

When Heidegger treats the wholeness of our life, in order to introduce the theme of death and being-towards-death, he qualifies it as the ability to be a whole (*Ganzseinkönnen*). This is introduced in section 45 (pp. 233–5). Have we brought *Da-sein* as a whole into view? But then, considering how we are all stretched out between birth and death, it may be that *Da-sein* never constitutes a whole at all. So the question can be addressed whether *Da-sein* has the *ability* to be a whole. *Da-sein* has to *accomplish* wholeness. It is through living under the shadow of death that we discover the ability to be a whole, *Ganzseinkönnen*, in sections 53, 61, and 62 (pp. 264, 266, 301, and 305).

A further phenomenon that is related to all the above is authenticity, expressed frequently as 'the ability to be authentically,' *das eigentliche Seinkönnen*. We discover this first in the introduction to the second division, pp. 232–3, and indeed it could be said to be the whole theme of that division: see, for example, the title on p. 267, which presents conscience as the testimony to our *eigentliches Seinkönnen*, which is fulfilled in the treatment in later pages (pp. 295–301 – we'll have some substantive comments on this treatment in chapter 4). It must be recognized that the term *eigentlich* is adverbial, not adjectival, and moreover that it modifies *sein*, not *können* – it isn't an authentic ability that is of concern to Heidegger, but an authentic existence, especially in the ability or capacity for existing authentically. More frequent is the related term that seems to alternate with it: 'our most intimate ability to be,' *das eigenste Seinkönnen* (e.g., pp. 277–9). Again, in that case, what is most intimate is not the ability but being.

These variants of the ability to be continue to be intermixed. For example, in Heidegger's discussion of *Ganzseinkönnen*, he will often qualify it as *eigentliches Ganzseinkönnen*, as in the chapter title on p. 301 and the text that follows. By this Heidegger means that authentic resolution that confronts death and that makes our being authentically whole or *ganz*. And our experience of guilt is treated not only as being guilty (*Schuldigsein*) but, more crucially, as the ability to be guilty, *Schuldigseinkönnen* (see p. 289). We shall have some substantive comments on this in chapter 4.

Another variant that plays a huge role in the second division is the ability to be a self, *Selbstseinkönnen*. This is usually qualified as *eigentliches Selbstseinkönnen* (see, e.g., p. 267), the ability authentically to be a self (but for an unqualified use of the term, see p. 268). This proves to be important throughout the whole inquiry, but specially in the second division. The ability to be a self operates at two levels, a complexity that arises from the formal character of what is called the self. Formally, what is essential to our being is the ability to be *a* self, and being *a* self is expressed in the term *Selbstsein* that occurs frequently, for instance, in the chapter title of the first division, chapter 4. But there is a further branching, in that there remains an alternative open even subsequent to the ability to be *a* self. This is the double possibility of the existing self, either to be *it*self or not to be *it*self. We have already quoted this from p. 12, where existence is defined as 'the possibility of the self, either to be *it*self or not to be *it*self.' This is the double possibility of authentic and inauthentic existence, what Heidegger often mentions as 'the possibility that is most of all our own,' or, perhaps better, as 'our most intimate possibility' (*die eigenste Möglichkeit des Da-seins*), pp. 42, 143–8, 187–8, 263, etc. This too will be more fully explored in chapter 4.

Having spent much of the first division outlining our being as being-in-the-world, Heidegger will at times reinterpret this as the *ability* to be in the world, *In-der-Welt-sein-können* (p. 191), here seen as the subject matter of our anxiety.

The auxiliary verb 'can,' *können*, also takes on a huge importance in the account of our cognitive reaction to our world. Heidegger treats our hearing existentially, showing how it incorporates not only acoustic sensitivity, but the activity of being open for a message (hearkening, *Horchen*) in such a way that hearing itself, *Hören*, is properly analysed as the ability to hear, *Hörenkönnen*, no mere potentiality given in advance of the actual hearing, but the very same thing. In *SZ*, section 34, Heidegger makes an analysis of it: to hear is to-be-able-to-hear (*Hörenkönnen*). Hearing is existent or self-surpassing, in being the ground for our paying heed to what is said, hearkening to it. Hearkening (*Horchen*) is rooted in the ability to hear (*Hörenkönnen*), it is 'more primordial than what the psychologist "initially" defines as hearing, the sensing of tones and the perception of sounds' (p. 163). A further transcendence achieved by the hearer is to be brought into contact with that with which the discourse was concerned: 'we are already together with the other beforehand, with the being which the discourse is about' (p. 164).

Seeing too is ability-to-see (*Sehenkönnen*), and it yields to a similar

analysis. I have studied it closely in the article 'Visibility.'[40] Every seeing incorporates the ability to see further. It contains the projection of a
further seeing beyond the current moment of stimulation. When I say
to you that I can see a flock of birds on the wing, I mean also that my
seeing will be prolonged into the coming moments, and that they will
still be visible then too, and I mean also that you too will be able to see
them if you take a look. These are some of the dimensions of the ability
or capability (*Können*) that lies within seeing. First, a futural seeing is
projected in the current seeing: you are able to continue to see. Second,
your seeing is capable of disclosing or discovering the birds. You can
penetrate to the thing as it shows itself.

The 'Letter on Humanism'

This is an appropriate point for brief remarks on Heidegger's own later
reinterpretations of *SZ*. The most prominent text is the 'Letter on
Humanism.'[41] Here it is above all the deepest bond of existence to being
that comes to expression in the reinterpretation of *SZ*, and this is certainly highlighting things that nobody would have been able to see
looking at the early text by itself:

> What the human being is – or as it is called in the traditional language of
> metaphysics, the 'essence' of the human being – lies in his ek-sistence.
> [Note the new spelling.] ... [T]he sentence says: the human being occurs
> essentially in such a way that he is the 'there', that is, the clearing of being
> ... [T]he fundamental character of ek-sistence ... is of an ecstatic inherence
> in the truth of being. (pp. 247–8)

The bond of our existence to being is further echoed and strengthened
in later pages of *HB*: 'In *SZ* (p. 38), it is said that every question of philosophy "returns to existence." But existence here is not the actuality of
the *ego cogito* ... Ek-sistence, in fundamental contrast to every *existentia*
and "*existence*" is ek-static dwelling in the nearness of being (p. 261).'
    It is *SZ*, not the later texts, that I have been expounding here, but in
offering these retrospective quotations, I mean to be faithful to Heidegger's deeper intentions, particularly to keep in mind his resistance to an
interpretation of *SZ* as a work of humanism, 'philosophy of existence'
or existentialism. There is no reason to ignore the guidance that later
works of Heidegger offer for an interpretation of *SZ* (usually distancing
him from 'existentialism'). And perhaps my *SZ*-exposition will have

been able to throw some further light even upon these gnomic remarks of the later Heidegger. Through the force of facticity in Heidegger's thought, it is not open to the agent to begin reflections by conceiving what the aim of life as a whole is, for instance, happiness, *eudaimonia*. We are too much woven into the fabric of history to exercise reason in quite that fashion; the reflection always comes too late. Every exercise of reason and choice is weighed down by the history of our lives, what we are already committed to in advance of the choice of action. In earlier versions of his work,[42] Heidegger used the term 'facticity' in a broader sense, not in contrast with 'existence' but virtually identical with it, as constituting our mode of being: thrown, situated, preoccupied, and finite. The title 'Hermeneutics of Facticity,' signifying the understanding that was accomplished by a finite, factical being, was to be understood as a subjective genitive.

Once we recognize the profound effect of attunement and facticity upon all our existence and projection, it becomes possible to see a continuity between *SZ* and Heidegger's later work. The common idea that he began with *Da-sein* and then dropped *Da-sein* for some tremendous and dark idea of being is not tenable any more. Existence was always shadowed by attunement, facticity, fate, and destiny. On the continuity in Heidegger's work, see two essays in the recent anthology edited by Polt.[43]

Excursus: 'Exist' in the Philosophical Tradition

From all our quotations, it is apparent that Kierkegaard and Heidegger do not understand 'existence' in the way that logicians and epistemologists generally do. Their discussion has little to do with the existence of classes and universals, or of microparticles and the other entities of physics. For there are quite diverse senses of the term 'exist.' We have already claimed that existence is only one sense of the term 'life,' and throughout this study we are seeing that it is only one sense of the term 'being.' But there are also diverse meanings contained in the term 'existence' that we can sort out by historical reflection on the languages of philosophy. When we say that craters exist on the moon, or that tame tigers exist, we are using just one sense of the term 'exist.'

After the medieval period, philosophy divided into distinct streams, one epistemological that used this specific sense of 'exist' and another, metaphysical, that used quite a different sense of the term that was then inherited by Kierkegaard and Heidegger.

The special sense of 'exist' in Kierkegaard is seen in its close link with *movement*. That was apparent in the texts we quoted from the *Postscript* and is evident in many other texts.[44] This is not just any kind of movement, and especially not a movement in nature.[45] To inquire further into that movement takes us back into a long tradition of philosophy, at least as far back as the medieval Scholastics who generally gave definition to existence by way of a contrast with essence, a contrast that left its traces not only on Kierkegaard but on many intervening figures – including Schelling and Hegel – who rethought the contrast and transformed it thoroughly without abandoning it. The late Scholastic Suarez[46] determined the concept of existence with a strong echo of the etymology of the word: *ex-sisto* = stand out, be placed outside. Something exists when it not only has causes but comes to *stand outside* its causes (*entitas aliqua constituitur extra causas suas*) and begins to be something (*ac incipit esse aliquid*). When a statue is no longer merely immanent in the craft and imagination of the sculptor, but, having been placed outside of the sculptor, stands by itself, it exists. The existence of the statue is its movement away from its immanence in its mental cause.

The central point is that Kierkegaard had a long-standing tradition behind him when he conceived existence or existing as a reaching-out or displacement, overreaching what was already constituted. But Kierkegaard never speculated about any such overreaching occurring in nature, or, for that matter, in God. Existence is the movement of the 'subjectively existing individual.'[47] This is a narrowing-in by contrast with the 'metaphysical' tradition that provided him with this important word. And on this point Heidegger, in *SZ*, remained true to him: existence belongs to the ontological constitution of ourselves only, human beings. I shall call the concept of existence that appears in Kierkegaard and Heidegger 'ecstatic,' signifying *moving outside*. We invoked it earlier in the chapter, mentioning the yoke between the life we have yet to live and the present reaching-out towards that life. Strictly this 'yoke' should be called 'ecstasis.' This interpretation is precisely what Heidegger wanted in his comments on existence-philosophy in *GA*, 49; his strong aversion to existence-philosophy there can be read as aversion to being identified with Jaspers and Scheler in the public mind.

In this light it is also apparent that what I am calling 'magnifying' and 'justifying' are to be grasped as movements of existence. They are not to be reduced to states, whether of greatness or justice; in this way they show how they pertain to existence in its ecstatic constitution.

The concept of existence that I call logical and epistemological arose out of the modern theory of knowledge. From Descartes onwards, it was seen as central to explain how the human understanding could come to know that which was *real* or *actual* or *existent* (varying terms in varying authors), but it was not an easy matter to say what these varying terms actually meant. While our cognition performed an out-reaching, such a movement was not attributed to the objects of cognition. What did it mean, then, to suppose that these objects existed? For example, Locke builds up the structure of our knowledge on the basis of his 'ideas,' and when the topic of existence arises,[48] he assures us that we do possess the idea of it. But it is always mixed with some other ideas, ideas of objects, in an inexplicable way. And his account is circular, for in trying to explain the idea of existence, he falls back upon the existence of the ideas.[49] The matter is no easier for Hume. Although, like Locke, he speaks with assurance of 'matters of fact and existence' throughout his *Treatise* and *Enquiry*, his account of how we acquire the idea of existence[50] is unintelligible. This idea supposedly accompanies every impression and idea, yet it has no distinct profile: 'The idea of existence, then, is the very same with the idea of what we conceive to be existent.' It remained for the logicians of a later age to give a convincing account: the framework of a logical analysis of discourse was able to express the specific character of existential statements. In his landmark article 'On Denoting,'[51] Bertrand Russell showed that existential statements could always be interpreted as asserting the truth of propositional functions (and negative existentials their falsehood); thus 'Unicorns exist' = '"x is a unicorn" is sometimes true.' This might be called the critical concept of existence, in contrast to the ecstatic, for it is existence (of an object) that is taken as the criterion for the truth of a conception or a statement. What verifies the statement is the thing or state of affairs to which it refers, which lies outside the statement. The inquirer has 'gone out' towards the thing to verify the statement, and this thing that lies out there exists. Much of Heidegger's phenomenology is worked out in encounters with epistemological theories of this sort.

Transition: Formalism and Application

The treatment of existence has been *formal*. There is no living person who is *the self*, but every 'I' and 'you' has selfhood as its form; neither do our everyday preoccupations directly focus on existence, being, authenticity, and so on – but these constitute the form of our everyday life, as revealed by phenomenology. The drive of care that constitutes our being is intertwined with all the concrete choices and actions and ends that preoccupy us throughout our daily experience, the specific conscious intentions. With our special focus on the care or concern about our being, our intent in the remainder of the book is to look for the embodiment of this care in our actual pursuits.

In general, our everyday attention is devoted to what we wish to say or accomplish; this is naturally the preoccupation of the ego or self. But there is the further action and presence of the *being* of the ego or self: its care and its existence, and these do not leave themselves without witness in everyday experience. The unthematic activity of our concernful being, *sorgendes Sein*, accompanies all the ego's choices. Our concern over our ability to be becomes expressed, not in what we do or say, but in the way in which we do things and say things. It becomes apparent not through what the self is pursuing, but how it conducts its pursuits; not through what you perceive but how you perceive it; not in what you think about or say but in how you think and speak; not at what we work but how we work; not for what we live (for what end) but in how we live – and so on. What appears along with the content of our action and speech is the magnifying of our being and the justification of our being. That is how the concern over our ability to be accompanies all our concrete perceptions, actions, and relationships.

To bring *together* this concern over our ability to be with the conscious choices and actions of the ego or self – that is what application means. We shall be turning to definite choices and deeds of everyday life, and in their midst find the traces of our being and our concern for our being. In our economic life, for instance, treated in chapter 3, we find that along with our duties in production or administration we are preoccupied with success, and that chapter will show that this is neither an end or *telos*, nor any company function, but a drive to magnify our own being. This application of the formal ontology of the self and its being will be followed by many further applications, dealing with communities and personal relationships. We all want a worthwhile life and we seek that and define it in any number of ways, but it is not a goal. We shall look in chapter 4 at a number of moral situations with a somewhat similar view: it will appear that in numerous cases the intent of the moral agent is the justification of his or her being. In both of these studies, I hope to show that a care about our being is the motivating force, not the requirements of the business firm or the moral requirements of the situation. The two chapters that follow will widen our view, but with a similar agenda: in an examination of community life we shall see that what is at work, in certain cases, is the magnifying of the community, and the justifying of the community. It is a communal care about our collective being that is operative here. These are applications of the phenomenology of existence and care, and can be regarded as the de-formalizing of what we have presented in this chapter.

3 Magnifying the Self

In our age, there is a dream of success disseminated through the media, the cinema, print, and the educational system. Nobody can escape its allure. On television and in popular magazines the pre-eminent person of our age, *the* success, is the celebrity. Business newspapers report on successful corporations, successful businessmen and businesswomen, and successful nations. In earlier times, we would read about 'powerful' corporations and 'wealthy' investors, but now a premium seems to be placed upon those who have succeeded in the struggles of the marketplace. And present-day discourse about education shares in this. In primary school as in graduate school, the system works to identify those who succeed, and those who do not, with less interest in older ideas such as education for citizenship or education for trades and crafts. The main site of success is the economic system, and for most individuals that means especially paid employment. But it is not the objective sociology of employment and social classes that concerns me here. Rather, it is the dream of success that is invested in the employment system. What I call a dream is more properly called a possibility, a possibility that may be open to us: to be a success. The great and successful figures that are displayed to us all on television really do exist, and their great successes reported in the press really did happen. Although for most people life offers something smaller, what counts here is the meaning that we derive from watching the spectacle. What possibilities for ourselves appear there?

People who grew up in the Western world during the twentieth century think of employment in connection with large corporations or public-sector institutions, with their escalator of promotions, but now at the outset of a new century, the realities of the economic system are changing quickly,[1] and younger people have new and different imaginary landscapes bearing upon their prospects. But that has not altered the idea of success itself. Great firms have fallen or disintegrated; others are fused internationally in globalism; new and small firms emerge with lightning speed; many entrepreneurs work alone or with a few temporary partners – all this is described by Reich, but his central point is that workaholism, drivenness, even monomania, are ascendent, especially in the United States. Capitalism is unrestrained, inequalities are growing, fewer people can expect steady jobs – a lifetime of insecure and unending work confronts more and more people. The result is an amazing array of excellent products, but less and less leisure. Reich's evidence is that this pattern will continue to grow in the United States, and will be exported around the world. It is success that reigns in this domain, with no rivals.

We need to avoid the temptation that can befall a social scientist (it did not befall Reich) of seeing this world as a pure structural system, ignoring individuals' motivations and responses, of assuming that the pursuit of success is a particular form of life characteristic of advanced capitalism that arose at some time in the recent past and will likely be superseded by some other form of life in the future. My purpose will be to show instead that the allure of success expresses something deeper and more universal. Obviously, no one of their toys or appliances or properties or vehicles is vitally important to the players in this system; thus, the system is wrongly grasped as 'consumerism.' The system has much more to do with production than with consumption. Movies, TV shows, and novels offer some insight into the individuals who live amidst the glitter of the present Age of Success. We shall be looking at a life in business, a life in journalism, and a life in the theatre.

Of course, most people do not shine in all this glitter. There may be successful farmers, I suppose, but not successful farm hands. The connection of most people to the glitter is two-fold. In the first place, we are all inundated with media representations of mega-success, and, up to a point, we enjoy watching it. When I turn to the topic of celebrity, I'll make a few comments on the disseminated excitement of success and glamour, and the possibility of our identifying, however fleetingly, with such figures. But then we shall see a second meaning of it, status anxiety.

In treating the phenomenon of success, I'll make the claim (*a*) that it is not a goal of action and not something we choose, and (*b*) that it is something we care about, a possibility for our existence. Let us examine this distinction. While philosophers and economists have devoted much attention to decision-making, the broader theme of care needs to be studied more. There are well-developed theories about individual and collective choice, that treat the ordering of preferences and the concomitant matter of the rationality of actions.[2] Arrow takes into account the finite set of alternatives that are available to agents in a given situation, and on this basis he is able to show what difficulties lie in the way of collective decision-making. It can never be simply an aggregate of individuals' preferences. But the case of success that we are going to study here cannot appear as one of the preferences that an individual would put somewhere on an ordered list. Success is not a goal of action, not something we resolve upon or decide upon. It is something we hope for. We do not pursue it as one of our preferences with an resolute, active intention. That is what the phenomenological study that follows will show.

Yet since success is something that we care about, we must try to say why. I shall say that it means for us a magnifying of the self, indeed a magnifying of our being. Prompted by care, success is not a rational goal in life, i.e., it does not have the nature of an end. Being a success can occur in many human activities, and we shall think about it here by focusing on making a success out of a business career. Already we can say that one kind of success occurs in the suitable performance of your function in some employment or other, the successful operation and repair of a machine, for instance, and that another kind would be advancing to higher and higher positions in your business firm. It is the second kind that matters in our discussion. Obviously, a business success has to occur within some particular business or industry, and all that business activity is as goal-oriented, as teleological, as it could be. The goal, the end, the interest, gives definition to the situation in which we act. But one cannot intend or aim just to succeed. One has to succeed in some venture, in some cause or with some product, so the success itself *supervenes* upon the cause or business in which one hopes to succeed. Now, given the contrast between success and goal-oriented activity, we'll need to see the way in which goal-directed activity is interwoven with our care about success. The salient point in what follows is to trace the drive to success to something within us that is not our purposeful intention: it is our being, our care about our being, the drive to magnify both ourselves and our being.

One of my points will be that the urge to success, or the hope of it, is not a curious by-product of an unhappy, anxious psyche, but springs from the very structure of our existence, what we have characterized as care, *die Sorge*, composite of existence and facticity. My way of showing this will be to look at several distinct levels of success: some of them belong to the most elementary strata of our life, and especially what I call pragmatic success. They then reach out into further strata of our life, for instance, professional success. All this variety expresses our care, and all the phenomena are deeply rooted in our being. De Botton (to be discussed below) has made a psychological study, setting out some causes of status anxiety, and then some possible remedies for it. As such it is an enlightening book, and I do not wish to take issue with it. But it leaves the question open whether there is an ontological grounding for these phenomena.

My study will show the gradations of success that begin from the pragmatic, and will then demonstrate how all the gradations are expressions of care. This will then lead us to examine whether there is some further horizon in which we should comprehend success, something further that it signifies. Here is the main conclusion of our investigation of the meaning of success – success signifies the magnifying of the self, and even, in certain cases, the justification of the self. We are then able to see how it is enlisted to contribute to the magnifying of our existence, and even to its justification. Whatever contributes to magnifying the person appears, further, as an increment in being. Mr and Ms Success live differently, their words are of a different significance.

Phenomenology and Hermeneutics

How then are we to establish such points that are admittedly subjective? Insofar as the study is not only phenomenological but also hermeneutical.

In our study focused on success, we shall look at some books reporting on lives that are marked by either major success or major failure. We shall be looking at a life in business, a life in journalism, and a life in the theatre. The study of this life and that life, highlighting the individuality of each author, will interpret the writings with a view to seeing what success meant to one or two of those who enjoyed it, and what failure meant to one of those who endured it. And we shall interpret them in the light of our understanding of existence: in what way do they exhibit an understanding of being, of temporality and selfhood? Though we are quoting from autobiographies, it is not a life in the sense of a *bios* that concerns us here – the plots, the narratives, beginning, middle, and end. Instead we look at these books for a sense of existence, so, in our terminology, we want to examine *being* a businessman, *being* a journalist, and *being* an actor, following, first, the narrative of an auto executive, Lee Iacocca,[3] then one by the journalist Jayson Blair,[4] then one by the actor Laurence Olivier.[5] In the following sections I attempt to show what all this clamour means to the participants.

The autobiographies are not here to offer empirical evidence for the claims I have made about existence – instead, I am looking here for what is original and unique in each; they are different de-formalizations of what we have already rendered in a purely formal way. The written work is precisely the locale where the meaning of a life or an institution is made most accessible, for the author expects the readers to internalize the material. Not only do the narratives of success and achievement communicate the self-magnifying that belongs to their lives – the writings themselves implement a further magnifying of the self. And we shall be asking whether the self-magnification is in the service of self-justifying, and if so how.

The Meaning of Success

Lee Iacocca's autobiography is a success story, recounting his origins from an immigrant family in Pennsylvania, and how he rose to become the president of the Ford Motor Company. He begins by announcing his main theme: 'People always ask me the same questions: "How did you get to be so successful ...?"' (p. xi). 'You're about to read the story of a man who's had more than his share of successes' (p. xiii). Looking at the book, we won't focus on the narrative (*bios*), but rather seek to learn from him what being a success was like.

But what *is* success? To elucidate the concept, we start out from common experiences that everyone has in grappling with the environment – getting a recalcitrant machine to work, for instance a computer printer. When the goal has been attained you have succeeded in your venture: a pragmatic success. The goal had some particular definition (to get a machine to function), but success itself was not the goal of the action. It was, rather, one outcome of the endeavour, the desired one. We want to succeed, we fear failure, we admire and sometimes envy those who succeed. But rather than being a goal, something we aim at, success is something we hope for. The goal is defined together with the specific means by which we can achieve it. This is the structure of rational action, and certainly the goal-defined action is not merely a hope that things will turn out well. So we should not try to comprehend success itself under the heading of 'rational action.' There are many phenomena in our life connected with success – ambition, competition, personal fulfilment, and such things as wealth and property. I suspect many of them have received more attention from philosophers than the present topic, but this one may have implications for those other matters as well.

Lying beyond various pragmatic successes is professional success. A manufacturer of computer printers who establishes a successful company will certainly have had many pragmatic successes (with this machine and that one), but professional success is not the mere sum of many pragmatic successes. It is a status attained by the self. Indeed, to 'be' a manufacturer at all, i.e., to have such a company, already signifies considerable success, which we may call basic. And to be a 'successful' manufacturer of computer printers signifies even more: for instance, to have prevailed in competition with business rivals, which we might call enhanced professional success. We can treat educational success as one branch of basic professional success. When somebody is a doctor or lawyer at all, that indicates the successful completion of a course of study.

Iacocca had his initial success in raising Ford's car and truck sales during the early years of his employment (pp. 30–40), and this fits our description of a pragmatic success: the goal was set (increased sales), and he was able to ensure that it was accomplished, and his narrative tells us how it was done. Success of this description is not one of the ends aimed at in action, not like wealth or power. Certainly, increase of motor sales was a good thing, and in succeeding as he did Iacocca accomplished something good, the matter or the cause in which he succeeded. But he could not aim just to succeed: it had to be success in some cause. His actions expressed his intention, but the success of the venture was not a part of the action, nor even part of the linkage connecting the intention to the goal: it lay outside that linkage. Expressions like 'aiming for success' or 'he intended to succeed' are perfectly acceptable in speech but are misleading philosophically because of leaving out the pragma, the particular venture in which the agent hopes for success. Aiming to increase sales and profits, and hoping for success in increasing them, expresses the matter more accurately.

Hope is one kind of care or concern that we have about the matter at hand. Instead of saying that Iacocca aimed to succeed, or intended to succeed, then, we say that he cared about success. And because hope and care are not rational intentions, it is preferable to say that success is an item of care rather than an object of care. Success, understood strictly, does not belong within the nexus that links an intention to its goal, and so the care about success also lies outside that linkage. Care is not an intention, but a movement of our being or existence. The rational thinking that posits a particular goal does not first constitute the care we have for our success. Care about our success is the broader context in which this or that practical action finds its place. We can put the point equally well in active or passive locutions: that he is concerned about success, or that success concerns him.

Now: basic professional success. In 1956 Iacocca was promoted to Ford's marketing division in Detroit and moved up quickly to become manager of the whole division (p. 46); the next part of the tale recounts how he became president of the whole corporation by 1970 (p. 92); we keep our attention fixed on the shifting phenomena of success that appear here. The incremental successes that Iacocca enjoyed brought an incremental magnifying of himself as measured by the increased scope of his authority and the usual signs of clout and status. Anybody who becomes the manager even of a division in such a large company has already succeeded: here it is the idea of professional success (not merely pragmatic) that has entered. Nothing is clearer than that Iacocca himself was always reaching. There is a reaching or a stretching that informs being a manager – a futural aspect, the effort of continuing to be a manager. Being a manager means *having* to be a manager. Just as an airplane requires the continual expenditure of energy in order to stay in the air, so being a manager is a project, an undertaking that requires active self-projection into the work that lies ahead. Since an anticipation of continuing day by day to manage the plant is required of anyone who *is* a manager, we can say that being a manager is an *ability* to be one. You extend your scope into the future and into the past as surely as being in the present. This is the 'stretch,' the stretching or self-extending of being into the possible, for which Heidegger used the Greek term *ekstasis* (standing out).

Iacocca succeeded again: his first major triumph as manager was to introduce the popular Mustang in 1964. This of course opened further horizons (see p. 78). Especially it renewed his focus on himself. This predominates especially in the futural direction of his existence.

In those days I was in a mad rush to the top ... I wanted the presidency badly, and I didn't agree that I had much left to learn. As saw it, I had been exposed to every test the company had to offer. And I had passed each one with flying colors. (p. 88)

So he was already a success before this, professionally successful: it was not merely the sales that succeeded – the manager has succeeded. Now the enhanced degree of professional success is at hand.

The enhanced success that Iacocca wanted was, however, not truly a goal of action. What is the motivation for success? What did this success have to offer Iacocca? Why did he reach? Why did he care? There are several occasions where he refers to this. Let us note what he says of the main crisis in his professional life: his painful struggles with Henry Ford and the governors of the corporation – why didn't he quit? (p. 120). He finds a mixture of reasons:

I enjoyed being president. I liked having the president's perks, the special parking place, the private bathroom, the white-coated waiters ... And I found it almost impossible to walk away from an annual income of $970,000 ... (p. 121)

Yet this matter is unclear, complex, ambiguous!

I've never had any qualms about getting a high salary. I'm not a big spender, but I appreciate the achievement a high salary represents. Why does a guy want to be president? Does he enjoy it? Maybe, but it can make him old and tired. So why does he work so hard? So he can say: 'Hey, I made it to the top. I accomplished something.' (p. 146)

Care is not to be understood as pre-eminently a goad to action. There is something more primordial: a care for the self. Our being concerns us (or, we are concerned about it). In almost every life, this concern is concretized in a form such as we noted in Iacocca's text: being the president. It can also be concretized as 'being a success.' This care or concern about being always incorporates an understanding of being, informal to be sure, e.g., an understanding of myself as a capable president. Did he have the ability to be president? Such a concern brings a retrospective appraisal of himself to see what strengths he may have brought with him into the corporation.

But what awaited Iacocca now was an even greater measure of success, a mega-success that shifted into outright celebrity. He was fired by Henry Ford, but his response was to move to Chrysler, at that time a failing company, and to raise the company virtually from the dead. In the course of the rescue operation, his dealings with many banks became so intricate that they afforded material for the daily papers and led him into memorable appearances before congressional committees. He appeared in *New Yorker* cartoons. He began to star in Chrysler's TV commercials. Now a celebrity, he is stopped everywhere on the street, and he can never dine quietly in a restaurant. Finally, President Reagan entrusts him with the project of renovating the Statue of Liberty, and he publishes his autobiography. He does comment on his new status with some irony:

> I certainly like being recognized for what I've done, but I'm always being reminded that my fame has little to do with my accomplishments. Am I famous for the Mustang? For guiding Ford through the most profitable years in its history? For having turned around Chrysler? It's a hell of a note, but I have a feeling I'm going to be remembered only for my TV commercials. Oh, that cursed tube! (p. 273)

Mega-success like this was not something he had sought, and perhaps, I suppose, he had not hoped for it either. But it was not distasteful to him, and in a moment we may inquire just what it meant to him. First, though, how are we to understand it? What does celebrity consist of?

The talk-show host or hostess, and the news anchor, are professional celebrities in that their métier is television itself – they themselves are perpetually displayed in the course of exercising the very function of displaying everything. If one of them makes an appearance at the local supermarket, they bring television's glamour into live presence in a space that beforehand had no glamour. But when a successful politician or author or scientist or business tycoon appears regularly on television, he or she is gaining exposure, which is something more than mere display. There is some work or achievement that gains exposure through their appearances: Iacocca is a 'somebody,' like Einstein, more so than the television host who interviews him. Bringing forth into the display his earlier successes – pragmatic, professional, financial – his appearance is now the very apotheosis of success itself,[6] mega-success. His fame rests upon his considerable achievements, an aspect of success to which we shall proceed a bit later on.

His celebrity status augments the status of 'being a success,' so that the self exists now in an even more magnified form. The words of the successful celebrity count for more than the words of others – Iacocca's book, a by-product of his celebrity, was studied by the ambitious, and the broad public drank in his words. His appearance in a restaurant attracts everyone's attention, so that patrons pay less heed to one another than they do to him. Knowing that he will appear on TV, people tune in, delighting just in having seen him, and when they tell others about the appearance they shine in his reflected light. And the self becomes magnified through other means as well: through great wealth and other possessions, through political influence, through influence in the industry. All this affords scope for action that is not open to other people.

This magnified self enjoys a magnified being or existence. We see here a signifying power of success and celebrity, reaching beyond all limited pragmatic and professional contexts. If wealth is among other things a signifier of success, still, success itself must be understood as a signifier of something else as well. It is not easy to differentiate some 'substantial' character of success from its signifying function. Yes, the success of Iacocca is a signifier of his considerable achievements, but there is more. I think this further meaning can be approached in a neo-Weberian way.

Weber's original thesis[7] was that those who followed the Calvinist religions built up their wealth and 'magnitude' as a consequence of a religious conviction. The accumulation of wealth and power that followed from their 'worldly asceticism' was taken as the sign of God's good favour, giving visible evidence of their membership in the elect destined for a heavenly salvation. Of course, Weber recognized that the specific content of this theology had tended to fade from view during the nineteenth century, but he maintained that the formal structure remained intact in modern capitalism, especially in the American version. And I believe that it is manifest in certain portions of Iacocca's book, so that his modern American success story took its essential plot from an older tradition. Owing to his celebrity, he was appointed by President Reagan to oversee the restoration of the Statue of Liberty and Ellis Island in New York City. He recounts both his work and the deeper emotions awakened in him by this project, restoring 'the Great Lady' and Ellis Island, the signifiers of America and the greatness of its mission.

> The island was part of my being – not the place itself, but what it stood for and how tough an experience it was. But my getting involved in the restoration of these two great symbols is more than just a memorial to my par-

ents. I, too, can identify with their experience ... the Statue of Liberty is just that – a beautiful symbol of what it means to be free. The reality is Ellis Island. Freedom is just the ticket of admission, but if you want to survive and prosper, there's a price to pay ... I go back to what my parents taught me. Apply yourself. Get all the education your can, but then, by God, *do* something! ... [I]t's amazing how in a free society you can become as great as you want to be. And, of course, also be grateful for whatever blessings God bestows on you. (pp. 339–41)

He has not talked much hitherto about his parents or God or America or freedom. These are things to which he is ultimately committed, which endow his life of successes with a transcendent meaning, a secular religion. The form of this meaning is Weberian. All the achievements and successes of his life have bestowed a magnitude upon him. Now this Statue of Liberty experience places him in the succession to all his ancestors, to all the immigrant Americans, and especially his mother and father. He shares in the blessings of God and freedom and America, and now it is clear that all his early successes and his present magnitude were the signs of being singled out for his place in that succession. His magnitude is now the proof that his very existence, or being, is *justified*: claiming its just place within the aspirations of his predecessors and the blessing of God.

A bit of caution is called for with respect to this last point. It emerged from a study of just one book about just one life and could not reasonably be extended to cover every candidate for success. The other matter, however – magnifying – would appear to pertain intimately to success itself, across the board.

Our study indicates that the meaning of success is, first of all, that it accomplishes a direct magnification of the self, endowing one with power, wealth, and repute. It is possible to add to this that the subject's life and existence are magnified, insofar as his words and presence now count for more than those of other people: he has more right to be heard, more right to be admired, emulated, and obeyed. And this has a further, indirect effect, the signifying of a possible justification of one's life or existence. This justification, however, is entirely subjective in the sense we mentioned in chapter 1, in that he sought to become justified through magnifying himself, and found his self-justification in that direction. But it is impossible to hold that someone's life is objectively justified through success and magnitude.

The book we have been reviewing gives us insight into what success, in all its levels, meant to the author Iacocca. But our topic, the meaning of success, must also encompass what success (as in his case) meant to everybody else who saw him or read his book, those who are not particularly successful themselves. Our devotion to celebrities is not an identification with them, for their very magnitude is what we worship, a factor that marks them off from ourselves. The radiance of their magnitude is akin to that of divinity, in that it reaches down upon us, not to make us great ourselves but to bestow on us, however briefly, an aura that can seem to justify our lives, a peak experience that tells us we have at least encountered something great.

This at least is part of the effect of Iacocca. But there is another response that counts for at least as much in our lives: people are frequently discouraged and dismayed by the display of other people's successes. What de Botton points out, however, following Hume,[8] is that we take in our stride the magnificence of those who are far, far beyond us in wealth and celebrity, like Iacocca, so that it can entertain us. It is when those who are or were close to us have surpassed us in success and achievement that we become oppressed and discouraged by the gap. 'Exposure to the superior achievements of those whom we take to be our equals ... generates anxiety and resentment' (p. 26). For de Botton, status anxiety is virtually a universal affliction, for it drives not only the responses of those who are left behind or who fear being left behind, but is just as powerfully at work in those who have succeeded, driving them to seek continually to succeed further. Above all it is manifested in those he calls snobs, who may or may not be successful themselves, but who are 'offended by a lack of high status in others' (p. 76). His chapter on snobbery aims to show how it is sustained by one's memory of the pain and anxiety that one has suffered at the hands of other snobs. So de Botton does not offer different motivations for the different groups (high-fliers, low achievers, and snobs), but finds a common aetiology in the conditions of life in modern society (meritocracy and high economic expectations), and above all in the emotional deprivation that is common in our age, an insufficiency of being loved. Remembering our mothers' love for us, we barely recover from the shock of the chilly climate in most adult experience. This brings him close to Adler's focus on the inferiority complex.

Failure

In our everyday understanding of things, success and failure are alternative outcomes of an undertaking, so we need some observations about failure. This polarity is most commonly understood, I suppose, to apply in the pragmatic domain: in attempting to repair a printer, we may succeed or we may fail. But though such concepts may apply in the pragmatic sphere, we are concerned here with an existential understanding of failure and its relation to success, i.e., our own failure and success, thinking of failure and success as possibilities for ourselves, that is to say as items of concern. We have at least three kinds of concern, and all of them can be identified as abilities: we are concerned not to fail (for the ability to avoid failure); we are concerned with how to endure failure (for the ability to endure it); and we are concerned to understand failure (for the ability to understand it), a concern that pertains to us now as philosophers.

We shall look more into the experiences of educational failure and professional failure – and into the question whether there is such a thing as being a failure *tout court*, some kind of counterpart of mega-success. For a start, it should be clear that professional failure is something more drastic than simply lack of professional success. There is a wide spectrum of experience that might fall short of success (an intermediate state that holds true for most people), but here failure means such things as bankruptcy, conviction for embezzlement or malpractice, being fired with no alternative prospects. The majority of those who cannot claim enhanced professional success or even basic professional success are not judged to be 'failures,' but what this point puts clearly before us is that the entire matter is one that calls for judgment. Any judgment of failure is unclear and questionable, and perhaps the only clear judgment would be the one that each of us makes about himself or herself.

The media do not bestow as much attention on failure as they do on success, but we have a vast documentation from fiction and dramas (e.g., *Death of a Salesman*), and nowadays from documentary books containing the record of the authors' own failures. I'll refer to a couple of journalists who have written about their fall from grace after their reportage was exposed as fraudulent, especially the book by Jayson Blair, formerly of *The New York Times*. Another case is that of Glass,[9] but here the story has been fictionalized so it is less forthcoming regarding his own motivations and experiences.

Blair's book appeared in 2004 in response to a scandal that had broken a year earlier. On 11 May 2003 the *New York Times* published a lengthy front-page story: *'Times* Reporter Who Resigned Leaves Long Trail of Deception,' detailing Blair's journalistic abuses over the previous months. It alleged thirty-six cases of deceptive reporting, concentrating especially on three of them: in a case of snipers in the Washington area in October 2002, Blair fabricated interviews with law enforcement officials; he wrote up supposed interviews with wounded veterans at Bethesda, Maryland, in April 2003 whom he had never visited; around the same time he plagiarized the story of a soldier missing in action from a newspaper in San Antonio, Texas. We learn from Blair's own book how he had succeeded up to then in deceiving his editors and colleagues in New York about these and other stories. He had secured information and photos through computer networks; he falsified travel records; he used telephone connections to make it seem that he was in Maryland or Texas when he was actually in his Brooklyn apartment. His book begins with the period in spring 2003, just when his superiors were uncovering his deceptions and calling him to account, particularly for the three stories mentioned above, and he was forced to admit his deceptions. The book then records how the *Times* story of 11 May exposed him to full public view, and how the scandal was taken up gleefully by other news organizations and TV networks. Though he tried to cover himself in further media interviews, every step he took only increased his disgrace, and we read what it was like to have a nervous breakdown (pp. 20–49), what it was like to read about himself in the press and see his picture all over New York City and around the world right over to China (pp. 52–64). Only after that does he go back to tell us how he first came to commit the deceptions and frauds. This way of composing the story permits us to follow, after the firing and after the nervous breakdown, what his calamity was like. Although we already know that he broke the rules and was then discovered and fired, we live through with him the experience of being publicly exposed and disgraced.

Blair begins the narrative with an abject confession: 'I lied and I lied – and then I lied some more. I lied about where I had been, I lied about where I had found information, I lied about how I wrote the story' (p. 1). The book continues with the firing, and the nervous breakdown he experienced.

> I walked in, shut the door to the bathroom, and stared into the mirror. I cannot remember what I saw; I was just thinking that I was tired, so tired, but not in the way one gets tired when they are annoyed or frustrated or physically exhausted. I was tired in the way one gets when they are done, when there is no more fight in them, when the numbness gives way to a feeling of total loss, to nothing but blackness. I remember seeing darkness,

I remember it enveloping me, and I remember giving in wholly, finding comfort in its lack of questions for me, its lack of disappointment, its lack of emotions. In a quick flash, I saw an image of myself hanging from the door hinge, the life gone out of me, the pain dissipated. There was no pleasure or joy in this image, but simply relief. (p. 20)

It is then, beginning in chapter 6, that he tells the fuller story of his life prior to the *Times*, and his career there over a period of four years. There is a lot of reflection on being black; there is a lot of whisky and cocaine all over New York, and a lot of anonymous sex as well as a relationship with one woman that seems to have survived it all: the book is dedicated to her. After many chapters on fairly routine stories in New York, we read of the first case in which he fabricated a story, on p. 181, one week after the airplane assault on the World Trade Center on 11 September 2001. The paper was packed full of terrorism stories and Blair was 'so desperate to get into the paper that I took the assignment to interview [some stock brokers]' and fabricated an interview with a made-up broker's name. He succeeded: this was his first *Times* by line. The circumstances of this kind of deed are those of the Age of Success. Dozens of bright young interns are hired every year by news organizations, hoping for major success: prominent by lines, a growing reputation, star status. The temptations are great.

In context, Blair emphasizes his excesses of whisky and drugs at the time, but he also begins to emphasize more and more the bipolar disorder he suffered from, background for those excesses and perhaps for the onset of his frauds. He also intimates that he had suffered from sexual abuse, of an unspecified nature, during his childhood. Now we begin to read of other frauds, and now he is on occasion tripped up by his errors. An editor suspected, correctly, that Blair had been drunk when he included false details about a benefit concert (pp. 198–9), and the paper had to issue a later correction.

The concluding chapters of Blair's book treat the three major fabrications of his last months, on the snipers, the veterans, and the plagiarism case. They are what finally pulled him down, and the measure of his failure was that he pulled down with him two of the most senior editors of the *Times*, Howell Raines and Gerald Boyd, as well as his own girlfriend, Zuza Glowacka. More and more, he dwells on his mental disorder and the old sexual abuse, searching, it seems, for causes of his behaviour. He speaks of his being withdrawn, dissociated, and even psychotic (pp. 278, 280, 287). But our concern in the present inquiry is not with the aetiology of Blair's behaviour, but what meaning he is assigning to his own failure by way of his written text. The impression conveyed by the final six chapters is a blur of uncoordinated activity. He is working on one story from his apartment, then he switches to another, then he is sick for two days, then he seems to have blacked out, without memories; then he sends in one story, and he tries to arrange for the correct dateline for another; then ... etc. There are no means and ends; everything is chaotic. I do not think this impression of aimlessness arises because of the *writing* at this point in the book; rather, the writing conveys truly the sense of a *life* lurched beyond aims and goals. The story concludes as he is summoned to the meeting with his supervisor that precedes the end of his *Times* career.

The existential truth about failure is not some final state called 'failure' – it is the very process of failing and living through that, which in this case meant living in a kind of temporality where goals had disappeared from life. The book does not try to justify his existence, and when he invokes mental illness and substance abuse, they do not appear as excuses. He does at times ascribe blame to some individuals, but only in passing, and they are not blamed for the frauds he perpetrated. The theme of race is a constant undercurrent, perhaps growing more prominent as we approach the end, but what is most notable on this point is Blair's interest, not in his own case, but in the experiences of certain *other* black men, notably the chief of police in the sniper case, and especially the juvenile accused in the sniper case.

> I identified with Malvo's apparent detachment and disillusionment, not excusing his actions, but fuelling a desire to understand him more. My other biases were that I identified with his anger and questioned the ethical notion of executing juveniles. (p. 258)

> It became clear that he was, unfortunately, no aberration in his family. He was the latest in a long line of intelligent malefactors – victims of racism, circumstance and shattered dreams, and perpetrators of crime. I wondered whether there was a connection, whether the roots of how it had ended for all of them could be found in the unique history of American slavery. (p. 273)

It seems that the theme of chaos and failure came to preoccupy Blair as he lurched through his own chaos and failure.

Educational failure is another pointer to the very process of failing as it is experienced existentially. In the midst of writing an exam (as I think we can all remember) there is the realization 'I'm failing this! I cannot remember the formulas!' This is quite a different thing from the judgment that you might render about someone's apparent 'failure' in business or in family life. There you only contemplate the end-state, failure, rather than the process, and that makes your judgment external and very fallible. But a first-person narrative such as Blair's brings the lived experience close to us, that I am failing and am continuing to fail.

There is a yoke between the current experience and the projected end-state, the failure that I am anticipating, and this yoke is the very structure of existence itself, as we described it in chapter 2 above: standing-out beyond yourself, standing out – towards an expected end. Except that this end is not really an end. Failing an exam is one of the dismal steps in failing a course, which is one of the steps in failing your degree, which is one of the reasons why you will not qualify in your desired profession. The history I am sketching here is the history of the process of failing. Blair made us acquainted with the business of continuing to fail. If there is an end-state, complete and decisive failure, that does not prevent a continuing progress towards that end-state: it is the sickness unto death that is never ended by an actual death. In the fevered mind, no doubt, there is an end-state: complete and unqualified failure. But that end-state is projected in the process of continual failing – it is not an ending of the process.

This brings us then to the question whether there exists a polar opposite to the superstar status we call celebrity. Does this 'end-state,' failure, exist? Is there such a thing as being a failure absolutely, being a worthless bum? Certainly we can say that, if there is such a thing, it must be conditioned by all the other kinds of failure, pragmatic, educational, and professional. We said that it was always a matter of judgment to determine failure, especially professional failure: it is never a self-evident fact. So the same thing would have to hold for being a failure. On what evidence, then, would we judge that someone had so calamitously failed in all respects that he or she could claim to be nothing more than a failure, a bum? Perhaps we do pass a judgment like that on someone that we see across the street, an unshaven panhandler with a bottle of cheap wine in his pocket. I warned against external and inaccurate judgments concerning someone else's failure – we do not judge it rightly when we take it for a end-state. It is the process of failing – the approach towards the end-state, even if the approach be never ending – that is the reality here. We do not often listen to the tales of the old pan-handlers that we meet on the street. If we do not, then we do not share in their truth, that failure is never more than the process of moving towards failure. And it seems clear from his that we cannot take failure as an indication that this existence is without justification. It would seem rather that the only one whom I am in a position to call a failure is myself.

This study has been an attempt to fulfil one of the existential concerns we have – the ability to understand failure. But now we have the opportunity to discuss another concern: do we have the ability to endure failure? Is there such a thing as the ability to fail? Since every worthwhile undertaking is one that might succeed or fail, the agent prepares himself or herself for failure. Since we are finite, all our ability is shadowed by inability, so that we can fail, meaning that we might be unable to avoid failure. On a small scale, this is the replica of our finite ability to be: for what is always possible for us is death, our possible inability to be. The experience of failing is to grasp failure as the imminent possibility, with little hope of the ability to avoid it. In this experience there is the projection of the end-state, failure; and with this appears the possible ability to endure the failure. Now, there can be an agent who is not prepared to accept failure under any circumstances, for whom existence without success is unthinkable. Through this insistent resolve, the agent is actually occluding an important facet of his or her existence. Recoiling from possible failure, insistent that life is possible only given success (and achievement!), the agent believes that success alone will equip him or her for being. Often we say that a young person is well equipped for success through happy circumstances in his or her young life. But the agent we are talking about here sees things the other way around: he or she considers that success alone could equip one for life, that a life without success is no life at all. But the contrary disposition incorporates the ability to fail (which is not the same as the pursuit of failure), and it will disclose to us much more completely the diverse possibilities for our existence.

Achievement

Iacocca's success story also indicated another element: throughout the book there are copious references to 'achievements' or 'accomplishments,' and it seems at times that they fulfil a standard that is something other than straight success, perhaps more important than it. Admittedly the distinction is not regularly expressed in these words. He refers at times to the 'achievements' of others (for example, Robert McNamara, p. 44, and Walter Chrysler, p. 149), at times to his own 'accomplishments,' though at other times he seems prepared to use the term 'successes' in that very same way (pp. 78, 223). Is there a genuine distinction here, whether or not Iacocca recognized it?

While pragmatic success has an objective character, a professional success may be attributed to 'office politics,' 'pull,'[10] or spurious reputation. But Iacocca, like many another, is saying in his story: 'I made my way on my own merits; I introduced the Mustang; I saved Chrysler Corporation' – his professional success therefore meeting a standard of objectivity just as in any pragmatic success. Achievements seem to be introduced as the legitimating factor that underlies his success, giving it authenticity.

Recognition and publicity are necessary parts of professional success – indeed, the successful seem often to be clamorous in calling attention to themselves. That very point is why we are investigating success as a strategy of self-magnifying. And in that proclamation what is usually uppermost is the claim to achievement. The most vociferous boasting can have the effect of awakening doubt and criticism in those who are forced to listen to it, and what they doubt sometimes are the boastful claims to great achievement. Here it is a kind of critical use of reason that we employ, looking for signs of genuine achievement. Of course it happens that persons of the highest and most impeccable achievements are as prone to boasting as those who have accomplished objectively very little in their professional life. Heidegger's section 38 in *SZ*, called 'Ambiguity,' has this as its main topic: the subtlety of differentiating a genuine accomplishment from something commonplace, however widely proclaimed. This is directly connected to section 35, *die Gerede*, that deals with the gossip and chatter whereby we elevate ourselves and set out to put others down. In extreme cases of the most intolerable boasting, we find the subject grounding his very existence on his achievements, virtually infinitizing the self. Our social rules may operate to discourage excessive boasting about one's achievements, but such etiquette has no sanctions to impose on the excesses of self-esteem in the privacy of one's own opinions. By contrast with such persons, the wealthy playboy has this to be said for him, that he does not weary us with his boasting.

To recognize an achievement is itself an achievement, for the achievement may or may not have the adornment of success, highlighted with publicity and acclaim. Above I spoke of the critical reasoning that we are inclined to exercise when we are exposed to someone's boasting. In fact, it is only because of a rational faculty that we are able to discern achievement at all – discerning its reality behind the clamour of success. The rational discernment of some achievement looks at the work outside of its relation to acclaim. It regards the work, not in relation to the public, nor in relation to the agent or producer, but rather in relation to the state of the world prior to the work at hand. If to build the Mustang was an achievement, that means that the world in advance of the Mustang was lacking. There was in the public a need for the kind of car that Iacocca then produced. Likewise, if a given work of art or a given book is appraised as an achievement, that means that all the prior works of art, or all the prior books, were in some way incomplete and in need precisely of the completion brought by this work that is now at hand. This discernment is rightly called an exercise of reason, I believe, because reason is the faculty by which we posit and understand the grounds (or reasons) of a phenomenon. It sees the justification for the work. And the acclaim that heralds a successful product and a successful manager is set aside for the purpose of a rational appraisal of an achievement.

The temporal horizon for achievements is quite different from that of successes. Since the appraisal of an achievement sets it over against all preceding (or possible) works of the same general type – the world would be lacking without it – it is in the broad horizon of world history that the achievement takes its place. The Mustang stands in the succession of the Model A, the Daimler, the Rolls-Royce, the great sports cars. We attribute the achievement to the manager and his co-workers, but personalities are not of ultimate importance in our recognition of an achievement. How, then, does success relate to achievement?

Success appears to have a dialectical involvement with it. There is a questionable character of success itself pure and simple, cases of success that may not be deserved, and other cases in which the success appears to be well grounded, well deserved. The cases of successful achievement are those in which the success itself is justified. A deeper-lying factor provides the success with its own justification. Sometimes this is clearly differentiated from success, sometimes not. These reflections lead into a complex situation. People seem to claim successes as giving a point and lustre to their lives, and they claim credit for them. But it is achievement that constitutes the grounding legitimation for success. Achievement is only discerned by a historical appraisal that leaves the producer or agent largely out of account. This has the odd result that we care about our successes, but, believing more strictly that it is only achievements that matter, we come to feel that it's wrong for someone to claim credit for either the success or the achievement.

It is certainly possible for someone to pursue greatness in some field – literary, athletic, etc. – with the hope that high achievement will justify his or her life; this is the idea that one's life will be essentially wasted without such achievement. As I pointed out before, it is common for persons of very high achievements to spend most of their conversation boasting about them – the sign that they have found a justification for their lives in these achievement. It is common too for other people to envy them and compare their own modest accomplishments with those of the paragon, acknowledging that this other life has truly justified itself. Nevertheless, the foregoing analysis points to a different conclusion. It is just the success that is justified by the achievement, not the life itself, and here 'justify' means as much as 'authenticate.' To say that a life is 'justified' through its achievements has no grounding according to this analysis.

But there is a second relationship we must note. Where someone's achievements are of a high order, we can say that this outcome has justified all the hard years of labour lying behind it; and that the person has 'more than justified' all the hopes and the expectations of his or her parents and teachers. What we have here is the 'economic' concept of justification that will be more fully discussed in chapter 4. An investment of time or money is seen to be justified by a rich pay-off – and so it is with labours and hopes as well: they become justified in retrospect by the achievement. Here there is a comparability of what becomes justified (labour and sweat; hopes and aspirations) and that which does the justifying (the achievements that are readily visible). We cannot endorse going beyond that to claim that an existence or a life could become justified in this way. We know that some of those whose achievements are of a high order do not spend their time boasting about them, and we can infer from this that they do not regard their achievements as having 'justified their existence.' Actually, there are several possible ways in which such people can differ from those who boast.

One way is an attitude of strict rationality: since it is only achievement that counts, all success is in principle despised. In this view, the dividing line between achievement and success is more or less absolute. Success is a matter for vulgar crowds to worship on television; it is the discerning few who recognize true achievement. In the hauteur of some senior common rooms, the very publicity of the world of success more or less qualifies everything successful as mediocre.

Another attitude is marked by irony. Someone who has had significant achievements, and enjoyed as well a certain amount of public acclaim, may smile ruefully whenever his works are praised or recognized. 'Yes indeed, they just keep piling these honorary degrees on me!' Someone who is as superb as that – diminishing the honours that most of the world holds dear – is as much a dissembler as a cleric or monk who is constantly lamenting his sinfulness: 'I am such a reprobate!' We know that this gesture is insincere, for the effect of it is to give you the impression that you are in the presence of a saint. And the academic ironist, appearing to disclaim both the honours and the achievements they recognize, has calculated carefully that most of his hearers have comparatively little to boast of.

Is it possible to hit upon a satisfactory balance between achievement and success? Authors and artists who are conscious of their achievements can certainly be gratified as well by some degree of (popular) success.[11] The critic who praises an achievement does not need to ignore and despise success. An author can be embarrassed by a success that is disproportionate to his or her achievement, but may enjoy the success just the same. One can be disappointed when a major achievement is greeted with indifference, but memories of past successes can be consoling. Perhaps the salutary effect of popular failure and indifference is the reminder it brings of the limits of any given achievement. These are some of the ways in which success (or its absence) is intertwined with achievement (or its absence), positive relations that surmount every priggish discounting of success in the name of pure achievement. Here we can draw upon the memoirs of Laurence Olivier for an illustration of their positive relationship, even where their difference is recognized.

Olivier's autobiography[12] conveys right from the beginning the atmosphere of superstardom and celebrity. There are some early passages about hard work, being exploited, and being out of money – yet these anecdotes are all set in the theatre where glamorous people are coming and going and often noticing the young Olivier favourably (see pp. 37–8, 50–1, 62–5, featuring Elsie Fogerty, Sybil Thorndike, and Noel Coward). His own star is ascending, and we know it will culminate in his opening of Britain's National Theatre and his being inducted into the House of Lords. Olivier's book does not divide his personal life from his professional life in the way that Iacocca's did. All Olivier's marriages and affairs were intertwined with his theatre business, and the outline of the book is framed essentially by his three marriages, all to star actresses with whom he played: Jill Esmond, Vivien Leigh, and Joan Plowright. There is not the slightest trace here of either the Protestant ethic or the spirit of capitalism, but a great deal of ecstasy, betrayal, love, and heartbreak.

Throughout the book, he shows that he is aware of his own extraordinary success as an actor, and his most constant refrain, which is convincing, is the extraordinary good luck that seemed to smile on him:

> From the last half of 1960 onwards life took on a pattern which, if it were not for my unbelieving gratefulness, might read like a steady crescendo of happiness and success, in danger of becoming tedious in its concern to avoid boastfulness on the one hand and a blasé nonchalance on the other. (p. 233)

> How lucky can you be? In mere gratitude I was bound to keep gloating upon my wonderful fortune: a new home life [with Joan Plowright] and a new profession [director of the Chichester Festival Theatre], at my time of life [mid-fifties]. (p. 239)

The present chapter has been exploring the relationship between achievement and success on the assumption that they are distinct from each other. But in the performing arts these two factors, while they are distinct, cannot be separated. The judgments rendered by theatre critics aim generally to identify genuine achievement (in writing and production and performance) and, like all actors, Olivier was intensely aware of critics (pp. 66, 70, 114), who treated him very well on the whole. But the nature of theatre means that success cannot be set to one side in a critical judgment. A show that was never applauded could hardly be esteemed an achievement. In the theatre, the success of the show is one part of the achievement. Olivier's career offered abundant occasions in which achievement and success were realized together:

> We opened *Private Lives* at the King's Theatre, Edinburgh; then in London we opened a brand new theatre, the Phoenix, which was a special distinction, and I experienced for the first time the incredible sense of being in a West End smash success – the thronged stage door and the parties almost every night. (pp. 83–4)

Obviously, this does not detract from the labours, the professionalism, and the skill that go into a production and valorize the achievement. Olivier recounts his labours in acquiring accents (pp. 66, 180–1), the physical risks he took on stage and screen (pp. 127–30, 151–4), and the sheer expense of energy in playing a major role (p. 274), and he records a lot of his failures (pp. 45–6, 70). These are the pragmatic successes and failures that underlie a successful career, even one that is to be blessed with extraordinary 'luck,' the success surely justified by the achievements in diction, characterization, stage business, and the like.

It is only the relationship between Olivier's theatrical achievement and his theatrical success that concerns us here, not the darker currents of his personal life: marriages, rivalries, and the brooding sense of guilt, selfishness, or even sin that hangs over these pages. By contrast with this multihued self-portrait, Iacocca's book seems one dimensional. It was quite fitting for Olivier, the parson's son, to open and close his book with a petition for forgiveness, taking his title of 'Confessions' quite literally. These deeper currents were at work in the life that was filled with so much success and achievement. Again we can confirm that, however greatly success and achievement magnify someone's life, they do not justify it.

Magnifying the Self and Magnifying Its Being

We conclude the chapter with a focus on a highly salient philosophical point. At the end of our account of the meaning of success, we found that it was not merely the self or ego of the successful person that was magnified, but his or her being or way of being. His or her words and presence count for more than others' do; the celebrity has scope for action that lesser beings do not. This is in keeping with the fact that the initial drive for success was a movement of care, a movement of one's being, not an ordinary goal-directed action. And the further possibility opened by success, certainly by celebrity, was a justification of one's being, even if only subjective, as we saw in the case of Iacocca's mission to restore the Statue of Liberty.

Achievement lends authentication to the magnitude associated with success. And, as in the theatre, it is not to be separated entirely from success itself. Those who discount acclaim or treat it with irony are not entirely forthright. So the achievement that gives grounding to success is a factor in the magnification of the self and its being. Still, it is clear that achievement does not constitute a justification of one's life, or one's being; the reason this is so clear is that the appraisal of an achievement is always rational and objective. We saw, however, that there is a very limited sense – we'll call it 'economic' – in which an achievement justifies all the efforts that led to it and all the hopes of teachers and parents.

Though failure in the pragmatic domain can be called the opposite of success, this is not true in existence, because here the truth of failure is the continuing process of failing: no end-state is ever apparent. It can be true, subjectively, that one's life of failing seems to remove any justification of one's existence, but it can no more be true, objectively, that failing and failure deprive a life of justification than that success affords justification. Certainly, however, one's being is robbed of magnitude.

Magnitude pertains both to the self and its being. In this way, we rediscover the double value of *Da-sein*, for we have seen that ontically it means as much as 'self,' but that it has as well the ontological value of the being or existence of the self. *Da-sein*'s care is for magnitude and justification and intensity; in this chapter, at least, we have discovered magnitude at both levels, ontic and ontological. The later chapters of this book will be examining quite distinct phenomena – morality, nationalism, and so on – but there will be a common emphasis on the ontic and ontological dimensions: both the self and its being will be magnified and justified.

4 Justifying the Self

In this chapter, it is not the individual's worldly interests that concern us but the interior self-consciousness, where factors such as the moral law and moral guilt are at play. Certainly these are items of intense concern to every individual. The point of this study will not be to develop a moral theory, i.e., promote one kind of moral theory over others. My philosophical references will be to Kant, but his theory is not really under discussion.[1] Our topic is a difficulty that arises from putting morality into practice in existence, a difficulty that is not theoretical. So, even while I am quoting Kant, the points I make would apply to other moral theories too.

Let me begin with one situation involving moral consciousness. We may not always know how we acquired the moral precepts that we hold, nor even exactly what they are, especially if we experience some mental turmoil and conflict over this matter. But in any case, it is in the circumstances of actual life that our moral precepts become applied, and that we are put to the test. We may hold to the moral principle that we are required to be honest in speech, for instance, but our intention to be honest, and our wish to be recognized as honest, do not always result in our actually being honest. One thing this intention does, however, is make us alert to the possible dishonesty of others. An ambitious person in some organization may spread rumours about a rival's questionable practices ('Have you seen how his reports always inflate his figures?'), and he may try to ensure that the rumours reach the ears of the CEO. Then his rival, hearing of this, says it's all lies: the gossip is being spread because the other one is intriguing for a promotion. Each is accusing the other, not only of saying some dishonest thing, but of being dishonest through and through, and the issue of argument is not just one deed or assertion, but the moral standing of the two persons.

Both of them are engaged in justifying themselves, even as they try to make the other look bad. There are many encounters of this type, in which, seeking to justify our deeds, we are caught up in the effort to justify ourselves.

These appear to be odd and unwholesome applications of morality. What lies at their heart is not only that a justification of one of our deeds is intended to justify our person as a whole – it is also that accusing others becomes a means of vindicating ourselves. How does it come about that moral principles take on such questionable applications? In exploring this, I'll introduce such phenomena as moralism and self-righteousness. My purpose will not be to criticize one version of moral philosophy or to promote another version. Although I'll refer to Kant, it is not with the polemical intent that has animated some of his critics, but only to raise a question about the application of morality that arises with any moral theory. My example has illustrated one kind of self-justification that pervades the human scene: through being moralistic. But there are other ways too in which we seek to justify ourselves, and I'll introduce them as the study proceeds.

Morality

The domain of morality is the central one for an account of justification. The experience of having your successes justified by your achievements, or in a different way having your early labours and sacrifices justified by your achievements, or the self that celebrates its magnitude through its successes, or even finding your existence justified through participation in the projects of your nation – these experiences are not nearly as deep as that of someone seeking to become free from moral reproach. Using just a few points sketchily presented from Kant's moral theory, we shall be showing how the dimension of existence, i.e., the understanding of existence, accompanies our moral consciousness.

Kant's moral philosophy has usually been interpreted on the basis of the *Grounding for the Metaphysics of Morals* and the *Critique of Practical Reason*, texts that were oriented to the foundations of ethics and devoted comparatively little attention to the practical applications of morality, legislation, and moral instruction. Recently, more attention has been paid to the 1797 *Metaphysics of Morals* (MM).[2] This work often recurs to the foundations of morality,[3] and accordingly it reinscribes the supremacy of the categorical imperative: 'The supreme principle of the doctrine of morals is therefore: Act according to a maxim that can at the same time be valid as a universal law' (6:226). Nevertheless, it has as its main content the study of legislation in the first part, *The Doctrine of Right*, and the development of detailed moral principles in the second part, *The Doctrine of Virtue*. Kant proceeds deductively, showing that the pure, abstract, formal moral law, the categorical imperative, becomes realized in more specific maxims, which then for their part are realized in moral actions. We shall focus on the doctrine of virtue, not right, and look at one of the duties that, according to Kant, every person has towards others. Beneficence, *Wohltätigkeit*, is that practical duty we have towards others that is the outward expression of the inner maxim of benevolence, *Wohlwollen*, that we have the duty to cultivate, and that is derived from the categorical imperative. The practical duty of beneficence is 'the maxim of making others' happiness one's end, and the duty to it consists in the subject's being constrained by his reason to adopt this maxim as a universal law' (6:452). The formal rationality of the moral agent includes the provision that all other rational agents, actual or possible, would be constrained by this imperative.

Given that we have made this deduction, we can now declare that the maxim of benevolence and the practice of beneficence are virtuous and right, and that their contraries, misanthropy and selfishness, are wrong. The categorical imperative was only partly de-formalized in the maxim of benevolence and the injunction to beneficence. It has been made more specific, but of course when we try to practise beneficence, we need the occasion, the beneficiary, and the concrete deed of benefit to complete the de-formalizing. If we undertake to make charitable contributions, for instance, we need to choose which charity we should endow. The categorical imperative applies to the maxims that we follow in our deeds, but it is up to each individual, in his or her moral responsibility, to find the deed that will show forth the righteous maxim, the deed of true beneficence. To entertain the categorical imperative opens out a lengthy lifelong ordeal of submitting our inclinations and our maxims to a test of reason. The self projects its life far into the future, expecting in effect an infinity of moral situations and moral efforts, where there is required the unending pursuit of purity of heart, an infinite effort to subordinate the faculty of will to the categorical imperative. Kant himself foresaw this in the *Dialectic of Pure Practical Reason*, where not even one lifetime could suffice for the project of submitting the will to this demand. This was the basis on which he was prepared to accept the postulate of the immortality of the soul, but a more elementary point is that we must remain ignorant of our ultimate status in respect of morality. We can never know whether we have brought ourselves sufficiently in line with the moral law to regard ourselves as morally justified.

The Concept of Justification

There is a link between the concept of justification and the idea of reason. To justify a deed you cite a reason for it. Sometimes this is because it was criticized, though sometimes the moral agent will think the matter through autonomously. Deeds can be wrong for many reasons that we need not explore here, so that any agent is at risk of doing wrong. When the agent or a critical observer weighs the possible detriments of the action against the reasons for it, and finds that the reasons outweigh the detriments, the deed has been justified. This is where a moral theory can enter in, to define the kind of reasons that suffice in such a case. Justification proceeds by reasoning.

But there are cases in which the problem of justification reaches beyond reason. When we turn to the self as a whole, it becomes more difficult to see how justification proceeds: reason cannot function in the same way. Consider a situation in which the agent undertakes to justify himself, and not merely this deed or that: it could be that your criticism of some deed of mine is not confined to that single case, but challenges a whole pattern of such deeds, putting into question my entire character, i.e., myself. If I have a reply to the criticism it must be to show not only that this single deed was right, but that I was in the right, I am in the right. It will become clear that no claim to be personally justified, as a whole, could ever be based upon a summation of all the separate deeds and words that had their own justification in the past. If it has any basis at all, that must be something equally general.

One practice that shows up all too often in real life is to seek to show that others are at fault, justifying myself thereby: moralism and self-righteousness. Here it is yourself as a whole, or your whole life, or your whole community, that becomes the subject of justification, and not merely some single statement, some single deed, or some investment. The same point can be made about magnifying: as we saw in the introductory sketch of success, we hope to magnify our life as a whole.

Since it is not merely singular deeds or utterances that we justify, but the self itself and its existence, we recognize too that the impulse to justify does not merely arise on one occasion or another where a fault or defect needs apology. Justifying the self is an *a priori* disposition, rooted in our existence. We recognize, of course, that in particular instances some particular deed or utterance requires justification. Particular experiences like that fit within the *a priori* disposition. Existence is a system of experience, open to novel events.

In all these cases, justification is something for which we *hope*, seeking as we do for what might afford a justification for our existence.

And besides these studies of the competitive life of success, and community, and morality, we shall also look at a religious relationship to God in which devout people have found the justification for their lives. Indeed, the theological doctrine of justification is the very prototype of any investigation of the justification of the self or the person. Here the central idea of justification is not that our righteousness becomes revealed after all, i.e., that we are *shown* to be justified in our works and our being. That assumes an original righteousness that was shrouded or covered up in some way, that could now be revealed by reason. Rather, the theological idea is that we have been *made to be* righteous through a divine redemption, that the status of our being, originally that of sinners, has been altered through a divine decree.

Not only in the moral appraisal of deeds do we engage in justification. People make knowledge claims for which they can be held to account, and they must satisfy a questioning audience and justify the assertion. For the vindication of a knowledge claim we adduce grounds for the claim, or evidence. One application of logical justification is in legal reasoning in its formal or procedural character, when a judicial verdict is justified by the evidence. In the case of cognitive justification, our whole person is just as surely involved as in moral cases: where I am able to show that my claim is sound, I have also justified myself as an expert or anyway a well-informed person, at the very least no dummy. But it seems that to justify myself in this way also goes beyond the capacity of reason.

In another standard sense of justification, we say that our efforts, or our expenses, are justified by their results. One might have devoted great time and effort to building an organization, and then if the organization succeeds, all the effort is said to be justified. Nowhere is the concept better exemplified than in a risky investment that proves to be justified by the pay-off. This belongs to the concept of 'justify' because of the match of outcome to the effort, the efficient adjustment of means to end. We call this the 'economic' concept in a broad sense: it gives the answer to a doubter who might have claimed that the effort was a waste of time or the investment a waste of money.

Inauthenticity

Here I return to the theme of existence. I shall make the claim that the existing individual, in understanding the moral law, pushes it away from himself or herself. In the usual understanding of the moral law, the categorical imperative, it swerves away from myself. I grasp it primarily as applying to others. And it is the 'left-handed' side of the law that I elevate: my understanding is focused on what these others do that is wrong. This swerving is not a logical necessity implied by the moral law. But neither is it an accidental matter that just happens to occur to one individual or another. It arises from the circumstance that our existence is inauthentic. Here we are investigating a matter that Heidegger did not himself treat in *SZ*: the inauthentic understanding of the moral law. Although this is a different application from Heidegger's own, the very concept of authenticity remains the same.

Authenticity and inauthenticity are central possibilities within human existence, and, since existence is deeply integrated with understanding, we can clarify what authenticity is by starting from authentic understanding. This is well explained in section 31:

> Understanding can turn primarily to the disclosedness of the world, that is, *Da-sein* can understand itself initially and for the most part in terms of the world. Or else understanding throws itself primarily into the [ends of its own existence], which means *Da-sein* exists as itself. Understanding is either authentic, originating from its own self as such, or else inauthentic. (p. 146)

This formulation is applied further on p. 148, where an understanding or interpretation of things in the surrounding world is said to be an inauthentic understanding. By contrast, our understanding of ourselves, and especially of the structures of our existence, is an authentic understanding: see, for example, pp. 279–80 and 302. Authenticity only becomes Heidegger's theme in the second division of the book. But the truly central issue opened up by his distinction is that our *self*-understanding can itself become inauthentic, where we understand or interpret what belongs to our own being inappropriately, determining it with concepts of substance or movement, for example, whose application is only to surrounding objects in the world. This appears in many passages of the second division (e,g., pp. 254, 281).

The very concept of authenticity was introduced purely formally much earlier, in section 9, pp. 42–3, and its application was to existence, not to understanding as such. This is the possibility of being oneself or not being oneself, which in section 9 is renamed choosing oneself or losing oneself. After that formal introduction we hear little about it until sections 25–7. What is to be said about authentic existence?

We have heard that *Da-sein* understands this double possibility, being itself or not, and that it is only through such an understanding that it understands itself. *SZ*, section 27, asks: who is the 'subject' of everyday life or existence? It is a customary thought, Heidegger says, that '*Da-sein* is in each case I myself.'[4] But 'it could be that the Who of everyday *Da-sein* is precisely *not* I myself.'[5] This is the self's not being itself: *das Da-sein ist zunächst und zumeist nicht es selbst* (p. 116). Heidegger opened his chapter 4 with the question: '*who* is it that *Da-sein* is in everyday-ness?'[6] i.e., 'Who is it that *Da-sein* is in everyday life?' or, even simpler, 'Who is the self in everyday life?' The question is asking in what guise or persona the self shows up in everyday life.[7] The answer is that self-hood in its everyday form has fallen under the dominance of a kind of mass subjectivity constituted by public opinion, mass culture, and economic pressure, that Heidegger calls *das Man*.[8] This is a specific formation of being-with, *Mit-sein*, that is constituted by anonymity, conformity, lack of responsibility, and alienation. This is *das Man* in its social expression, but what concerns us mainly here is the ontological point that where *Mit-sein* takes on this specific form of collectivity, it is mirrored in the self as the specific form of *Selbstsein* that Heidegger calls *Man-selbst*. The 'Who' of everyday *Da-sein* is *Man-selbst* (p. 129).

The pronoun *man* enables Heidegger to expound inauthenticity. It is the German equivalent of the French *on*, the indefinite pronoun so often used as the subject of declarative sentences, and for which as a parallel expression in English we sometimes use the subject 'one': 'One does rather think, doesn't one, that ...'; *On peut supposer que ...*; *Man ist doch der Meinung, daß ...* The device is ingenious because it exhibits the suppression of the first-person pronoun in discourse, to reflect the displacement that, according to Heidegger, occurs in our everyday life: the occlusion of the 'I.' Within the framework of *SZ*, the terms 'authentic' and 'inauthentic' are not properly applied to the self or to *Da-sein*. They indicate ways of existing, ways of being. We need to treat the German words as adverbs: existing authentically, being authentically. Note as well that the German *Sein* is a gerund, a verbal noun, and to capture it in English we should treat 'being' gerundively, i.e., modify it with adverbs like 'authentically,' not adjectives like 'authentic.' Heidegger does not usually apply his term *eigentlich* to a normal substantive term. Only once in the book, I believe, does he use the term 'authentic self' (p. 129), and once only the term 'inauthentic self' (p. 181). The term 'authentic *Da-sein*' appears only on p. 43.

In the sentence we quoted in chapter 2, '*Da-sein* always understands itself in terms of its existence, in terms of its possibility to be itself or not to be iself,'[9] the differentiating factor is the pronoun *es* that precedes the word *selbst* in the final clause. It would come through in English as the alternative between 'being *you*rself or not being *you*rself,' and in Heidegger's treatment this is an alternative enjoyed by *the* self. We learn from pp. 42–3 that this alternative is between existing authentically and existing inauthentically. Because *Selbstsein* is a highly formal structure, it incorporates both the latter possibilities. The fourth chapter of the first division shows how the two possibilities of existence play themselves out; but never should it be supposed that inauthentic existence (which we'd express in English as 'not being *you*rself') is in any way selfless, i.e., bereft of *Selbstsein*. The inquiry instituted in the second division concerns the grounds for the second possibility, of being a self authentically. Where Heidegger speaks of *Selbstseinkönnen*, the *ability* to be a self, he means the ability authentically to be a self; there is no reference in the text to any ability to be a self *in*authentically. Nevertheless, the indifferent *Selbstsein* is also a matter of ability; it is one form of *Seinkönnen*. The two possibilities are granted to the self by its existence. To exist in Heidegger's sense means that being yourself is never a mere given but always an achievement; it stands under the rubric of possibility. One expression of *Seinkönnen* (ability to be), then, is *Selbstseinkönnen* (the ability to be yourself). The term *Selbstseinkönnen* does not actually show up, I think, until section 38, p. 179, but it becomes very prominent later on in the second division, especially section 54 and following. This alternative is something understood. It is not external to us, a mere hypothesis entertained by Heidegger about possibilities lying within human life. This two-fold possibility is already comprehended within everyone's pre-ontological understanding of being. Moreover, it is out of this alternative that *Da-sein* achieves self-understanding. Heidegger says in section 4, p. 12, that either you have already chosen one of the two possibilities, or else you have stumbled upon one of them or else grown up in it all along. In section 9 he has more to say about this possible choice: 'And because *Da-sein* is always essentially its possibility, it *can* "choose" itself in its being, it can win itself, it can lose itself, or it can never and only 'apparently' win itself' (p. 42). These are the possibilities that matter to us most of all.

Now I add the point on which the present argument turns: to be itself includes understanding that the moral law applies to itself. It is the state of being, existing authentically or inauthentically, that governs how the moral law is understood, authentically or inauthentically. In inauthenticity, I find the way to apply it, not to myself, but to others. Who is responsible here? Not me: it's him. 'The man said, "The woman whom you gave to be with me, she gave me fruit from the tree, and I ate."' (Genesis 3:12).

There is a *swerve* in our existence, or a swerve that comes into effect just by virtue of our existing: the inauthentic understanding of our being, and therefore inauthentic existing. This general point is precisely Heidegger's, though not the application to the moral law. It is vital to understand that this is not an analysis of immorality. As we shall be seeing below in further comments upon Kant, inauthentic understanding of the moral law is quite a different matter from forming maxims that flout the moral law. Kierkegaard's work is full of references to the inauthentic understanding of morality manifested in our daily practice. Though his language did not include an equivalent to the word 'authentic,' *eigentlich*, the very point at issue is the subject of one of his finest discourses, best known in English as *Purity of Heart Is to Will One Thing*.[10] A little later, we'll quote several passages from this text. The swerve is expressed in fault-finding and blame, for nothing concerns the self more than morality. There is comparison with others, and then blame assigned to them. Thus when the norm of beneficence itself becomes identified with some particular organization, easily described, and where my group, our group, are those who practise this, we have now found a source for self-justifying in the moral sense. It becomes evident as moralism when we consign others, who fall outside this same description, as immoral. 'Why don't they contribute? Because they're too selfish!'

Of course, to derive from the categorical imperative some such claim as that – those who do not contribute to my particular charity (the March of Dimes?) are failing in the duty of beneficence – is utterly fallacious. And the moralist is not *that* deficient in reason. We have to attribute it rather to the 'swerve' of existence into inauthenticity. We'll study a few examples to try to confirm this thesis. The point of the swerve is the justification of oneself. Before proceeding, I should say that moralism is not dependent on special features of Kant's thought, such as the role of imperatives or duty, the place of formal rules, the analysis of maxims, laws, and so on. In my view, the advocates of a 'virtue ethic' and the advocates of utilitarianism have not proved any more adept in making their way around the shoals of moralism.

The Phenomenology of Inauthenticity

Moralism

Those who have organized a charity, and those who support it, regard it as a realization of the moral law (not as a business investment or mere entertainment), and, rationally speaking, they can account themselves righteous through their actions. Now they constitute a group: 'This is our cause and we've made sacrifices for it.' And now they can *use* the moral law for the purpose of justifying themselves. This is moralism. Supporters of this charity – talking among themselves, we may suppose – express their judgments about all other people: 'they won't contribute to our cause because they're too greedy.'

The moralistic judgment concerns other people's motivations as well as their deeds. The moralists' reasonings are claiming for an evident fact something that cannot be known in this way – the inner maxims and motivations of the others: 'too greedy to contribute.' Kant made this point but too pessimistically. In his view the noumenal personality of others was quite inaccessible to us. More to the point is the view of Kierkegaard and Heidegger that discussions about existence (and that includes motivations and maxims) are necessarily *formal*. Greed, therefore, can be known only as a *possibility* that arises in existence: whether any individual or group is actually greedy in the required sense cannot be known. This imputation is precisely a device for justifying oneself and one's group – nothing more. And here I must acknowledge that this limitation holds for the present argument too. Though I am dissecting the thoughts of moralists, I am no more able to peer into their souls and motives than they are into those whom they criticize. Whether any individual or group is actually moralistic in the present sense cannot be known. Like greed, moralism is one existential possibility.

What chance is there of discussing this possibility if we cannot know whether or not anyone exhibits it? One source for us are the literary works in which essential possibilities for human existence appear in an inexhaustible array of shapes. We are not likely to find autobiographies that lay bare for us the intrigues of the author's own moralism, but we have in vast abundance plays and novels where moralism stands unmistakeably before us.

The twists and turns of moralism that contaminate morality are a phenomenon of great interest to novelists and playwrights, especially in the Victorian age and its aftermath. In *Jane Eyre* (1847),[11] the life of the heroine is lived from the beginning and as a whole under the shadow of moralism. Orphaned at an early age, she became the ward of Mrs. Reed, an aunt by marriage whose jealousy of Jane's family led her to a loathing of the child. Seizing on a few contrived pretexts, she condemns the little girl as perpetually disobedient and a liar (19–25). Added to this disorder in family life is the nightmare of a cruel school supervised by the ambitious Rev. Mr. Brocklehurst. Invited by Mrs. Reed to take Jane to his school, he submits the child to an interrogation regarding her opinions on scripture and religion. Thereupon he declares her to be a reprobate with 'a wicked heart' (42–3). Thus, through their combined agency, Jane's life at school becomes nothing but a punishment for the wickedness and deceitfulness that they have attributed to her (78–9).

Victorian novels often took as their subject the disorders of the church, a counterpart to the disorders of family and education that loomed so large in *Jane Eyre*. Often, the stories turn upon the hypocrisy and moralism of those who had found preferment in the church, and of their hangers-on. The wife of the bishop of Barchester, Mrs. Proudie, is a great comic figure in Anthony Trollope's Barchester novels, but the comedy is fused together with her real menace, and without that oppressive menace there would be little comedy. In *The Last Chronicle of Barset* (1867),[12] Mr. Crawley, one of the lesser clergy in the diocese of Barchester, has been charged with the theft of twenty pounds. While everyone is awaiting the trial of Mr. Crawley, his case becomes the subject of endless gossip throughout the diocese. The deepest wish of the bishop is to escape hearing about the matter – though he still has a residual sense that he owes some help and succour to his subordinate. Not so Mrs. Proudie. In the first place, Mr. Crowley, nothing but a 'perpetual curate,' is certainly a very poor man, and therefore would have committed the theft. Even if he were acquitted, she insists to her husband the bishop, he must get rid of the incumbent:

He has been disgracefully involved in debt ever since he has been here; you have been pestered by letters from unfortunate tradesmen who cannot get their money from him ... He cannot come to the palace as all cler-

gymen should do because he has got no clothes to come in. I saw him once
about the lanes and never set my eyes on such an object in my life ... I feel
sure of his guilt and I hope he will be convicted ... But if he escape conviction, you must sequestrate the living because of the debts. The income is
enough to get an excellent curate. (p. 54)

Mrs. Proudie thinks that her own protegé, Mr. Thumble, would be ad-
mirably suited to do the work.

It was not only English novels that dwelt on moralism during the
Victorian age – it loomed large in the American literature of the same
period and later. Think of Nathaniel Hawthorne's probing of the grim
history of the Puritans of Massachusetts, especially in his great sym-
bolic novel, *The Scarlet Letter* (1850). There the moralistic persecution of
Hester Prynne was carried out by the established authority, the theo-
cratic government of the state, so the topic goes beyond the sort of moralism that drives individuals in their quest for self-magnifying and self-
justifying. But we find our topic in clear, sharp form in the later Victorian age and moving into the twentieth century.

Sinclair Lewis's novel *Main Street*, from 1920,[13] presents the manner
in which a small town in the U.S. Midwest closed itself against a young
woman, Carol, who was newly arrived from a big city after she had
married the town doctor. She was not 'one of us' and because of her cit-
ified ways was suspected of all kinds of immorality and outrageous-
ness. It is established that she seems to be irreligious (p. 67); she detects
faces watching her behind curtains (p. 83); it is regularly hinted in con-
versations that she is extravagant (p. 85); it is made clear that she is too
indulgent to her maid (pp. 178f.). Her cultural interests are regularly
denigrated as proud and highfalutin, and when she finally reaches out
to her neighbours with some practical suggestions for charity work
with the poor, it is made clear to her that she has absolutely no understanding of the town, because (*a*) such work would be unnecessary
here: we don't have poor people (p. 137); but also (*b*) this work would
be harmful, because those people are shiftless and lazy (p. 138).

We need to note that, however we appraise moralism, it is not in itself
the violation of the Kantian moral law or of any of the subordinate
duties in which that law applies itself. Moralism is therefore not like an
evil will that makes into its maxim the contrary of the categorical
imperative. The murderer fails every test of morality that Kant sets up.
But the moralist is, if anything, more punctilious than anyone else in
acting according to the moral law. It would be wrong to call the moral-

ist immoral, therefore, for moralism is a kind of excess that belongs to morality, some kind of degeneration that has befallen morality itself. It is the embodiment of morality in an inauthentic understanding and inauthentic existence.

To look more closely at Kant, we see that there are no grounds in his thought to find this moralism to be in violation of his moral law, the categorical imperative in any of its formulations. Moralism, the disposition to make negative judgments about the morality of others, is not directly regulated by the categorical imperative. To harm others, or to treat others only as means to my own ends, does violate the imperative to regard others as persons, as rational autonomous ends in themselves. But where I condemn the morality of another in a moralistic spirit, I *am* regarding that other as a moral person, a deficient one. There can be no moral obligation in Kant to recognize others as morally good and worthy. Where the agent is conscious of practising beneficence – through a charity, for instance – Kant does not find an obligation upon that agent to respect the motives of those who abstain from the charity ('the altruistic maxim of beneficence toward those in need is a universal duty of men' [*MM*, p. 453]). Though Kant is fond of quoting the Gospels from time to time,[14] he never cites Matthew 7:1, 'Judge not, that you be not judged.' On these grounds, then, we need to look outside the Kantian ethics for a closer critique of moralism.

And on other grounds, too, Kant lets us down at this point. He found it quite in accord with reason for the active moral agent to be pleased with himself or herself. In the *Critique of Practical Reason*, there is justification for self-esteem in a moral agent who has some (realistic) sense of his or her righteousness. It is a part of existence, we said earlier, to magnify ourselves, and if success and achievement are steps towards that, surely it can seem that moral success, or moral achievement, should claim as much as any other. That is a *rational* conclusion. And Kant seems to have seen no problem with moral self-approval: the moral agent was entitled to a pleasant feeling of satisfaction with himself or herself. In the *Dialectic of Pure Practical Reason*,[15] he recognized that the highest happiness ought to be the reward for anyone who had adhered faithfully to the moral law, but that this does not occur in our imperfect world: only in eternity would this highest of goods be achieved. Nevertheless (reading further in the same text), the virtuous agent is compensated in this life by the right to be contented with himself or herself: *Selbst-Zufriedenheit*. This is a 'satisfaction with existence ... which necessarily accompanies the consciousness of virtue' (p. 117). A bit earlier we read, 'A man, if he is virtuous, will certainly not enjoy life without being conscious of his righteousness in each action' (p. 116). From virtuous living, he can expect 'satisfaction with one's condition, i.e., contentment, whose source is contentment with one's own person' (p. 118). Thus, if the moral code comes to us from reason, and if it is reasonable to accord esteem to self and others in proportion to merit, then one should esteem oneself highly for moral excellence. But this is a conclusion drawn on the basis of reason alone, without taking existence into account. Is it as rational to be as proud of one's moral status as of scientific or artistic achievements? It would seem that Kant thought so. But one relevant difference is that moral life is lived as a whole, as a continuing effort of existence, where there are no 'works' to display but only an ongoing life to live, only a work in progress. Thus, on two different grounds, we see that Kant is not equipped for an analysis of moralism: on the one hand, he would be ready to endorse those who criticize others; on the other hand, he gives his approval to self-approval.

Indignation

We all make pronouncements on racism and sexism, or on prostitution and gambling, in a moralistic spirit. Judgments on these matters are frequently made in indignation; this is that type of anger, as Hobbes said, that does not spring from an immediate hurt to ourselves, but from witnessing 'a great hurt done to another, when we conceive the same to be done by injury.'[16] Indignation over government or corporate abuse is most commonly expressed on behalf of others, though usually arising from situations in which we are close enough to feel compromised. We Canadians were indignant when we learned of the abuse of First Nations children in residential schools, particularly because the governments and churches that ran the schools were seemingly acting on behalf of Canada. My particular point here will concern a special form of this that is usually called 'righteous indignation.'

The history of residential schools in Canada for Native children seems to show that they were designed to eliminate the culture of the Native peoples through assimilating their young to the Euro-Canadian standard.[17] The impact of the attempted cultural assimilation was indeed terrible. There was often harsh physical discipline (p. 204), poor housing, clothing, and food (pp. 300–7), and psychological suffering in most of the children: loneliness, confusion, and self-hatred (pp. 204–5), resulting all too often in adulthood in alcoholism and drug dependency (p. 205). Besides that, there are many well-documented cases of sexual abuse (p. 520). The serious investigation of this only began in the 1990s with commissions established by the Canadian government (pp. 325–30).

We can differentiate a number of distinct reactions to this history and to the developing revelations of it in the press, in government reports, and in scholarly literature. The most important response is that of the Native population and their leaders, many of whom endured this schooling in their youth. They usually speak of these experiences with terrible sadness and anger, indeed white-hot rage.[18] Second, there have been repeated apologies and proposals for restitution from the churches who were complicit in this history. This is a chastened response. Third, the governments in Canada have been slow to react, beginning with vague regrets and some finger-pointing at the churches (p. 433), but showing more recently a serious effort to document the history and begin a process of restitution to the affected population.

What interests me here, however, is the viewpoint often expressed in the press and by Canadian citizens as a whole. As the author Miller argues, the fault is to be shared by the Canadian public as a whole, yet frequently in the press, those who expressed concerns for the Native children were content to demonize the churches. They slipped away from responsibility themselves (p. 435). This superficial secular response must be contrasted with the deeper religious one. The press and general public in Canada usually combined their indignation towards churches with the further proviso, 'I at least didn't have anything to do with *that*.' An indignation of that character, on the whole unreflective, is truly *righteous*: indignation lacking in any element of shame or guilt. Where shame or a sense of complicity accompanied the indignation, it became inherently a deeper, more complex thing, but the common secular righteous indignation operated as a close cousin of moralism, little more than a prop for self-esteem.

I have treated one issue for the purpose of illustrating my point. But righteous indignation is an immensely widespread phenomenon, exceptionally common in political parties, press editorials,[19] and universities.

Self-Righteousness

Further along the road where we find moralism and righteous indignation lies the phenomenon of self-righteousness. But this is an exceptionally slippery topic, for any disquisition on this subject is likely to condemn itself. To speak of self-righteousness is to denounce it, seeking a kind of blame to fix on somebody, obliging one's hearer to seek refuge from this accusation, to appeal, 'No, never in word or deed have I exhibited self-righteousness!', so that one is exhibiting with textbook clarity the posture of self-righteousness oneself. If self-righteousness is a fault, who is in a position to cast the first stone? This is one of the cases in philosophy where a theme can be discussed generally or formally but not made applicable to individuals. The way we treat the matter existentially is to think of self-righteousness as a possibility lying on the pathway of moral existence, one whose actuality can never be known.

The phenomenon does not seem accessible to pure reason, as we may confirm from the case of Kant, who found no fault with being satisfied about one's righteousness. It is in relation to existence that self-righteousness shows its darkness. It becomes an ally of moralism, indeed, the very heart of moralism, because of the comparison with others. Hypocrisy is not the same as either moralism in general or self-righteousness. If the moralist makes use of a moral consciousness towards the particular end of self-justifying, the hypocrite is a moralist who also offends against morality itself in practice.[20] It might be possible to see that self-righteousness is the deeper ground for moralism and indignation: these latter are expressions of the self in particular judgments and circumstances, whereas self-righteousness should be seen as a fixed disposition of the self that finds expression in these ways, their very essence. Self-righteousness is the stout and hardy core of an existence that resists any recognition of shame and guilt, that is invulnerable, that will not examine itself, that assumes it is *always already* justified.[21] This rests on a conviction about one's own being, the conviction that merit and innocence are bestowed on all one's deeds and thoughts because of the primordial innocence of one's own being, just because one is who one is. But the deeper ground of this conviction is the movement to *establish* one's own being as innocent, or justified, so that it is able to radiate justification on all one's words and deeds. The move to justify one's being is therefore the sustaining core of self-righteousness.

Kant regularly expressed his disgust at the contamination of moral counsels with self-interest. One text of many appears in the second section of the *Grounding*: 'I am willing to admit out of love for humanity that most of our actions are in accordance with duty; but if we look more closely at our planning and striving, we everywhere come upon the dear self, which is always turning up, and upon which the intent of our actions is based, rather than upon the strict command of duty.'[22] The contamination by self-interest results from efforts to give an empirical foundation to morality, as is common in popular moral discourse. The popular rhetoric that confuses motives earns Kant's scorn where prudence and inherited habits are mixed up with morality in the strict sense. 'Such a procedure turns out a disgusting mishmash of patchwork observations and half-reasoned principles in which shallowpates revel because all this is something quite useful for the chitchat of everyday life' (p. 409).

The matter we are treating here is analogous: not a counsel to you that appeals to your self-interest, but an effort to vindicate my own self through the discourse of morality. It is Kierkegaard above all who shows his genius in probing inauthentic moralism and our efforts to justify ourselves. The meaning of his title is that willing the Good, i.e., a will obedient to the categorical imperative, is the only circumstance in which the will is single-minded, not split into a manifold of secondary intentions. Here inauthenticity appears as the double-mindedness of a will that – claiming to will only the Good – is in fact submitting that will to many conditions and qualifications that pull in other directions. He introduces the case of a lover who seems both to love his fiancée and to love her money, for she is rich: how can the lover become quite clear which it is that he loves? Kierkegaard probes into the appearance of a good will (willing the Good) that has attached a condition: the reward.

> The double-minded one stands at a parting of the ways. Two visions appear: the Good and the reward. It is not in his power to bring them into agreement, for they are fundamentally different from each other ... So he stands pondering and reflecting. If he is wholly absorbed in his pondering, then he continues to stand – a symbol of double-mindedness. (p. 74)

A similar ambiguity (what we call the swerve) appears in one who seeks to will the Good, but who is nevertheless also imbued with a fear of punishment (pp. 79–98). How to treat this 'also'? One of Kierkegaard's sharpest insights is into the case of one who wills the Good, but who nevertheless wishes above all that the Good should triumph through him,

> that he shall be the instrument, he the chosen one. He does not desire to be rewarded by the world – that he despises; nor by men – that he looks down upon. And yet he does not wish to be an unprofitable servant. The

reward which he insists upon is a sense of pride and in that very demand is his violent double-mindedness. (p. 100)

Kierkegaard is also attentive to the danger that lurks in his own discourse, like the danger that haunts any treatment of self-righteousness: how could he be sure that his own discourse on double-mindedness is not double-minded itself?

> Oh, that the talk would not seem to wish to judge or accuse others. For to wish to judge others instead of oneself would also be double-mindedness. Oh, that the talk might not seem to press demands that are binding upon others but that exempt the speaker, as if he had only the task of talking. (p. 68)

If the essence of this entire sequence (moralism and righteous indignation) is really self-righteousness, understood as an inner disposition, then we need to probe into it. It is precisely the posture that holds that I myself am already justified in all cases just because of who I am. It is my being that affords a constant justification in advance.

Shame and Remorse

Someone is being *blamed* – but for what? A formal discussion must leave that matter open. But we can see a difference of level. Though moralistic blame and fault-finding can at times seem to be confined to one particular deed or omission that caused reproach, more common is the extension of blame that reaches into the entire character or life of the offender, especially insinuations that come to take on a wider scope. Consider someone being criticized for being strict and stern with a child. Very likely it is suspected that the agent had always performed actions of this type; the question would not be about circumstances of one occasion – rather, the question would concern his whole life and character. A general fault appears more sharply. And all the more so if he defends his accustomed hardness with children. For this person, like all of us, can sense if a rebuke is aimed only at one small act we performed, or if it has the deeper force touching on our person. So the person under criticism here may say something like: 'You know you've got to keep these brats in line!' This is not only justifying a current deed – it's speaking up for his whole mode of life, his whole conduct with children (and perhaps everyone).

There are many ways of justifying a single deed (e.g., 'I didn't do that') that are not of interest to us here, but we want to consider certain devices whereby we refuse the imputation of blame. (*a*) Most common is the counter-attack: 'But you – you're just constantly pampering that child!' (*b*) Or I may say, 'Sure I did it, but it wasn't wrong.' Or, more belligerently: 'So what?' This response commits the one who was blamed to justifying whatever deed it was that provoked the accusation. And of course, this is in principle an entirely suitable line of defence. We are entirely right to want to justify ourselves and our actions. (*c*) Then there is the stance of defiance: 'I don't need to apologize to anyone; who are you to be blaming me?' In such a response, we notice the complete lack of shame, perhaps even an incapacity for shame – i.e., shamelessness. Though we are right to want to justify ourselves, this shameless response does not undertake to do that: it is refusal to justify oneself, an indifference to justification, kicking off any and all restraints. Such a stance assumes that one is always already justified.

The acceptance of blame includes the reaction of shame: this is what we call remorse, always marked by shame. But another response to blame is not complete in that way: while seeming to accept blame, it actually does not, and especially it avoids the experience of shame; this is the response that we call 'regret.' Nothing is more common than for a public figure in our day, particularly politicians, to respond to the imputation of blame by declaring his or her 'regret' that such-and-such happened. This expresses an unfavourable judgment on a deed or event ('It's too bad') while distancing it from oneself: it is as impervious to shame as righteous indignation is. Here one's justification is never put into doubt. This is an evasive form of reacting to blame. And the analysis of the 'politician's case' will be pretty close to what we said about self-righteousness. What counts is the conviction that one's own character is beyond discussion. One's righteousness derives straight from one's being, as an ontological certitude.

Another response, however, is that humble posture that is penitent in all cases, that has renounced self-justifying in advance, a crushed self, a battered ego. And in a related point, there can be forms of remorse that are overreactions, that absorb blame out of all proportion to the intended reproach. You complain mildly over some small matter, and I go ballistic, feeling condemned for everything I ever did in the past. This overreaction is a common type of neurosis that infinitizes the ascribed blame. It is the extreme opposite of the politician who cannot accept blame, who reacts on all occasions with mere 'regret.'

First, however, we need to distinguish the shame that is inherent in remorse from several other experiences of shame that we can leave aside in this study. I may be ashamed of my body, ashamed of my appearance or of my poor accent in French. This whole array of experiences could be classified as aesthetic rather than moral, for what is salient in the present context is that they involve essentially a shame before others. Were nobody to see me or hear me, my body and my accent would not be occasions of shame. The shame that is a part of remorse, on the other hand, reaches deeper within, because we have accepted the blame for something: we know ourselves to be blameworthy, and we do not dismiss the blame as some other person's opinion. We are fully capable of blaming ourselves for what we have done or left undone, not needing external reproaches to lead us to remorse.

The remorseful acceptance of blame brings the recognition of a fault in oneself. This term can be used in a lesser sense, equivalent to agency or responsibility ('Yes, that was my fault'). But it is an ontological sense that I intend here – there is something faulty in my constitution, just as there can be a geological fault on the West Coast, or a structural fault in the metal sheathing of a plane. The reaction of remorse cannot confine itself to just the single occasion of the deed that incurred reproach and blame. That I was capable of the offence betrays something pervasive in all my conduct, an underlying, universal characteristic. Here there is the ontological shift proper to shame and remorse: it is not just this or that deed of which I am ashamed; I am ashamed of myself. With this we enter into a deeper level of discussion that has its impact on all the phenomenology we have reviewed so far: moralism, indignation, self-righteousness, shame. Fault is my interpretation of what Heidegger calls guilt (*Schuld*). Guilt is not merely a guilt-consciousness; it is a factor in our being. Because of that, it is not an option for anyone to be entirely free of guilt.

The remorse, and the shame that dwells within it, need not concern only one's own individual deed: we can feel shame and remorse for a collective action (Canadian maltreatment of the Native population, for instance).

To summarize so far: absence of shame characterizes both righteous indignation and regret. It is the presence of shame that differentiates remorse from regret. Many of our strategies for self-justifying, such as moralism and self-righteousness, serve to block our shame and make us incapable of remorse. The neurotic overreaction arises because one senses that there is more to be ashamed of than one small deed. Guilt neurosis disables one from a remorse appropriate to the occasion. But where remorse is achieved, it does open the door to something further, something that occasions shame but is still harder to acknowledge: the fault in one's being. We are often prevented from acknowledging the fault because of the anxiety that arises within our shame and remorse, of which neurosis is one expression. What is required here is a more powerful experience than is ordinarily achieved by the usual occasions of blame. Heidegger has shown how the recognition of guilt (or fault) is induced by what he calls conscience (*Gewissen*).

An indignation that is no longer unreflecting, no longer righteous indignation, arises through your recognition of your own guilt, for instance, your share in your nation's guilt. This is felt subjectively as remorse. Remorse and the recognition of guilt are the remedy for moralism, for they keep alive a sense of shame. Kant thought there was a justified moral self-approval, even though in his philosophy of religion he did recognize a 'radical evil' in human nature (how that might be rendered compatible with his usual blandness about self-approval seems to be a difficulty in Kant-interpretation). Moral self-esteem is particularly noxious when it is expressed in public because there is the comparison with others, though it is not usually by direct boasting that we give public expression to moral self-esteem. It is accomplished usually by insinuations about others and their many failings, where my own moral goodness seemingly supplies me the warrant for despising large groups of people. Still, quite apart from any public display, we have shown that moralism and its kin are lacking a sense of shame, lacking therefore the possibility of remorse, lacking the possible consciousness of fault or guilt, lacking therefore in conscience.

Conscience and Guilt

The incapacity for remorse springs from the inability to be guilty. What is it then that bestows on the self the ability to be guilty?

Heidegger's account of conscience (*das Gewissen*) in *SZ*, division 2, chapter 2, treats, first, the call of conscience and then the response of the self.[23] Heidegger's is a rigorously phenomenological account, and, for that reason, the connection between conscience and morality is left indirect, one of the surprises of his study. He treats conscience as one form of discourse (*Rede*), the form that we know as calling (*Ruf*). A voice that calls out, seemingly unsolicited and original, reaches you with the assurance that it is you, and nobody else, who is intended. But

Heidegger does not present the conscience as the 'voice' that calls, nor indeed as a caller at all – rather it is the very call itself, something phenomenally more evident than a caller 'behind' the call. Since Heidegger is presenting existence as being in constant movement, we can suppose this to be a call back, one coming from behind, that opens to us the possibility of stopping the movement, or moving in a different direction. (In this I liken Heidegger's account to the stories we hear of the 'divine sign' of Socrates.)[24] It does not prescribe some new direction for our movement; indeed it prescribes nothing at all, and we might imagine the phenomenon (this is not in Heidegger's own text) just as the calling out to you of your name. The call, rather than prescribing a direction for you, only permits you to pause, to be open to some other possible pathway. The way Heidegger makes this point in his own text (p. 273) is to stress the 'silence' of the call, which means not only that it is not an outer acoustic phenomenon, but principally that there is no message in the call, no content, no command. This implies a certain gentleness of the phenomenon that differentiates it from a categorical imperative or a judicial injunction. You are free either to respond to the call or not, though you cannot doubt that you in particular have been called. For the call puts you yourself in the spotlight (p. 272). Not that you were ignorant of yourself and your goals and doings prior to the call, but the call puts them all up for discussion, as if to pose the question, 'Wasn't there something else you had to do?'

Who then is calling to you here? It is important to acknowledge that, just as there is no determinate message relayed, so the caller of the call must be seen, first of all, as indeterminate: the source of the call is unknown. The obscurity of the caller is a positive element in the phenomenology of conscience, a point that permits Heidegger to eliminate several putative subjects as having no warrant in phenomenology: to suppose that the caller is God, or a social collectivity, or an authority figure, or a father (pp. 269, 275). We adhere to the phenomenological evidence by heeding the phrase *Es ruft*, something is calling, someone is calling (pp. 276–7). To sense this blank is to begin to do justice to the phenomenon.

Yet the further phenomenological elucidation will show that it is your being, *die Sorge*, that is calling to you. The call comes from within even though the caller withdraws from scrutiny. Now, phenomenology will examine the very hiding and self-concealment of the caller, that is, the phenomenology will permit this very concealment itself to stand forth into view. There is a depth within ourselves that escapes our scrutiny, a resistance, which is so intimately a part of the phenomenon that it must be recognized explicitly. Here is one of the connections between conscience and anxiety: we become anxious when we attempt to peer into these depths. And we need now to reflect on that very point. Why are we so constituted that in our daily life we cannot draw near without anxiety to our own constituting depths? To accept that will be *inter alia* to concede that the phenomenological study itself cannot be conducted without anxiety. The call does not summon me from without, in contrast, say, to Lévinas, for whom the call proceeds from the face of the Other person.[25] It proceeds from our being, which is also of course our being in the world and our being with others.

What we experience as the call is, in its origins, a disclosure, for a call is one kind of discourse, and the essence of discourse is disclosure. The care or concern, *die Sorge*, that constitutes our being is interwoven with the anxiety that belongs to this phenomenon. We are finite, vulnerable beings, imbued with an ability to be that brings us concern and anxiety about our being. It is through this unshielded concern that our being is disclosed to us. In our *Sorge*, we are impelled into a future that we worry about with innumerable possibilities: we disclose all of them. Yet, in this, we have already been modified, shaped, affected, and constituted by a whole world in advance of any of our projections. This interaction of being-affected with projection is care, and it is what calls out to us, laden with anxiety, as conscience. Our own very being is at work in the calling. Conscience is the call of care.

Section 58 completes the study of the discursive, disclosive character of conscience. Heidegger first treated conscience as a calling, and now the other half of the phenomenon is our hearing, and heeding and understanding, the call. In Heidegger's reasoning, it is evident that conscience belongs to everyone.[26] Since conscience speaks only in the mode of silence, says Heidegger, commanding nothing and communicating nothing, what it calls is simply that there is a call. To hear such a 'silent' call evokes a similar response – not doing-*X*, not being-*X*, not fulfilling a command. The 'hearing' of the call that truly understands it issues in nothing more than the will to have a conscience, the will that the call continue. Nevertheless, this will becomes further interpreted by Heidegger as resoluteness (*Entschlossenheit*). But this will, that conscience continue its call, is never without an interpretation that we make. Every 'understanding'becomes completed, in Heidegger's fundamental ontology, by an interpretation, *Auslegung*. What is first understood – here, we mean the call – now becomes interpreted, and that occurs in our life and action. The role of interpretation in Heidegger is the guarantor of our freedom, spontaneity, in the response to the call of conscience. This call is no less formal than Kant's moral law. Conscience is not a commanding voice that constrains us towards this or that course of action.

Conscience expresses the power of *Rede*, discourse. The call is a summons to the self that 'summons it to itself, that is, to the ability to be that is most of all its own, calling it forth (ahead of itself), to its most unique possibilities' (p. 273). 'The call directs *Da-sein* forward toward its ability to be, as a call out of uncanniness' (p. 280), awakening the authentic ability to be a self (p.298). The authenticity towards which the self is summoned is not an already subsisting 'true self,' slumbering in some way during our everyday life. That would force some kind of content into this call of conscience, a point that Heidegger insists on denying. To hear conscience is to be summoned to a possibility: 'another kind of hearing is aroused' (p. 271). The will to have a conscience, *das Gewissenhabenwollen*, means persevering in relation to the call, a continuing heeding of the call, a life lived in proximity to conscience, as the self undertakes its life. We do not bid this call goodbye, moving forwards to start out on our own. Rather, we are shaping a life in conformity to the call. It is as if we responded to the call of our name by replying 'Here I am.' Conscience is 'the attestation of an authentic ability to be a self' (*Bezeugung eines eigentlichen Selbstseinkönnens*, p. 267).

Now we can clarify that the call of conscience does not summon us to be moral. Rather, it calls us out of our inauthenticity – the inauthenticity of our existence and our understanding, and in particular, of course, out of our inauthentic understanding of the moral law. Its address needs to be assimilated and understood, and just as everything that is understood needs also to be interpreted, *ausgelegt*, there is the vast scope for the self to interpret the call, and its own will, in action in the world. Called into authenticity, it can confront its moral situation without self-deception. Discourse is completed in interpretation. The prior intimate resolve, the will to have a conscience, could in this respect be read as a pre-understanding. When you then proceed – in utter freedom – to act upon an understanding of that sort, you frame your own interpretation of it, and are able to be a moral agent.

Our conscience reveals to us that we are guilty, and Heidegger's account of that leads into one of the deepest studies in the whole book in section 58. He reviews a number of senses of the word *Schuld*, and singles out for his attention the kind of case in which something has gone wrong and you bear the blame for it. This includes a concept of ground or grounding: being guilty is to be blameworthy for a wrong, *Grundsein einer Nichtigkeit* (p. 283). To take blame or guilt upon yourself is to assume responsibility, which is an act of freedom projecting into the future, signifying your ability to be, i.e., to persevere, under the burden of that guilt. Thus, understood existentially, *being* guilty signifies the *ability* to be guilty, *Schuldigseinkönnen*. Now Heidegger wants to reveal an *a priori* guilt, an ontological guilt that shadows us all quite in advance of any deed for which we might assume the blame. He argues at this point that we can see here the ground of the possibility of moral guilt. Indeed, *a priori* ontological guilt is the ground of the possibility for all moral experience and all moral discourse, including moral philosophy. Just as scarcity is the ontological ground for any possible economy – the reason why there is an economy of any sort – so ontological guilt is the grounding for any possible moral code.

The call of conscience makes us anxious because it is the breakthrough into consciousness of an anxiety that for the most part lies hidden in our depths, expressing the exposure and unshieldedness of being. The call begets in us a conscious anxiety that now takes on the specific form of an effort to protect ourselves. Especially in this form: here is the reason why I ought to exist. Our response to a threat to our being is the effort to ground our being; we want to give reasons for ourselves; we want to justify ourselves. But as Heidegger sees it, our effort to take responsibility for ourselves means further: to shoulder the blame for ourselves. I make myself guilty by assuming this primordial responsibility, giving myself grounds for my being: to be a cause, or to stand in for a cause.[27] (Here we can see the basic position of Sartre's *Being and Nothingness*. The world as a whole and your own facticity, including your birth, are taken within your responsibility and you assume the blame for them. 'In a certain sense I *choose* being born.'[28] This is an extreme expansion of responsibility to encompass all of being, as if facticity were only one department of our projecting. This arises from Sartre's infinite expansion of autonomy.) Heidegger, however, grasps that our facticity, though it belongs to our care, is not superceded by the projection of ourselves (as guilty). The irrecoverable facticity, expressed as thrown-ness, is manifested in all the phenomena, like unexpected sickness and unwelcome visitors, that express an original passivity. Facticity itself is an original matter of anxiety, so that as we attempt to gain control over our being, we are always thrown back on our exposure, our unshieldedness. The anxiety that makes us first of all try to give a reason for ourselves, to gain control, is further augmented through the inevitable experience of being thrown and unable to be our own grounding. The experience of guilt is strictly speaking the *ability* to be guilty, the ability to be, 'while never gaining power over our own being from the ground up' (p. 284). We have the ability to be, without this maximal power. Therefore, Heidegger says, in the ability to be guilty, '*Da-sein* is released to itself from the ground, *an es selbst entlassen aus dem Grunde*' (p. 285). Through the intensity of our projected ability-to-be-guilty, we are released into a non-responsible disclosure of our being, a phenomenon not noticed by Sartre.

And what arises in this circumstance is a unique intertwining of guilt with justification. This indeed is the major inference I want to draw in this discussion: that precisely where I (the self) am guilty, I must recognize that my being, on the other hand, is justified. In one respect, that is because my being (care) has been the author of the call of conscience. In another respect, i.e., to analyse this in a different way: though it is certainly I myself whose guilt has been thoroughly disclosed, still, the persistence of our facticity, and not being accountable for our being or our existence (what we cannot take under our responsibility), reveal that our being or existence itself is now justified. We cannot do any more to ground it. What we see here is not a new passivity in the self, for this is still a resolutely self-projecting self. Rather, we are viewing the complex constitution of the being of the self, showing a firm difference between the status of the self (guilty) and that of its being (justified).

The will to have a conscience, and the ability to be guilty that it engenders, are the permanent markers of the self that exists authentically, permanent in the sense of accompanying the self towards its death. Though the self takes on its guilt, there appears to be in Heidegger no place for acts of confession. Conscience is a form of discourse, *Rede*, that is assimilated by our understanding (and, as I have stressed, interpretation). But there is no counter-*Rede* that we enact, except for the silence that is expressed in our resoluteness. Our possible confession to one another is not mentioned, and it is a worthwhile question to Heidegger whether it is excluded in principle. (As we shall see in a moment, there can be no confession to God in the present account.) In the absence of a place for confession, there would appear to be in Heidegger no place for forgiveness. There might be a confession to one another of this or that deed, and, in such a case, the other would be in a position to forgive us. But the ontological guilt, it seems, allows neither confession nor forgiveness – only silent acknowledgment on one's own part. This proves to be, from my point of view, a major difficulty in

Heidegger's account of conscience, and in a later chapter I begin from this point to introduce an account of spiritual existence that is able to account for confession and forgiveness.

Returning to the text of Heidegger, section 58 discusses conscience as *Gewissenhabenwollen* and guilt as *Schuldigseinkönnen*. Their relationship is summarized in the opening sentences of section 59: 'Conscience is the call of care from the uncanniness of being-in-the-world that summons *Da-sein* to its most intimate ability-to-be-guilty. We showed that wanting-to-have-a-conscience corresponded to understanding the summons' (p. 289). To proceed further now, we want to see the consequences that Heidegger himself draws from the discussion, particularly in sections 60 and 62. Then we shall see what further consequences we can draw from the discussion in view of our own questioning concerning self-magnifying and self-justifying.

Sections 60 and 62 are devoted to showing how the possibility of our authentic existence, that is, our ability to be authentically, is revealed or attested, *bezeugt*, by the experience of conscience. Heidegger introduces now the possibility of resoluteness, or a resolute existence. We are existentially resolute insofar as we project our possible being (and therefore understand it) strictly and solely upon our being guilty (pp. 295 bottom, 296 bottom, and 305). Thus, wanting to have a conscience implicates us in an unending condition of guilt, accepting our inability ever to be free from it (p. 305). Certainly, as Heidegger says on pp. 296–7, such a posture embodies anxiety. It also engenders reticence, *Verschwiegenheit*, respecting the possibilities open to our lives insofar as conscience has spoken: we do not give utterance to the intimations of conscience, nor to our response. But this generic resoluteness is constituted only through ever-renewed moments of resolve, in specific decisions made in this situation or that (p. 298), though it is Heidegger's claim that a resolute existence has a power mostly lacking to us in our everyday existence: of opening up original and unprecedented possibilities (p. 298). This is owing to the fact that resoluteness is a special mode of disclosure – an argument vital to Heidegger, but that I shall not pursue here. The creative possibility of resoluteness derives from the very nullity that constitutes our guilt: where I understand myself as the null basis of a nullity, I have wiped away the conventional understanding of my world, and my resoluteness lies precisely in holding fast to the disclosure. Earlier, I commented on the gentleness of the call of conscience, differentiating it from a categorical imperative or a judicial injunction. We should also understand that the posture of resoluteness is, despite all appearances, an equally gentle orientation to the world. It is open to questions; it is a rule of the self over itself, not over others; thus it is misunderstood when it is equated with a hard or militant drive.

Now we need to understand just why resoluteness is a key to authenticity. The terms 'authentic' and 'inauthentic' are not properly applied to the self or to *Da-sein*; the two possibilities are ways of being: being myself or not being myself. In existing inauthentically, where *Da-sein* is *das Man*, I am not myself. It is not that I have become someone else instead or something else instead, some sort of non-I. What arises in everyday life rather is that we permit *das Man* to take over and act in our place. It is not that *we* have become something else or someone else, but rather something else or someone else has taken over being us. We have *permitted das Man* to take over being us, take over the *ability* to be that was in each case our own, take over the singular life that it had been our singular task to lead. *Das Man* has moved into the subject-position; the subject-position is now occupied. We have become nothing at all. This is inauthentic existence. Though this is existence reduced to its lowest point, *Man-selbst*, living in *das Man*, may well have a feeling of inflation or magnitude, being carried along by a mass of like-minded others, like the chattering moralists in *Main Street*, and may occupy a position of eminence, like Bishop Proudie.

What then of possible authenticity? Here we return to the context of sections 58, 60, and 62. We see the role of anxiety, being towards death, and the call of conscience – all these three convergent in that resoluteness whereby we project our being as the constant ability to be guilty. And that is authentic existence.

Anxiety is an attunement the effect of which is to break down the self of everyday (*Man-selbst*), so as to disclose the *Da-sein* and its being that lies under it. 'Anxiety reveals in *Da-sein* its own being toward its most intimate ability to be, ... its own freedom for the authenticity of its being as possibility' (p. 188). This does not transport an isolated subject out of the world into a vacuum; it 'brings *Da-sein* in an extreme sense precisely before its world as world' (p. 188). The uncanniness (*Unheimlichkeit*) that belongs to anxiety is the world disclosed as alien, but with this world-disclosure we have the disclosure of our own 'authentic ability to be-in-the-world' (p. 187), the uncanny world-disclosure accompanying the unshieldedness of a self that has been reduced to its pure, naked ability to be. The self is dislodged from the familiar ways of its everyday life. *Das Man* is unseated from the subject position. You are prevented from being the person that you have usually been. You are now reduced to your own bare-bones ability to be and nothing else.

A further possibility for authenticity is described in *SZ*, Division 2, Chapter 1: *Da-sein* anticipates its possible death. Death is that special possibility in which *Da-sein*'s very ability to be is at issue (pp. 250–1). Now the ability to be is projected into the possible *inability* to be. Death is the possibility of being impossible, of being unable to be. To confront death means projecting your own ability to be into its greatest extremity, into that point where the ability to be will fail and must fail. Such anticipation of death is the authentic understanding of your ability to be a whole, an authentic existing endowing you with the 'ability to be that is most intimate' (*eigenstes Seinkönnen*, p. 263). Here too, *das Man* is ejected from the subject-position (p. 263), and, as the title and concluding section of this chapter indicate, we have in this the self's authentic ability to be a whole (pp. 235, 264). There are many further treatments of *das eigentliche Ganzseinkoennen*, for it forms the groundwork of the study of temporality in the second division, chapters 3 and 4.

In all this, the most vital point of all is that there is a continuity of authentic with inauthentic existence, a movement back and forth between them. This is foregrounded in section 38, devoted to *das Verfallen*, translated by Stambaugh in two different ways, varying by context, 'falling-prey' or 'entanglement.' But in earlier lectures,[29] Heidegger had employed the Latin-based word *Ruinanz*, ruination, and perhaps that word is more telling for the point at hand. '*Da-sein* has always already fallen away from itself, i.e., from its ability to be itself authentically, and fallen upon the "world."'[30] It is lost in the public, lost in the kind of community that is guided by idle talk, curiosity, and ambiguity. Both in section 38 and in the earlier lectures on ruination, what Heidegger has in mind is the very movement towards *das Man*, the movement that he characterizes here in section 38 as a lurching, plunging, and eddying (*Sturz, Wirbel*). This movement is not to be attributed to the self; it is a movement within the being of the self, a movement within existence, the movement whereby existence becomes inauthentic. The ontological radicalism of this discussion is pronounced. It brings forward the element of nothingness that constitutes inauthentic being.

Inauthenticity ... constitutes precisely a distinctive kind of being-in-the-world ... Not-being-its-self functions as a *positive* possibility of beings which are absorbed in a world ... This *nonbeing* must be conceived as *Da-sein*'s proximal way of being, in which it mostly maintains itself.[31]

The absence of God is not a contingent factor in this phenomenology, but central to its meaning.[32] Though *SZ* recognizes that here could be a theological discourse that would treat God and a possible human being-towards-God (see section 3), this 'science' would have nothing to do with philosophy. The stringent separation of phenomenology from theology is made even more categorical in other texts, early and late. The early text *The Concept of Time* (1924)[33] locates God in eternity, and says that philosophy knows nothing of either. *Phänomenologie und Theologie*, contemporary with *SZ*, says that *'faith*, as a specific possibility of existence, is in its innermost core the mortal enemy of the *form of existence* that is an essential part of *philosophy.'*[34] And the *Introduction to Metaphysics* (composed 1935, published 1953)[35] says that Christian belief makes it impossible for one even to ask philosophical questions, urging again the strict separation of theology from philosophy. In interpreting authenticity in Heidegger we must keep these clarifications in mind. In the coming chapter 7, we shall look at another possibility for being, a possible existence as spirit, that would grant a place for confession, forgiveness, and justification, and in that light we shall have to look again at Heidegger's views on authenticity.

Ascetic Autonomy

Meanwhile, we shall apply Heidegger's discussions of authenticity to our own guiding questions in this book: what implications do they carry regarding the efforts at self-magnifying and self-justification that we have been tracing in human existence?

The study of guilt was ontological, not psychological: it did not concern guilty feelings, and that means that the self may or may not have achieved an understanding of its guilt; the self can remain in inauthenticity, avoiding any suggestion of guilt (and therefore also shame and fault), seeking reassurance in any number of ways. But where this guilt is not only understood but, beyond that, where the self lives in the resolute self-projection upon its ability to be guilty, it is quite apparent that the posture of moralism and righteous indignation is broken forever. A resolute existence can never find a justification for itself in that way. And, as we described moralism and indignation above, they were nothing but the instrument of self-justifying. So it is ruled out that the self that is able to be guilty might somehow persevere in moralism and righteous indignation. But could the other possibility arise, that while the moralistic route to self-justification was closed off by the resolute ability to be guilty, there would be other means at hand by which the self could justify its existence? For instance, could it do so through success or achievement? That suggestion does not reckon with the radicalism of guilt: being the null basis of a nullity. The ability to be guilty spreads further, leading ultimately to the point where the self undertakes to exist without any justification at all, where it must recognize that its existence is totally unjustified and unjustifiable.

Formally, it is not only the self that now appears unjustifiable, but being and existence too – so that we attain a cosmological reach. This extreme possibility surpasses the double possibility of guilt and justification that we saw above in *SZ*, section 58. Not only is the being of the self unjustifiable, but any embodiment of being: the universe itself. This extreme result is not prompted merely by the ability to be guilty, for as we saw earlier, that ability first arises in a disclosure of being in which being is fully justified. The radical development we see here arises from the firm declaration or conviction of a guilty self that, finding itself unjustified and unjustifiable, extends its condemnation upon being, and upon the universe. That is not a necessary phenomenon, but only one interpretation of guilt.

The ability to be guilty incorporates a readiness for anxiety (*Angstbereitschaft*, p. 296) because the existing self is now exposed, not shielded by any mandate, uniform, or identity to which it could appeal as giving the reason for its presence in the world. And when we view this, not only as a moral situation but as an ontological structure, we are led to rethink the very character of selfhood. Heidegger undertakes this especially in section 64, where he shows that selfhood is reducible to care. There is nothing at all of substance in the being of the self (p. 318). Even Kant, who exposed the paralogisms of metaphysics concerning the soul, that it is unitary, simple, and therefore immortal, did not go far enough in the *Destruktion* of metaphysics, for his account of the apperceptions of the 'I' retained the principal features of the traditional idea of substance: a self-same subject lying at the basis of a succession of representations, a *hypokeimenon* (pp. 319–21). As against Kant and the tradition, Heidegger affirms that 'the self that is revealed by the reticence of resolute existence is the primordial phenomenal basis for the question of the being of the "I"' (p. 323). It is from this point that Heidegger makes the most important transition in the argument of *SZ*: to the analysis of ecstatic temporality that was made possible by his study of existence and care.

Our interest in the present inquiry, however, is something different – to grasp how this account of selfhood and care impinges on the self-appraisal of the self, its magnitude and its justification.

We have in Heidegger a resolute authenticity that has left behind any metaphysical foundation for the self. I should like to offer the claim that what he has established phenomenologically is nothing less than the guiding idea of twentieth-century culture, operative not only in phenomenology but in all philosophy, science, and cultural criticism, not just in continental circles but, if anything, even more forcefully in the English-speaking world. It is sometimes suggested that 'authenticity' is an obscure or arcane idea,[36] but actually the matter is otherwise – it is the core idea of recent times, generally assumed without reflection and often left unexpressed.

This ascetic modernism divested itself long ago of theological authority, with its world-picture of the creator's providence and human destiny. And the ancient philosophical idea of the soul and body proved to be unsustainable in the light of modern science, so that the way was opened for a scientific psychology that was empiricist, naturalist, and often behaviourist. This tendency is still dominant in the philosophy of mind, and I shall cite one or two examples to undergird my main claim. Galen Strawson, in his essay 'The Self: A Fallacy of Our Age,'[37] challenges what he takes to be an academic consensus of recent times, that being a self is constituted essentially by a narrative consciousness of the life that I have lived and intend to continue. Some people, and many authors among them, he says, have a strong conviction of narrative, and possess a 'diachronic' view of self: personhood persisting through time. But according to Strawson, it is just as possible to exist in a non-narrative way, and indeed to grasp one's life as only episodic (not diachronic); moreover, this is every bit as good and ethical a life as the other; in fact it's clear that Strawson praises it as a superior view of life, less weighed down by a portentous presentation of one's ego. We can safely divest ourselves of the stories we tell about our being. (He includes Heidegger among the diachronic narrativists. It may be that Heidegger inclines more to the diachronic view of life than the episodic, but in fact both these alternatives apply only to the conception of life that I was calling *bios*. Neither would be applicable to the actual matter of concern to Heidegger, what actually constitutes our life: existence.)

Let me cite another English philosopher of our time, who shows us that we can divest ourselves of our so-called personal identity: Derek

Parfit.[38] As I sketched in chapter 2, he undertakes to show weaknesses in our common view, and its philosophical ancestors, that each of us is an identical person throughout the extent of his or her life. He has many arguments against this view, some of them of a hi-tech, science-fiction character (persons dividing like amoebas, transplanted brain hemispheres, and so on), some based on more familiar material. This argument certainly has a Humean background. But what sustains Parfit's position is not a mere methodological preference for observable data. It is the will to be rid of the self. *Reasons and Persons* is a venture in travelling light, a demonstration of what we can do without: soul, personal identity, narrative and continuity. The force of this book, and of so very many others, proceeds from the intuition that a metaphysical girding for the self, a soul or some other interior landscape, a hope for immortality, are *unworthy* of us in modern times. We have the duty to avoid consoling stories of the soul that intimate that we are important in the universe. Only a thinking that honestly faces the absence of the gods and the soul, that sees the heaven now scraped bare, that confronts the vastness of the universe, grasping the human condition as that of animals crawling on the earth, is permissible. This is thinking that is resolute. Although many people believe that such modern philosophy is shaped above all by science, my argument is that neither scientific experiments nor mathematical calculation undergird its deepest commitments. The deep commitment is to a kind of stripped-down honesty, and Doing-Without, that is opposed most of all to spurious dreams about humanity's dignity and special place in the universe. The key motive is an ideal of authenticity.

The kind of thinking I call ascetic modernism is in general not merely irreligious and anti-religious but positively atheistic. We saw that authentic existence in *SZ* was godless. But here we need to note that there is another atheism that is not authentic in terms of the present discussion. I want to differentiate an authentic form of atheism from an inauthentic form. The understanding or interpretation of a phenomenon is authentic when the phenomenon is brought closely into connection to the self; it is inauthentic when it is disconnected from the self. We see an example of this at the end of the first paragraph of *SZ*, section 32, where understanding and interpretation are said to be inauthentic when they focus on the world around us rather than upon the self itself. There is certainly an etymological strand in these terms (*eigen* signifying something appropriated by the self, just like the term *autos* that is the root for the word 'authentic'). Using the term in this sense, we can differentiate an inauthentic atheism from an authentic one. Where someone merely notes the circumstance that the age of faith has passed away, that we live in an era of unbelief, this is an inauthentic understanding. Supposedly something just *happened*. Faith has ebbed away, churches stand empty, *man glaubt nicht mehr*. The contrast I have in mind is with an atheism that is authentic, which affirms that it is not fit for me to believe in God. To believe in a God is incompatible with my sense of myself, my intellect, my autonomy. I cannot, I will not, bow to a God.

Now I should add that a very common viewpoint today ascribes the weakening of religion to science. It alleges that with the advent of science, religion has been placed under siege. But with respect to this opinion I shall also differentiate an inauthentic from an authentic atheism. An atheism is inauthentic if it argues that recent astronomical studies leave no place for God, or that recent biological studies (evolutionary perhaps) have ruled out God. This understanding of things supposes that the results of scientific research have come into conflict with certain doctrines of religion (creation of the universe, separate creation of distinct species). But these scientific results are not germane to those doctrines. These sciences gain no access to that immaterial and eternal domain into which the thoughts of religion conduct the believer. Biology and astronomy cannot prove that there is nothing immaterial or eternal; they simply exclude such a domain from their fields of study, and so no inference from them to atheism is valid. By contrast, authentic scientific atheism expresses the resolve to adhere solely and strictly to a scientific kind of *thinking*; it is the resolve to limit one's thinking in practice to sciences like astronomy and biology; it is a certain resolute posture of the self. When Heidegger said that philosophy's mode of existence excluded faith, this was an authentic atheism on his part (though it had little to do with science).

The recent book by Dawkins[39] is full of inauthentic arguments for atheism, i.e., ones based on the findings or results of recent scientific studies, especially in chapter 4. We have more and more evidence for Darwinian evolution, but this requires no God (therefore God does not exist: *non sequitur*). Cosmic regularities do not establish intelligent design (therefore God does not exist: *non sequitur*). Soon we shall show that life has a chemical source (therefore God does not exist: *non sequitur*). Such counterarguments depend on Dawkins' view that belief in God is a scientific hypothesis – 'God's existence or non-existence is a scientific fact about the universe, discoverable in principle if not in practice' (p. 50) – that came about to explain phenomena of that sort. But historically this is certainly not true. Moreover, logically, it requires that one reframe every religious belief into the form of the scientific method. But that is a completely arbitrary proposal. It is like saying that from now on musical criticism must be based on physical studies in audiology; from now on the science of optics will exercise the functions of the art critic – and perhaps of the artist too, for that matter. This exposes the weakness of a scientistic philosophy that is not aware of the multiple possibilities of disclosure, and the limitations of each. Inauthentic atheism, then, is supported here only by the weakest of arguments. But the book has another strand: authentic atheism, meaning that it expresses the resolve to employ only scientific argumentation; any other form of thought is repugnant and unworthy; there is really only one form of disclosure. The remark cited above from p. 50 is his resolve, meaning 'I *will not* consent to allow my mind to chase after religious notions.' This underlies the strongly rhetorical character of his book that seeks to awaken a similar resolve in the reader by a torrent of sarcasm and abuse aimed at the Bible and theologians, and mockery aimed at philosophers. Here the person of the author stands forth in his own right, a person engulfed in emotion. It is certainly his emotional eruptions, rather than the calibre of his thought and argument, that gained him his readers.

I shall conclude with a remark concerning ascetic autonomy in general, not only its atheist form. There appears to be a paradox here that arises when this kind of thinking is given expression in discourse. From Heidegger, we derived the point that a resolute and authentic self-understanding has eliminated not only moralism and indignation, not only a preoccupation with success and achievement, but the very idea of justifying the self. And the stripped-down ascetic philosophy of our time has the purpose of undermining the spurious paths we have followed in justifying our existence. Now we see the paradox: that to reveal human existence as utterly unjustified and unjustifiable, the posture of Mr Tough Guy, proves to be one further means of self-justification after all. Ascetic autonomy becomes a means of self-justification when it is given the inauthentic turn, when it becomes the means of asserting the superiority of the Tough Guys over all those others who cling to childish beliefs. *We* are resolute and authentic because we have been able to face the spectres of meaninglessness that cowed both philosophers and their public in the past. This is a justification of the self that also accomplishes a magnification of the self. Ascetic autonomy differs from self-righteousness because of the breadth of its scope. The self-righteous agent is resolutely self-focused, but ascetic autonomy dismisses all possibilities of justification: the world itself is unjustified. The few who can know and accept this truth form a kind of league of their own (Dawkins calls them 'the brights'), so the autonomy is not entirely self-focused. The existential genealogy of ascetic autonomy, as we have traced it here, proceeds from authenticity – so it should not be likened to the different forms of inauthenticity we treated earlier in the chapter: moralism, righteous indignation, the refusal of blame, incapacity for shame, or the inability to be guilty. All this it puts beneath itself, resolutely eliminating any question of justification at all. But we can see its dialectic. The 'brights' have indeed, by their own lights, justified their existence, and magnified it.

We shall return to ascetic autonomy in chapter 7, where we shall appraise it from the point of view of spirit.

5 Magnifying the Community

Social and political thought studies the many forms of community. Our inquiry into existence is not concerned with this variety, but with the character of our attachment itself, the ways in which we belong to a community, be the latter what it may. What is important to everyone, ancient or modern, is an identification with one group and a separation from other ones. Is it too much to say that belonging in a community affords a 'justification' for our life or existence? When we consider it, not from the viewpoint of reason but from the viewpoint of care, this is true. A national community or a religious one or some smaller local community is often held together by judgments made about or against other communities that are perceived as rivals and threats. All such communities share a world with rival communities: club versus club, church versus church, and above all nation versus nation. It is in this relationship that a community is obliged to magnify itself – thereby magnifying its members – and also to justify itself, inasmuch as rivals cast into doubt its accomplishments and principles.

Being in a community is not just a belonging to it, but an identification with it, and identification (identity) opens out the way to self-magnifying. If we are convinced of the greatness of the community we are attached to, this makes for a vindication of our own greatness. Each of us has the further concern for the justification of that community to which we belong, and this too recoils back upon the singular self. Our justification through the community must encompass a justification *of* the community. There has been a huge literature on this in recent years, over the 'politics of identity.'[1]

The present chapter treats the magnifying of the community, and the following one treats the justification of the community. We begin by showing how a philosophy of existence naturally extends into a philosophy of the community, drawing on *SZ*. Then we offer two illustrations of the magnification of the community: one drawn from the world of Pericles and Athens, and one drawn from modern nationalism. We then turn to Heidegger's own involvement with nationalism in the 1930s, posing the question whether it was the inevitable fulfilment of his existential-phenomenological project. We conclude this chapter with some observations about militant religion in our own times. The following chapter on the justification of the community will offer some counterposing illustrations drawn from ancient times and from Heidegger's philosophy.

Existence and Community

The account of existence in chapter 2 above did not manage to treat a factor that is just as decisive and primordial in our being as anything else: our being-with, *Mit-sein*. Existence is the ability to be, but this ability cannot be realized in separation: it must incorporate others as well, i.e., incorporate an ability to be with others, incorporate an understanding of that ability, and thus incorporate an understanding of the others themselves. The thesis of chapter 4 of the first division of *SZ*, sections 25–7, is expressed in the chapter title: 'Being-in-the-World as Being-with and Being-a-Self,' a double structure bringing together into one account two equal aspects of being-in-the-world. So being-with is not a mere circumstance of how we occur in the world. The presence of other people in the world is anticipated in the constitution of our being, and in our understanding of that constitution. It is not by agreement or convention or contract that we form an association with them – belonging structurally together with them is inscribed in our constitution: it is ontological, not conventional. With readers like Philipse, the very idea of authenticity has been misinterpreted to imply an ideal of solitude and heroic aloofness.[2] Such readings err in failing to see that *Mit-sein* is ontologically constitutive and irremovable. And the idea of authenticity, for its part, is realized both in being a self and in being with others. Sections 25–7 discuss our being-with-others in the inauthentic mode and in the authentic mode, as well as our being-a-self in the authentic mode and in the inauthentic mode: being yourself authentically is accompanied by authentic being-with-others, and inauthentic selfhood is accompanied by an inauthentic collectivity. It is a constant error in Heidegger readings to suppose that authentic existence necessarily implies solitude, so that inauthenticity arises from our social being or is equivalent to that.[3] It is not only our understanding that is given over to being with others; the others belong to our facticity as well: that is, the social world is an *a priori* condition for the self's projecting of itself, a condition for its existence. Chapter 4 discussed authenticity in detail.

A similar tendency has arisen in the reception of Kierkegaard over the years, suggesting a completely asocial vision of the 'singular individual,' a philosophy where there is and can be no community. This is an understandable reaction to Kierkegaard, but it is an incomplete one, for this reading is based only on his texts in existential philosophy, separating them from all the Christian discourses. Those discourses were addressed to a religious community and were unthinkable without it.[4]

Because of the formal character of Heidegger's treatments in *SZ*, there was little or no opportunity in the treatise to investigate the different forms that being-with can take in actual life, such as collegiality, friendship, joint ventures, marriage, parenthood, community organizations, nationality, statehood, internationalism, and so on.[5] But given that the question of existence pertains to fundamental ontology, i.e., belongs to the preparatory inquiry that is to lead to the question of being in general, we might ask if there is truly a lacuna in *SZ*. What ought to have been added? Certainly there are many types of community, but it does not seem that it was necessary for Heidegger to differentiate them or appraise them. But of course we can do so, and are doing so. Heidegger's account always speaks of 'others' in the plural: this is not that magnified Other, spelled with a capital letter, that we read of in Lévinas[6] and his followers. Rather, these others are those among whom we exist (*unter ihnen*), among whom each of us is also reciprocally one among others; it is not that we confront them over against us or above us.

An essential supplement to Heidegger's account of being-with is the treatment of communication in sections 33 and 34. It is evident that all understanding, interpretation, and utterance have been realized within a social framework, and should be taken from the start as an articulation of our being-with.

To consider the application of the philosophy of existence to social and national life, we need to absorb the main contents of Heidegger's chapter on temporality and history (second division, chapter 5), treating the temporal and historical determinants of our life. History is certainly the venture of countless millions of people, but to approach the very constitution of what is historical, Heidegger begins, in section 72, with some reflections on the temporal being of the singular self. In our resolute being-towards our own end, death, we bring into play the other marker of our finitude, our birth, because of the ecstatic constitution of death, our ultimate futurity. It reaches back into our past in the sense that every initiative and project that we have undertaken since our birth finds its nullification here. The shadow that falls backwards on our life discloses that life as a forwards stretching into the shadow, a tensile stretch in which everything we did and experienced shows itself as the mere Between: between birth and death. The self that is mortal must also be natal (p. 374). Existing, i.e., the ability to be, is precisely this stretching (p. 373). Conceived ecstatically, neither birth nor death is an event; rather, they concern us. Just as we are always en-route to death, we perpetually retrieve our birth (p. 374), and in this way we run our life's race. I use the latter phrase to render Heidegger's difficult phrase: *das Da-sein geschieht*, literally 'Da-sein happens.' For an ontological comprehension of our life, then, we need to grasp this race more fully, i.e., the course of the race, which is the structure of *Geschehen*. This alone will open up a view of the broad currents that appear in the course of every life's race. The very coursing of these essential currents constitutes the vastness of temporality itself in its totality. This is what we usually call history (*die Geschichte*). German differentiates *die Historie*, a narration, from *die Geschichte*, the happenings that become narrated (the latter term is related to *geschehen*, 'to happen'). But Heidegger's phenomenology is not a study of *Geschichte* as such, but rather of what constitutes it, its essence, *die Geschichtlichkeit*. This term is often translated as 'historicity' or 'historicality,' but our present usage renders *Geschichte* as the currents that course in every life's race, and *Geschichtlichkeit* as the very coursing of the great currents, never detached from the race run in everyone's life.

We are looking at the running of life's race to find how the course of it defines our existence (p. 382). The race consists of our choosing and acting, but we do not derive our possible choices from the death towards which we race. Others have preceded us in the race, still others accompany us now, and someone got us first started in some direction: our finitude also means that we are surrounded by all these others (p. 383). Their lives are patterns among which we choose. And the choices we make will determine our fate (*Schicksal*), i.e., how we fare in the race, what fate we are capable of (p. 384). But fate does not only befall each of us individually. Those with whom we run (*Mitgeschehen*, p. 384), those who ran before us, those we followed and those who follow us, all share with us in a common outcome (*Geschick*). A *Geschick*, such as victory or defeat in war, is the crucial component in the coursing of the great currents, in *der Geschichte*. 'By *Geschick* we mean the course taken by the life-current of a whole community, a people. It is not merely a product of the fates of singular individuals.'[7] Whether we are referring to the fate of an individual, or the destiny of a people, the essential mark of this category is that it confirms our finitude. What we attain is not simply the goal or *telos* of action postulated by ourselves in our autonomy, but a counter-*telos* or anti-*telos*, that stands in the place where we had installed our *telos* but rebukes our assumption of power and determination. We are overpowered.

Now we must see that fate, whether singular or collective, is essentially a possibility, and must be comprehended phenomenologically primarily out of the future. This basic structure of everything historical is determined by the future, and not the past. The possible choice that I can retrieve from a past hero's life is futural, for it is a past that is understood as something possible. It is something to be retrieved, or repeated (*wiederholt*). That structure makes possible our different relations to the community, i.e., our forerunners, our contemporaries, and those yet to come. It makes possible our loyalty (*Treue*) to the community, and also our possible opposition to it or to some of its members, a struggle (*Kampf*) for them or against them (p. 385). That is what historical existence consists of.

We can examine phenomenologically the manner in which the self confronts its own historical *Schicksal* and also confronts the *Geschick* of the nation, for that is what Heidegger's *Volk* or *Gemeinschaft*, or later *Volksgemeinschaft*, is. (On the latter term, see note 14 below.)

First, there is the possibility of identification. The self is projecting itself into its possible future. In doing so, it will continue in a confluence with the historical movement of the entire nation. But it reaches back, in the life of the nation, for a prototype or hero for repetition. It draws this out for itself, and then, as Heidegger says, it hands it down to itself; it does not merely 'receive' a message, but takes it over and gives it to itself. This possibility, drawn out of the life of the nation, it now projects as its own futural possibility, making its own project possible by way of this 'heritage' it has taken. It faces the world, draping itself in a project that it has inherited but made now to live a second time. This is what I called identification, and I see in it the ground of the possibility of nationalism, to be discussed below. But we shall examine a second possibility in the next chapter.

Magnifying the *Polis*

While politicians no doubt engage in justifying themselves as well as their nations or communities, we need to interrogate their words to find out how they suppose that *all* the citizens can find their place within the nation and within its collective glorification. This theme appears with striking clarity in some speeches that come down to us from classical Greece, precisely where the tradition of political philosophy finds its origin. We shall look at Pericles, who elevated his *polis* to great heights, but seemed to submerge its citizens. Then the community on which I shall focus is the nation, which has been in modern times the most important and comprehensive community, formative for those others (clubs, churches, families) that lie within it. It is, moreover, of all communities the one most directly committed to the justification of our existence.

Thucydides' *History*[8] offers portraits of the small-scale ancient *polis*, presenting rhetorically the very way in which individuals and subgroups belonged to the *polis* and identified with it. One should not call a Greek *polis* a nation, but still there is a sufficient parallel here for my purpose. Here we have a famous example of magnifying the *polis*, which seems to magnify everyone in it – and perhaps also to justify them. In the *History*, book 2, chapter 4 (2:34–46), we read of the assembly held in Athens in the year 431 B.C.E. to mark the end of the first year of their war against Sparta: a funeral held for the soldiers who had fallen, those whose bones had been recovered and those whose remains could not be found. The funeral oration on this occasion was pronounced by Pericles, the democratic leader. Eulogies, and especially military ones, are perhaps the occasions most conducive to thoughts of human greatness, and so the funeral oration of Pericles (which Thucydides probably reported with some verisimilitude) has often been read as a pre-eminent document of the Greek ideal of greatness. Here the manner in which the youthful fallen soldiers belonged to the community appears, not in their own testimony, but in the rhetorical performance of the older statesman.

Pericles begins his oration by expressing the fear that his hearers may become jealous when they are made to hear about the dead mens' great deeds (2:35), but in fact none are recounted. The theme of the funeral oration rather is the greatness of Athens herself as a *polis*, and the effect is to present the greatness of the fallen soldiers as their being the citizens of such a city. The first topic (2:36) is what the current generation's ancestors had accomplished in building the city up and acquiring wealth and empire: such a city in its glory was then able to raise up such young men who were ready to die for her. Pericles then begins to praise 'our constitution and the way of life which has made us great' (2:36), as a democracy that is 'a model for others' (2:37), combining freedom with respect for law. Athens is the richest in culture and education (2:38–9), wisest in policy, and most generous to outsiders (2:40–41). Pericles makes us think that Sparta with all her allies must have been small-minded indeed not to defer to Athens in all things. 'This, then, is the kind of city for which these men, who could not bear the thought of losing her, nobly fought and nobly died' (2:41).

It is startling to hear Pericles speaking in praise of the famous dead without mentioning any of them by name. He speaks of their great exploits in their pursuit of the war, but he does not recount a single one in any detail. Only in the greatest generalities does Pericles recall their 'gallant conduct' and 'risks most glorious' (2:42). 'Famous men have the whole earth as their memorial,' says Pericles, but perhaps we can read this to refer even more to famous cities such as Athens. In fact, Pericles has praised the fallen soldiers for being Athenians. The oration is far more insistent on 'us' than it is on 'them' – they were great because they were a part of us. Greatness devolves upon the soldier from the *polis*. It is true that 'what made her great was men with a spirit of adventure, men who knew their duty' (2:43), yet we have also just heard the final word of praise that soldiers can expect – the summation of their greatness is to be 'worthy of their city.' This communitarian logic would seem to be that you are able to achieve greatness if you have the good fortune to belong to a community which is itself great. The corollary is that your role is to repeat the great deeds of the mighty ancestors whose exploits founded the great community. Such an ultra-communitarianism could hardly be found expressed in any modern political world, despite the conventional reverence that we often hear expressed for both Thucydides and Pericles.

Pericles brings his fellow citizens to stand proudly confronting the world outside with their incomparable identity: Athenians! And they possess the substantial token of their stature: the bodies of those who were ready to die for Athens, her witnesses, her martyrs. It is in their defiance that the citizens experience their own strong justification, arisen through that of the city itself, now enhanced by hearing of the sacrifice of the fallen, who are now incomparably justified. Their incomparable justification lay in the mighty deeds that magnified the great city, and the citizens experience a vicarious justification through membership in a common city with those martyrs. It could seem from Pericles's address that a city so greatly magnified by those who were justified would itself be justified – its war with Sparta now clearly a righteous cause.

The Nation: Magnitude through Justification

In many ways, the discipline of philosophy and the problem of nationality are not well suited to one another, and philosophy has to pay heed to history and sociology for insight here. For one thing, there is no firm set of criteria by which we could acknowledge that X is a nation while Y is not. This is evident to everyone who has thought about the problem, and has been expressed very well by Max Weber in an essay called 'The Nation.'[9] Moreover, political philosophy since antiquity has been preoccupied with government, the state, regimes better and worse, questions that cut across the existence of the nation. Modern political philosophy considers the origin and justification of the state, liberty, justice, welfare – issues that lead to a correlation of state and society, society and the economy, leaving largely aside the question whether a given society is a nation. Nationalism has often been looked on with suspicion by philosophers. But this is an awkward circumstance, since the huge political issues that confront humanity in our age, at the outset of the twenty-first century, involve nothing as much as nationality. This is pre-eminently true in Canada, which confronts the claims of the Quebecois nation and of the First Nations. It is true of Europe, whose *patriae* or fatherlands, states and nations at once, seek to accommodate members of other nations within their borders. It is national questions that agitate the entire Middle East and account for much of the violence in India, Pakistan, and Afghanistan, and as well the Chinese confrontation with Tibet. The United States confronts its external enemies whose agendas are far more national than economic, and it too has growing national diversities within its borders.

The principal thrust of Weber's account of the nation is the dynamism that is inherent to it. It is a community that overreaches family, clan, and tribe, and, though it may not have a government of its own, i.e., a state, for Weber there is above all the subjective sense of community in a nation, a solidarity, and this subjective sense of solidarity shows the inherent dynamic of tending to build up a state. This tendency is not motivated by desire for good administration or economic rationality, but by a solidarity based on prestige, the prestige of a community that has some unique mission in the world, a cultural prestige. This can be founded on a common language (but need not be, for different nations have shared one tongue), it can be founded on a common religious faith (but need not be, for creeds often cut across nations), and it can be founded on a common racial heritage (but need not be). The key idea of a common history can be tied up with any of those factors. It is typically intellectuals who bring national sentiments to expression, and in hoping for a national state they seek to work with politicians whose métier is precisely the domain of the state.

To add to Weber's analysis, one could say that the very idea of 'nation' is a rhetorical one rather than an analytical or scientific or philosophical one. I do not use the term 'rhetoric' in an unfavourable sense, nor do I suggest that there is something illusory about the nation. The elders seek to imbue the young with a passion for the nation, and point the way to activities that, in strengthening the nation, will confer a justification upon their lives. In doing so, they also communicate the conviction that the existence and mission of their nation find their own justification within the horizon of world history. The nation extends itself through history by being passed down in rhetorical communication, and here, least of all, is any idea of a mutual social contract tenable. Here is the perfect case of a community that belongs *a priori* to the facticity of the existing self who is born into a historical community that uses every possible means to enlist his or her loyalty.

A central fact is that there are, and always have been, many nations. And we have reason to think that there always will be, though this is not a matter that reason could demonstrate. Very likely reason's preference would be for a single world community without diverse nations, but as it happens this pluralism is a part of our facticity, our history. 'Nation' is not an idea of reason. And what appears equally central to human facticity is the rivalry among nations. As we proceed to consider the matter further, we shall conclude that an existential analysis is obliged to operate without the hope of the ideal worldwide community.

What we shall bring forward is that the essential drive of the nation is to magnify itself (and indirectly its citizens). But this puts the phenomena in a different order than what we saw in the case of individual success: if Iacocca's drive was to magnify his being so as then to justify it, we see that in national contentions the effort of justification is undertaken as a means to self-magnifying.

Two documents come to us from the height of the Cold War. In the

first, President John F. Kennedy is addressing the American Newspaper
Publishers Association in New York, April 1961:

> Our way of life is under attack. Those who make themselves our enemy
> are advancing around the globe ... We are opposed around the world by a
> monolithic and ruthless conspiracy that relies primarily on covert means
> for expanding its sphere of influence – on infiltration instead of invasion,
> on subversion instead of elections, on intimidation instead of free choice,
> on guerillas by night instead of armies by day. Its preparations are con-
> cealed, not published. Its mistakes are buried, not headlined. Its dissenters
> are silenced, not praised. No expenditure is questioned, no rumor is
> printed, no secret is revealed.[10]

In the second, Premier Nikita Khrushchev is writing in retirement,
sometime after 1964:

> The main thing I noticed about the capitalist West when I was in New
> York, which Gorky once called the City of the Yellow Devil, is that it's not
> the man that counts but the dollar. Everyone thinks of how to make
> money, how to get more dollars. Profits, the quest for capital, and not peo-
> ple, are the center of attention there.
>   The ruling quarters of the United States describe the so-called American
> way of life as a model for the 'free world.' But what kind of freedom is
> that? It is the freedom to exploit, the freedom to rob, the freedom to die of
> starvation when there are surpluses, the freedom to be unemployed when
> production capacities stand idle. Freedom in the United States is a free-
> dom for monopoly capital to oppress the working people, to bamboozle
> people with the bi-partisan system, to impose its will on their partners in
> military blocs. Such a society provides the basis for wars between coun-
> tries because the tendency toward reaction inside the country and towards
> expansion and aggression outside is characteristic of monopoly capitalism
> and imperialism.[11]

We see in both these documents the language of justification. But we
need to ask: to what end? It is manifestly to the end of self-magnifying.
   Kennedy had been dealing with continued Soviet pressure on Berlin,
and just weeks before had authorized an unsuccessful invasion at
Cuba's Bay of Pigs. Now he is telling the world that these actions were
justified; more, he is offering justification in advance for further actions
of the United States to contain communism (and the Cuban missile cri-

sis would loom up before long). But he invokes the communist threat here for an even deeper reason: it is not just the military actions that are justified, but also America itself: the 'way of life' that he is committed to defend is to have its complete justification in its achievement of individual freedom, the progress towards equality, and the rule of law. The founding ethos of the republic bestows justification on it – that is why actions in defence of it are justified.

Khrushchev's memoirs constitute in part a self-justification, showing how the career that he spent in pursuit of power, and then exercising it until his fall, contributed to the growth and security of the Soviet Union. The present passage explains the views of the Communist Party concerning capitalist nations and in particular the United States. To undermine any self-justification of capitalist ideology by pointing out the glaring faults of the system is to justify the communist movement and most of all its leading power, the Soviet Union. In the light of this fundamental justification of communism, all the Soviet diplomatic and military initiatives receive their own secondary justification.

Not the vast descriptive manifold of forms of community, but the reciprocal interaction between the self and a community (of whatever description) is the theme here. One clue to the existential character of a community or nation lies in the rhetorical means by which political leaders and other speakers propose the justification of them. We noted that Khrushchev's memoirs (like those of most politicians) were a work of self-justification. And in the passage I quoted, in offering a justification for the communist movement and repudiating any justification for capitalism, his own self-justification continued. Anyone who stands forth as speaker or writer to vindicate his own community bathes in the radiance of this work: Khrushchev and the Soviet Union have some community of being, whereby its justification implies his own, and vice versa. It is his identity, his being a Soviet citizen and secretary, that is endorsed – both justified and magnified – through the rhetorical celebration of the Soviet Union. This is particularly evident in the speech or writing of a statesman, but the very same point applies to every member of a nation: the justification of oneself, through identifying with the nation, is accomplished in the same breath with the justification of the nation.

We may take a look at Heidegger's nationalism in the 1930s. What we see in *SZ* is not nationalism, but the orientation of a phenomenology that could be put into the service of nationalism. The following years, especially 1933, show how this played itself out. In those years he often lectured to students on the German idealists,[12] intimating the revival of their vocation as universal teachers and guides to the people. As Germany was entering the years of its most tormenting struggle between left and right, Heidegger would often refer to Germany, never a theme in his phenomenological decade. Above all, the precision, finesse, and exactness of phenomenological work begin to vanish as a headier historical and ideological mission comes to dominate Heidegger's utterances. Then, in a rupture that completely surprised his older students and friends in 1933,[13] he threw his influence towards National Socialism, and joined the party after acceding to the Rectorate, on which occasion he offered an inaugural address, *The Self-Assertion of the German University*,[14] whose exoteric message was that academic freedom was an outworn concept and that the faculty and students would be obliged to serve the German people and the new movement of National Socialism under the guidance of their philosopher-*Führer*, Heidegger himself. A new kind of philosophy, non-phenomenological, challengingly Teutonic with references to national heroes, Nietzsche above all, and figures from the heroic age of the Greeks, especially Heraclitus, has completely displaced the Kierkegaardian theme of the self and its existence. Though he calls for the university to assert itself, and though this requires the knowledge and recognition of its essence, and though this essence is science – we hear his national passion when the university has to be the *German* university.[15] This entire history has now been presented in detail, far more than I have been able to show here, in a recently published book by Radloff.[16]

Another statement of this new philosophy is in the *Introduction to Metaphysics*[17] (lectures of 1935), where we can read, for example:

> This Europe, in its unholy blindness always on the point of cutting its own throat, lies today in the great pincers between Russia on one side and America on the other. Russia and America, seen metaphysically, are both the same: the same hopeless frenzy of unchained technology and of the rootless organization of the average man.[18]

Heidegger's strength was not political wisdom, but he did possess a rare conceptual power, hardly equalled among twentieth-century philosophers, which means that his studies devoted to history (like his other studies) still reach out beyond the tragedy of his times and of his own involvement. We shall take up this positive possibility in the next chapter.

Militant Religion

Very different from the 1930s, when fascism and communism flourished, are our own times, which seem to be marked by a revival of vigorous and conflicting religions. The religions are embodied in communities that are articulated in completely different ways – the worldwide sense of Islam, the diversity of Protestant churches, the organized hierarchy of the Catholic Church, the unique commitment of secular and religious Jews together to the State of Israel, the national expression of Hinduism, a new militancy of Buddhist monks. Both the public rhetoric and the believers' consciousness celebrate the greatness of their communities and their traditions, a magnifying of the community that we cannot ignore here, for millions of people find in these communities the foundations of their being. Perhaps our inquiry will permit certain clarifications to be made.

Popular discourse calls these newly invigorated religious communities 'fundamentalist,' yet I believe that is a misnomer. Whether in its original Protestant context[19] or in its current application to Islamic, Jewish, and other religions, this term merely designates a certain theological preference (literalism, narrow orthodoxy, etc.) that in itself carries no implication of militant aggressiveness towards the world outside (the Crusades and the Inquisition were not 'fundamentalist'). What is salient about the militant believers of today, intolerant of other religions and infidels, is that they are prepared to use armed power to strengthen their cause and to weaken others. It seems that the greatness of God must require the magnifying of the community of believers, and of each individual member – and the fateful step comes when force is employed to confirm that greatness. This is not a structure unique to Islam, nor is it logically implied by the Islamic theology of a unified community (*umma*) and state, with a *sharia* law. That is to say, the Western-Christian tradition of the separation of church and state is by no means the uniquely rational constitution. History offers evidence of *sharia*-governed caliphates that were not militant and aggressive towards outsiders or minorities within, and it offers as well darker evidence of aggressive militancy within the Christian West. It is where we must magnify ourselves and our community (and God!) by such aggression that we may speak of militant religion.

Militant religion starts from the greatness of God, and finds it inconceivable that the faithful community, devoted to God, should not itself be great. Greatness then devolves upon all the believers; the Victorian

Christian version can be seen in the hymn 'Onward, Christian Soldiers.' Nevertheless, we need to recognize two points. First of all, there are three differentiations and relationships here: (*a*) the relation between the self and the religious community; (*b*) the relation between the religious community and the state; and (*c*) the relation of both of them to God. But where the greatness of God stands unequivocally in first place, the community is only magnified in a conditional and derived fashion, like the magnification of the self. And thus, to magnify God does not by any means imply a magnification of the community and the self – indeed, in much religious consciousness, we are abased in front of the greatness of God. In the second place, every religion also contains a potential remedy against this militancy. Nothing is more clear in history than the possibility of prophets like Amos and Jeremiah who appealed to God in a struggle *against* the state and against the official religious community. We can see an analogy to the role of conscience in the analytic of existence – the call of the prophet to his or her people breaks into the communal discourse like the call of conscience, and calls the people out of the inauthenticity of their religion.

6 Justifying the Community

It is not only in moral situations that the issue arises of justifying oneself as a whole, or one's life as a whole. One can find one's justification through one's community (national, religious, or whatever). This depends upon the prospect of justifying that community itself – this is the moral society, a society endowed with a great culture, with a historic mission, and so on. On that assumption, the leaders of the community can appeal to youth to dedicate their lives to the service of the community – this is a promise of justifying one's life, leading a worthwhile life. But how could the community as a whole receive justification? And how could the single self participate in that? It offers me nothing to belong to a community if I am unable to find it excellent and right, especially in relation to other communities, ones that I must oppose and reject because of my commitment to my own community. In the speeches of community leaders we see how the whole community is justified, especially in its relations with other communities, in war and in its internal life and practice. The individual who hears and believes such addresses, finding the whole community justified, thereby finds an anchor for his or her own life: the justification of the community member is accomplished together with that of the whole – this is inherently a double work. This is the background for what we call the 'identity' of the self as citizen or believer. The justification of the individual is now framed by his or her whole world; the broadest conditions for the being of the self have now entered into the justification. Both the magnifying of a community and the justification of it have their impact on the individuals: to magnify and justify their existence.

We shall begin by stepping back in time again to pursue a contrast between the philosophy of Socrates and the rhetoric of Pericles, turning precisely on the interaction of the citizen and the *polis*. Then we turn again to Heidegger, who shows us the temporal, historical constitution of the nation in interaction with the temporality of the self. Heidegger will point us to a deeper concept of civilization in which the limits of each historical nation can be explored.

Caring for the *Polis*

In a speech delivered about thirty years after Pericles', we hear from Socrates a radically different rebalancing of the relation between the self and the *polis*-community that incorporates the intervening influences of sophistic and philosophy. In Plato's *Apology*, 36b–c, Socrates, having been found guilty of the charges brought against him, will, it seems, be put to death. But Athenian law and custom required the accused to make a counterproposal, his own suggestion for a sentence. This leads Socrates to offer a retrospective assessment of his life – at this climactic moment he is setting a value on that life so as to justify the sentence that he is proposing to the jury. (First, he proposes that the Athenians should 'sentence' him by providing him with a lifetime's worth of free meals in the town hall of Athens. Later, in a more serious vein, he proposes a small fine.) Meletus, his accuser, had proposed the death penalty.

> He assesses the penalty at death. So be it. What counter-assessment should I propose to you, gentlemen of the jury? Clearly it should be a penalty I deserve, and what do I deserve to suffer or to pay ...?

What kind of life was his? What was its point and value? We recognize that Socrates also speaks here of an assessment that he had already made at the beginning, when he first set out to be the gadfly of Athens. He did not fall accidentally into his life of probing and questioning; he resolved upon it out of deliberation (*mathōn*), embarking on it in contrast to other kinds of life he could have undertaken.

> I have deliberately not led a quiet life but have neglected what occupies most people: wealth, household affairs, the position of general or public orator or the other offices, the political clubs and factions that exist in the city.

This vast range of activities that he has excluded from his life includes just about anything that claimed eminence or importance in an ancient community, the means by which citizens would claim some significance, some justification for their lives. To this we can add a point made early on in the *Apology*, that Socrates did not claim to be a sophist, a professor either; he differentiates himself sharply from such persons and such activities (19b–20e). Socrates has also sketched his difference from the poets and the artisans of the city as well as its public leaders (21b–22e). So Socrates had no profession at all! But he is making the provocative claim that all those who do follow one of these other ways of life are having an easy time of it compared to him: these are all forms of the 'quiet life' (36b). By contrast to them, Socrates's life is one of exposure and unprotectedness. In the present summing-up, and in his earlier reflection and choice, there was no reference to any goals that he might have been aiming to achieve, economic, literary, or whatever. Goals would have been something distinct from the pathway of life that pursued them, but instead of that, his original choice had been to live in a certain kind of way, to be a certain kind of person, and that is how he expresses his self-assessment now that he is just about at the end of his days. 'What do I deserve for being such a man?'

He says that he was not really equipped anyway to lead a life like any of those other ones. A reflection on his own nature gave him his direction in life, a sense of the singularity of his being. Though Socrates' choice was justified for himself, he does not question the value of all the kinds of life people lead other than his own, the value of a political, military, or economic life. His mission had not been to turn the Athenians away from the commitments they had made to all their affairs, so that they might come to lead a life like his. Nor does Socrates say that there should be no business or households or public offices:

> I thought myself too honest to survive if I occupied myself with those things. I did not follow that path that would have made me of no use either to you or to myself, but I went to each of you privately and conferred upon him what I say is the greatest benefit, by trying to persuade him not to care for any of his belongings before caring that he himself should be as good and as wise as possible. (36c)

This is the first of the two 'cares' that Socrates is appealing for in the present speech. He says that there is a gift that he alone can give them, and other work would have hindered him in giving it. 'I went to each of you privately' – as we see in the *Euthyphro* or the *Laches* – putting a focus on one other singular self in an encounter with the singular self of Socrates. The benefit that Socrates can offer is not conversion to the philosopher's life, but attention to a matter that ought to accompany and affect whatever life that person is already engaged in, politics or business. It is an appeal to the priority of a care for the self. With all the 'cares' demanded by a profession or a household, this is the further 'care' that ought not to be evaded.

As Socrates expresses it here, along with the care for 'all that which is yours,' *tōn heautou*, there is a care for 'you yourself,' *heautou*.[1] 'All that which is yours' embraces just the economic management, military struggle, and the other matters Socrates has set aside from his own life. (See note 2 below for a justification of this reading.) The Socratic challenge is that his interlocutor should be able to find, behind all that which is His, the self that is to be called He. As an interlocutor, I am asked to care that I myself should be as good and as wise as possible. These are not attributes pertaining to that which is merely Mine, they pertain to the self. These are the cares for and about existence. This is not making a sharp separation between what is Me and what is Mine, as if there could be a separation! It is a correction of the limited viewpoint of the citizen who is utterly given over to wordly affairs with oblivion of him or herself. The self is the grounding for the manifold of its possessions and affairs.

Now Socrates introduces an illuminating parallel and a further extension. He says that 'I went to each of you privately' for a further reason:

> nor to care for the city's possessions more than for the city itself, and to care for other things in the same way. What do I deserve for being such a man?

Socrates is also concerned that his fellow citizens should 'not care for the city's possessions more than for the city itself.' The grammar emphasizes the parallel: Socrates wants to awaken, not just care for *tōn tēs poleōs*, 'all that is the city's,' but also care for *autēs tēs poleōs*, for 'the city itself,' just he awakened care not just for *tōn heautou*, but for you yourself, *heautou*. As in the first case, there is no idea that the city could be disentangled utterly and exist separately from all that belongs to it, all its affairs. Socrates is voicing the corrective to bad politics and management, for which Athens is nothing but its walls, its navy, its treasury, and so on. What belongs to the city itself? I believe that the further study of 'the city itself, 'as distinct from its paraphernalia, is above all preoccupied with the laws of the city. This is apparent from the text of the *Apology*, for in recounting Socrates' justification of his own life, it focuses on his extreme, scrupulous regard for the laws, in contrast to the casual lawlessness of both the main 'political clubs and factions' in the city. It is also apparent from the literary context of the *Apology*. After the close of this text, Plato opens his next work, the *Crito*, in the prison where Socrates is being held in anticipation of his execution. Urged by his friends to make an escape, Socrates replies with a stout and inflexible vindication of the rule of law, expressed as an imagined dialogue between himself and the personified laws. The laws stand in the same relation to the city that the soul does to each of us, both taken as the object of a philosopher's care and contemplation. It is law that bestows justification upon the political undertakings of the city, and the highest undertaking of philosophy is to probe into the further justification of the law itself, a matter Plato undertook again and again, right up to his final work, *The Laws*.

To care for 'the city itself' would also be to care for the gods of the city, as Socrates had discussed with Euthyphro in the dialogue that usually precedes the *Apology*. It would include care for its history, so notably narrated in *Menexenus*, *Timaeus*, *Critias*, and other works. It would include a care for the future of the city: a theme of the *Republic*.

Though Socrates' main concern in this dialogue is with the self, he has added the supplementary phrase 'and to care for other things in the same way.' It is a universal kind of thinking that this speech brings before us. What are these 'other things'? The text does not mean that we should devote a similar care to the 'wealth, household affairs, the position of general or public orator or the other offices, the political clubs and factions that exist in the city.'[2] For my part, I would see in this an anticipation of the whole Platonic philosophy that searches for what things truly are, for their Ideas: the Ideas of all the virtues, for instance. The elaborate doctrine of the *Republic* is not, of course, implied by the *Apology* speech of Socrates, but something of that nature would be the outcome of his insistence, here and in the *Crito*, on the rule of law. To take the city into his care means finding that principle whereby its life and actions are justified: law. And if we do allow ourselves a reference to Plato at this point, we see that the Idea of justice, and laws that are appropriate to it, are precisely what justifies a *polis* or any type of regime, separating it from corrupt regimes. What is contained in the *Apology* itself is the double movement of care. We take the city into our care by seeking the law of justice by which its life becomes justified. And a care for the self will see how it belongs in this city. So it is able to find a possible justification for its being by a participation in the city that is finding its own justification. While Pericles had magnified his city to justify the soldiers' death, Socrates shows us how a single citizen has a responsibility, not only *to* the *polis* but *for* the *polis*. This route puts emphasis on the justification of the city rather than its magnification. And so, what the self gains from participation in such a city is not magnification. Indeed, this self may be ever so small and insignificant. What has become justified is actually the being of the self, understood as its membership in such a community. In caring for the city's own justification, the self may discover a justification not only for itself but for its being as both participant and guardian, for the city's laws permit the self to become a guardian. This justification is in principle capable of being shared by all the citizens together. That constitutes a striking contrast with a justification gained through the magnifying of the self, what we saw in our study of success in an earlier chapter.

Existence and History

Earlier, we treated the nationalistic writings of Heidegger from the 1930s, showing that they did not realize all the potentials of his phenomenology of history. The prevailing tone was celebration of the nation, much like Pericles in his time. We suggested that there was a different kind of possibility implicit in *SZ*, which was not an identification with the nation and its past heroes. In the other possible posture, the self reaches into the future with its projected possibility, and likewise aims at a confluence with the current of the whole nation. In expressing its care for the city itself or the nation itself, it recognizes this now as the *possible* city or nation. Here it has differentiated the city or nation Socratically from all its affairs and possessions. This futural community does not function as a source for the identity of the self. The self does not feed off the city. Rather, the city is an item that the self takes into its care. But the self does recognize its own facticity and *Geworfenheit* (guilt and encumbrance), which pertain to its own past, rather than that of the city or nation. This gives it leverage in confronting the guilt and encumbrance of the nation or city itself. It is just this Socratic posture that Heidegger himself did not achieve – he remained purely nationalistic, and in this way his stance is like that of Pericles rather than Socrates.

So in looking more closely at *SZ*, section 74, we discern that while *Schicksal*, fate, expresses what is historical in each one's life, it is *Geschick* – which we may translate as 'destiny' – that constitutes history proper, what lies in the coursing of the greatest currents of all, those of peoples or nations. We can pursue this further by referring to later writings of Heidegger (composed some years after the rectoral episode) that give more clarity and depth to the *Geschick–Geschichte* connection.

Particularly salient here is the 1946 article 'Anaximander's Saying.'[3] Near the start of the essay, Heidegger is commenting on the essence of history, *Wesen der Geschichte* (300/245), because he wants to preface his discussion of this famous fragment with reflections on the very difficulty of interpreting something separated from us by a twenty-five-hundred–year interval. What is our own current situation in history? And what should we say about the early history of the Greeks? He disputes the common representation that history runs its course in a continuity of time, marked by 'chronological distance and causal sequence,' *die chronologischen Abstände und die kausalen Aufreihungen* (311/254). He shows that an epoch of history is constituted by its *closure* against both prior epochs and later ones, applying the term 'epoch' in the sense of the ancient Stoics and Sceptics, the *epoché* that is a withdrawal or a withholding (311/254) that also yields a concealment. There is an *epoché* of *being* operative in each period of history. Thus what was given to Anaximander, or rather *sent* to him (*geschickt*), was a decisive but finite disclosure that revealed the dawning of the destiny (*Geschick*) of the Greeks, that which governed their existence in history (*Geschichte*). 'What is Greek is that dawn of destiny as which being itself lights itself up in beings, and lays claim to an essence of humanity, a humanity which, as destined, receives its historical path, a path sometimes preserved in, sometimes released from, but never separated from being.'[4] What is essential to history then is not at all its continuity or perdurance, for beginnings and endings are the stuff of history, and so are surprises. This idea opposes any view of 'history' as a hyper-entity. Though the Greeks lived out their destiny, much of their destiny was concealed from them, and even more of that was concealed from later epochs of history. Thus *erring* or *errancy* – *die Irre* – is the rule in history (310–11/254) both within one epoch and between epochs. 'Each time that being keeps to itself in its destiny, suddenly and unexpectedly, world happens. Every epoch of world-history is an epoch of errancy.'[5] The manifold *Geschicke* do nonetheless accumulate though they do not constitute an order or a story, and so we too in our time are fated to fall within the destiny of the Greeks, even as we confront our future, our 'coming, more primordially destined, history,' *der kommenden anfänglicher geschickten Geschichte* (300/245)

A people that lives in history, moves in it, are utterly committed to it, given over to it – so much so that we must say they course, they run – but not that they *are*. We should not attribute existence to a people. *Existenz* is in each case my own, but peoples and nations run, move, course. (Perhaps in Heidegger's later diction we could say that *sie sich ereignen*, they eventuate themselves.) We must not conceive them as substantial or ontic. This is just as important as avoiding the substantial view of the self. The historical conjunction, the *Gegeneinander* of the many nations, is the entire vastness in which each nation has its time and place, each one constituted by its *Geschick*. We cannot substantialize either *die Geschichte* or *das Geschick*.

Though the *Geschick* is limited, shadowed, by the *epoché* that belongs to it, it does bequeath a heritage. The disclosure of being to Anaximander lives on in its way, though modified by epochal concealment, to constitute the civilization of the West. This is the long interval that constitutes Western history itself. Heidegger thinks in an eschatological fashion about the West, *das Abendland* (301–2/246–7), stressing that it is the land of the evening, of the setting sun. What the West experiences as its destiny was ordained in the primordial disclosure and the heritage that lasted over two thousand years. In philosophy, this *Geschick* set the agenda for Heraclitus and Parmenides (323–5/264–6) – and we have further parallel texts in Heidegger that deal with these two and the reigning *Geschick* in both of them[6] – and Plato and Aristotle and the whole later tradition followed in their train.

Heidegger seems to see in the philosophy of Nietzsche our modern *Geschick* or destiny. Nietzsche formulates a counter-utterance to the Saying of Anaximander: 'To stamp becoming with the character of being – that is the *highest will to power*' (306/250). So we are able to see that *das Abendland*, that huge interval between these two *Geschicke*, is guided by them both. First, it is guided by the first *Geschick*, embodied as it is especially in the negative form of the concealed *Geschick*; and second, it is guided by the eschatological readiness for the destiny (*and its epoché*) that pertains to our own modernity and that is expressed by Nietzsche.

What then shall we say about this long interval itself? It is the time of metaphysics (336/275), and by this Heidegger means precisely the predominance of the *epoché*, oblivion both to the destiny and to what has been destined or sent in it. A central aspect of his reading of the fragment of Anaximander is that it has, as it were, a prophetic character corresponding to its eschatological character: Heidegger is able to read *in* the fragment itself the true diagnosis of the long history to which the thought of Anaximander would be exposed in the 'epoch' of metaphysics. What the fragment says is that a disorder, *adikia*, is committed, where a reckless disregard prevails, and yet there must be a *tisis*, a compensation – for that is demanded according to the ordaining order, *to chreōn*.[7] Central to Heidegger's reading is that this authentic *Geschick*, obscured during the twenty-five-hundred-year history of metaphysics, included the forecast of that very oblivion, for therein lies the most reckless disregard of all, the disregard of being in favour of a field of beings that we could master in both our thought and our practice. Still, metaphysics is that by which we lived. Our *adikia* was no mere whim; that is expressed, for instance, in the counter-discourse of Nietzsche. We need to grasp the character of this epoch of metaphysics.

I do believe that this carries the discussion of *SZ* forward,[8] forming a stable conceptual whole in Heidegger. It constitutes a formal treatment of the structure of history, which may invite a more concrete application, a de-formalization that leaves to one side Heidegger's particular preoccupation with the interpretation of pre-Socratic texts. My thought is that one concrete embodiment of the relation of *Geschick* to *Geschichte* is the relation of the nation to civilization. In applying Heidegger's text in this way, I am not of course attributing the application to him.

Nation and Civilization

As we spoke earlier about the nation, it was particularly clear that individuals find themselves cast, thrown, fated, into a national community. From the individual's standpoint, the national community has the character of facticity and heritage, a point captured by the lexical link of *natio* to 'natal.' It, least of all, could be derived from some sort of compact or social contract. And this is not a merely a subjective feeling of individuals about the nation. The nation was never an intentional community, a product of some 'making.' It always pre-existed any intention to give directions to it. There is an obscurity about the origination of any nation. Myths of origin circulate throughout its lifetime, and perhaps no form of scientific history or anthropology could give exact information on the origination of any nation. Important as that fact is, there is an even greater import in the passing away of nations, an event that cannot be foreseen during the lifetime of a nation, and that would often be dismissed during that lifetime as 'inconceivable' (a form of death the thought of which is more thoroughly repressed than that of the individual). Likewise the terrestrial borders of a given nationality are vague. Philosophy has not even any criterion for 'nation,' and our best thought is that nationality is a matter of degree (the French are more of a nation than the British). This vagueness does not generally apply to states, and in much of our practical thinking we focus on nation states, not looking beneath the well-defined constitutional states to the nations that underlie them. Tempting though it might be for some philosophers to dismiss a matter so indeterminate, the truth is that nationality is as powerful a force in history as the economy or war or statecraft or science-and-technology.

So it is appropriate to think of the nation as arising by fate or destiny (*Geschick*), passing away by fate, and experiencing fate in the course of all the currents that run through its life, especially victory and defeat. Human intentions do not rule here. The members of a nation are likewise aware of their *Geschick* when they think of a mission proper to their nation: a mission or assignment is what Heidegger was thinking of in his comments on the early Greeks. Indeed, the literal meaning of *Geschick* is something destined or sent, which becomes the sending or the obligation of the people. Myths of founding will often personalize the national mission: it was destined by a god or a primordial founder. It is in the destined mission that the people of a nation represent the justification of their nation. This does not need to be foreign missions or exploration, but can be accomplished within the nation itself, if the nation feeds and educates all its members and confers on them the cultural acquisitions of the nation, which vary of course from nation to nation (opera, mountain-climbing, worship, development of agriculture, commerce, sexual liberation, military arts, athletics, and so on). One highly important mission of a nation is to accomplish some reign of justice among its people, and some form in which the nation may govern itself. The study of the nation's destiny thus leads into questions of law and the state. Philosophy has rightly recognized that being a nation is not a necessary condition for state and law, but in fact the nation has more often than not been the mediator that has brought the state and law to a certain people. Heidegger's idea of the *Geschick* foregrounds the multiple offerings of the *Geschick*. In the case of the Greeks, their *Geschick* brought them the craft of sailing, the taming of the land, the management of horses, capture of all the creatures of land and sea, military virtue, medicine, the understanding of the justice of gods and of men, the arts of speech, drama, and persuasion, the life of the *polis* – and philosophical thought.[9] A key implication of the idea of the *Geschick*, then, is that some political form, some form of government and law, is given, but not separately from a kind of culture, a kind of economy, and other concrete forces in the life of the nation: all these things belong together.

Heidegger's idea is that to every *Geschick* there belongs an *epoché*, a withholding, that brings some limitation and some concealment or erring. The nation has therefore a beginning and an ending, and a bias in its institutions that closes off any view of possibilities that were not given it. The *Geschick* delimits and confines a nation, in such a way that a nation *is* the very confinement ordained through its *Geschick*. But what is it then that becomes confined or delimited in the national *Geschick*? It is civilization. Rival nations all hover within that encompassing whole, and in particular their codes of law and government are delimitations of it.

The concept of civilization can bear a sense that is inherently plural: Eastern and Western civilizations; Arab and Chinese civilizations. In this usage, it has a logic similar to that of nations with their *Geschicke*. These civilizations can be thought of as families of nations, or, more commonly perhaps, as prototypes and ancestors of nations that then became states, such as Saudi Arabia. But there is another concept that is inherently singular, referring to a process that has occurred all over the globe, the transition of human groups to a form of life marked by agriculture, property, the regularizing of relations between the sexes, between parents and children, and much else. Philosophers from antiquity to modernity (Plato, *Republic*, book 2; Hobbes, *Leviathan*, book 1, chaps. 13–15; Engels, *The Origin of the Family, Private Property and the State*) have represented the transition from barbarism to civilization. This is at once a descriptive and a normative concept, resembling in this way other concepts such as culture, learning, *Bildung*, *paideia*, and so on. Not the 'transition' but the state of being civilized is what I intend here: each nation's *Geschick* has brought a specialization and delimitation of civilization. This enables us to differentiate two factors in history: on the one hand, civilization, on the other hand, the nation. Civilization itself does not bring forth a state, but through the *Geschick* of a historical nation, some kind of law and state emerge, always given in connection with a certain economy, culture, and so on. The concept of civilization is resolutely impersonal; nobody here is an author or hero.

Civilization has always pre-existed each historical nation, but it does not cease to be alive after nations form. It is thus both 'pre-historical' and 'historical,' continuing to influence each national life, even though not confined to the limits of each, each *epoché*. As one expression of the temporality proper to civilization itself, acting within nations and their states, I shall pick out movements. Currents in historical life that call for this name are different from state and national institutions but act upon them in many different nations. Great movements in modern times are the Enlightenment, the Renaissance, Romanticism, the democratic movement, socialism, conservatism, feminism, the civil rights movement (especially in the United States, but not confined to it), the Protestant Reformation. There are movements in the arts such as cubism, surrealism, and postmodernism. There are movements in philosophy such as positivism, existentialism, and any number of others. Some of these movements may have become institutionalized (the Protestant Reformation generated many churches), but others have not. In general, movements carry individuals along in their current, but did not originate with the self-conscious reason of those individuals. They were not mandated by decisions of the state. They are not identifiable with the genius of one particular prophet. Thus movements have the character of fate and destiny too, though not in quite the same way as nations. They pertain in a different way to history. I have mentioned movements in order to give some profile to the kind of currents in history that can be marked off from the currents we call national. Movements too are historical in the sense of *Geschick*, but now as a *Geschick* of civilization.

Let me offer a few examples indicating how civilization may be a grounding for a given community and especially for its law or laws. We think of the foundation of marriage laws in the ancient historic observation of marriage, the incest prohibition, and the rules of kinship. We think of the ancient observance of respect for human life as a foundation for legislation respecting murder, rules of war, and so on. I believe we can see that very, very ancient literatures – assuming a life at the very beginning of history – give testimony to the customs and wisdom of civilized people who were not yet in a society marked by law and the state. Here are fragments from the Greek poet Hesiod, writing in the eighth century BCE:

> Those who give to every man,
> those from abroad and those from home,
> straight judgments, and do not transgress

the just – their city flourishes,
their people prosper too.
Peace, the children's guardian,
patrols the land, and Zeus, far-seeing,
does not plan cruel wars against them.
Upon the men who judge with honesty
famine and disaster never wait;
they work at their appointed tasks
with merriment.
For them the earth brings forth
a plenteous livelihood. (*Works and Days*, pp. 225–33, trans. J.M. Robinson)

It is not that there were no powers and kings in Hesiod's world – there surely were – but he is able to see in the thoughts and judgments of ordinary peasants a discernment of justice and right. He is aware of an informal culture in which, apart from state and law, true judgments of justice could be made. The point here is not only that there was such a civilization; in addition to that, the poet himself was aware of it and could use it as a standard by which to measure the overweening pride of kings and conquerors. The power of civilization itself was recognized in remote antiquity. Another citation:

Best of all is the man who considers everything himself and sees what is going to be right in the end. Good, too, is he who obeys another man who says what is good. But the man who neither understands for himself nor takes another's advice to heart, he is a useless fellow. (*Works and Days*, p. 293, trans. Werner Jaeger)

Nearly two centuries later Solon arrived, the one who was remembered by the Athenians as their greatest law-giver and the founder of their constitution. But, we are asking, whence did that constitution stem? In particular, what was Solon's own view of the essential sources of these laws? He was also a poet, and what we read in his lines is testimony to the dependence of his law and constitution upon the primordial informal civilization. As Jaeger cites it in his *Paideia*:[10]

Solon ... was impelled to demonstrate the existence of an immanent order in the course of nature and human life, and with it an inherent meaning and an essential norm in reality. He is clearly presupposing a law connecting cause and effect in nature, and expressly setting forth as a parallel to it the rule of law in the social order, when he says elsewhere, 'From the clouds come snow and hail, thunder follows the lightning, and by power- ful men the city in brought low and the *demos* in its ignorance comes into the power of a despot [Solon, fragment 10].'

I am seeking to show that in the pre-Socratic period (Solon was the approximate contemporary of Anaximander), there was a historical, social grounding for laws and constitutions, not one merely envisaged in the transcending thought of a philosopher.

There is a similar conclusion we can draw by looking at the records of the very early life of Israel, and here it is not the history of fact as such that concerns us, but the understanding and interpretation of history conveyed by the documents of the Bible and the editing to which they were made subject. We know the story from the book of Exodus of how the children of Israel were made into a people by the great adventure of their flight from Egypt, the wanderings in the desert, and the theo- phanic revelations at Sinai that grounded their covenant with their Lord. Here is the foundation of the law, the constitution, and what became the kingdoms of Judaea and Israel. Here and in Leviticus is the law regarding marriage and kinship, for example. And yet, with that in mind, we must ponder all the materials that precede this founding event – first, of course, the prehistory (creation, Noah) but especially the life of the ancestors of the people of Israel starting in the twelfth chapter of Genesis and recounted up to the end of the book. This is the record of a wandering nomadic family, Abraham and his offspring, who move through several lands from Ur to Canaan, encountering other tribes and families. Though Abraham surely had a covenant with his Lord, there was as yet no state, no temple, no priesthood, and, I should say, no king and no law. Although it is Exodus and Leviticus that lay down the laws for marriage, there was still marriage among the generations of the patriarchs, a marriage, I would say, that was regu- lated by civilization rather than by law. Just *how* Abraham took Sarah (and Hagar) to wife is not told us. Though Abraham sent his servant to find a wife for Isaac at the abode of his kinsfolk in Mesopotamia (Gen- esis 24), we are not told how kinship was determined, or how the wed- ding of Isaac and Rebekah was performed. It is not until Exodus (chapter 2) that we learn of priests who perform marriages (verse 21). Besides the record of kinship and marriage in Genesis, we read much about oaths and inheritance (Genesis 24:2–9, 25:29–34f), normative pro- visions of custom that preceded the covenant of Sinai. They are not presented in Genesis as divine commandments, unlike the sacrifices and circumcision that we find in Genesis 15:7–11 and 17:9–14, for instance.

This concept of civilization constitutes an alternative not only to a covenant-theology; it is also an alternative to the entire tradition of philosophy that vindicated the measures of the state or the nation by reference to a natural law.

The duality of nation and civilization, two kinds of current in *Geschichte,* helps us to think about the beginning and endings of nations, as well as the patterns of justification that we see within the lives of nation. Take Canada. What is clear to everyone is that it is a state with a federal constitution. But its national status remains unsettled. The idea that Canada was a 'Dominion,' i.e., a branch of the British Empire, is vanished beyond recall. Its citizens usually call it a 'country,' *pays,* less often a nation. The older idea that it was or contained two nations, *deux nations,* has been abandoned because, on the one hand, the country also contains a group of First Nations (of indeterminate number), and on the other hand, nobody outside Quebec identifies with such an entity as 'English Canada,' an English nation within Canada. Canadian history was often presented in the past as the conquest of New France by the British Empire, that – after long, painful, intervening years – was succeeded by a compact or contract: Confederation in 1867. But those are only military and political representations. With a view to the existence or life or being of Canadians, a more adequate appraisal grasps Canada as the prolongation of the civilization of Europe and the civilization of native North Americans. Agreements and conquests do not reach deep enough into the matter. Canada is the historical prolongation of a number of nations who are, for their part, limited crystallizations of civilization itself. Whether its *Geschick* will ever be to become a nation unto itself is unclear, but the country is well aware of the demands of civilization. Perhaps fate will make it a nation, but if not, it can still be a confederation that is attentive to civilization. Social contract ideas have even less relevance to Canada than to India, a country that *is* a civilization.

One of the deepest studies of the Canadian constitution is that of Doull.[11] He shows that Canadian reality is not to be grasped on the contractarian principles that hold sway in the United States, nor on the European model of a 'postmodern' federation of national states. Canada is not a nation, in any classic sense, nor is it a federation of *deux nations.* Its federal division of sovereignty – between federal and provincial entities – does not diminish the common spirit of Western freedom that actuates the common life of both French and English populations in Canada. 'To know how the common polity of these peoples which now exists, if imperfectly, came to be, one must attend not only to the events of their common and special histories, but to the spirit moving in them' (pp. 436–7). Doull is confident that preoccupation with the constitution will not in the long run stand in the way of the recognition, on the part of the whole people, of this philosophical or spiritual principle that he has articulated so well in this article. It may be that my concept of civilization is not so articulated, from a legal point of view, as Doull's concept of Western freedom, but I do think that the two are akin.

Political philosophy, especially in the modern period, has been concerned with the problem of the justification of law in general and of particular laws. That means that it has also had to approach the question of the right, or justification, of the state and its institutions. While I would never claim that a philosophy of existence like Heidegger's, oriented strongly towards history and its constitution, could replace the mainstream of modern political philosophy, it might be able to offer a corrective to it, drawing on the idea of history that we have developed here. The mainstream philosophical project has been to show, in this way or that, that state and law are justified by being the embodiment of reason (Aristotle and Hegel) or the result of rational deliberation (Rawls and the social contract tradition). But if we can show through the historical argument that the state derives its justification from civilization, precisely as the *epoché* brought by a *Geschick*, we might then be able to show how particular laws, rulings, and measures, undertaken in the framework of a state and judiciary, actually derive their justification from ancient and informal provisions of civilization.

Earlier we saw that Socrates's care for the *polis* was a search for its justification, and moreover that a justified *polis* would have a still further justifying power – for the being of the self. What we have traced now in the Heideggerian account of *Geschichte* and *Geschick* is a modern alternative to Socrates and to the Platonic account of justice. The nation's *Geschick* is a finite embodiment of the universal civilization. The latter constitutes a grounding for a nation's laws and practices that justifies them. And the self that participates in such a community through political practice can find there a justification for its being. It is not merely the self but its being that finds justification through all the constructive and critical interventions whereby the self investigates the laws and institutions of this *Geschick* against the older backdrop of civilization.

7 A Spiritual Existence

It is now one kind of existence that we shall look into – existence as spirit. The general points that we established about existence in chapter 2 will remain in place: it is the ability to be, marked by the possibility of being a self, and a possibility of not being itself, marked by being-with, and by temporality. We shall certainly need to explain the term 'spirit,' but thereupon succeeds the main task, to fill in the general concept by showing how spirit is realized within existence. This will then bring us to some questions about God and theology, in particular the divine act of justification.

Spiritual existence is through and through marked by possibility, which means, first of all, that it itself is one alternative versus many forms of spiritless existence. Being spiritual is always the *ability* to be, spiritually. And many of the postures of existence that we have reviewed in this book are in effect existence without spirit, for everyone also has the ability *not* to be, spiritually. But more than that, spiritual existence always stands open to further possibilities, is always poised on a knife-edge, always in crisis – for example, what I shall be discussing here, the crisis between an autonomous existence and a devout one. Moreover, there are many forms of spiritual existence in addition to these: my title 'A Spiritual Existence' means that just one spiritual existence will be studied in this chapter. It is a devout existence I shall treat, but this is not to be understood as 'religion as such,' religion in general, for the religion under consideration here is the one that enters into struggle with autonomy, while innumerable folk religions, liturgical and ethical religions, and so on, fall outside our consideration. And religion is not by any means the only manifestation of spirit or the privileged one. We are not going to be treating art in this chapter, but whatever we understand by spirit, it cannot be isolated from the arts. And, in view of the present overall topic, Nietzsche surely said something true when he remarked that 'it is only as an aesthetic phenomenon that existence and the world are eternally justified.'[1] It is possible to see history too, and family life, and love, as manifestations of spirit, as has been the case in the Hegelian tradition. But our study will be more narrowly focussed.

This chapter will seek to explain and justify the concept of 'spirit,' which is largely absent from contemporary philosophy, and then bring into discussion the human relationship with God, following Kierkegaard and also some of his religious sources. Clearly, Kierkegaard's account goes some distance beyond Heidegger's because of his spiritual grounding and the theological expression it calls for. While I believe that Heidegger did grasp many of the themes of existence more deeply and more accurately than did Kierkegaard, it is not my purpose to draw a balance between them. I wish only to record, here at the beginning, my agreement with some of the commentators who point to Kierkegaard's strengths: among others, Habermas has highlighted some of those strengths.[2]

Kierkegaard did not think of spirit as a part of the self or a faculty, and certainly not as some cognitive faculty. Spirit is a way of being or existing, which, when it is realized, encompasses the whole self, including the body and the soul. We shall follow him in regarding spiritual existence as a *possibility* for us, that is sought with struggle and arduously maintained in being (many lives are lived without any access to spirit or any relation to it). We are understanding Kierkegaard to be giving an account of the existing spirit. In this, Hegel took a less modest view – for him, every form of life was just one of the shapes taken on by spirit, the universal substance and grounding for all. Kierkegaard's most penetrating treatments of spirit (*Aand*) are in *The Concept of Anxiety*[3] (henceforth, *Anxiety*), 1844, and *The Sickness Unto Death*[4] (henceforth, *Sickness*), 1849. Although he refers in many texts to the spirit, these are the ones in which he penetrates to the ontological heart of the matter. Anxiety and despair are passions that disclose to us, if we have eyes to see, the greatest truth about human life – its existence as spirit.

Existing spiritually, in the sense we take from Kierkegaard, involves the continuing activity and agitation of becoming spirit. That of course is the implication of existence: spirit *is* the ability to be, spiritually. And as an existential possibility, spirit puts us always before further, subordinate possibilities – there is always an Either-Or. Our study will be focused on existence, the existing spirit, existing *as* spirit. Kierkegaard offers concrete studies of anxiety and despair that he shows to be manifestations of spirit, and that will make our grasp truly phenomenological. No doubt Kierkegaard depends to some extent on the concept of spirit that was worked out in prodigious detail by Hegel, and in my own studies I have often drawn upon that pre-eminent philosopher of spirit for the purpose of gaining a concept of spirit. But it has become apparent to me that in his presentation of the *existing* spirit, Kierkegaard moved beyond the Hegelian sphere of influence.

The treatments of guilt, conscience, and fault led us in chapter 4 to study the posture of autonomy and asceticism. But in this chapter, we are following a different development that starts out from the same basis. Spiritual existence develops from moral existence in a different way. Existence as spirit brings a certain activity and dynamism that are different from the phenomena of ascetic autonomy. And when we establish just what a spiritual existence is, we shall scrutinize two major possibilities for it. The first is a devout, religious existence. Spiritual existence is not so hospitable to atheism. But the second makes its appearance through a contrast with the first. It is the very ascetic autonomy that we have already treated, but now it is understood retrospectively as a form of spiritual existence, in an antagonistic relation to devotion, even though of its own accord it did not recognize its own spiritual character.

The problem of justification arises within every form of existence – we have seen considerable evidence for that – and it is central to our present topic too. Ascetic autonomy seems to abandon any claim to justification (though chapter 4 showed at the end that this was ambiguous). But a devout existence is in search of justification above all. We shall also be seeing the prospect of a magnifying of our being through an association with God (see below, 'The Problem of Grounding').

What Is Spirit?

But can we understand or apply the idea of spirit? Though the word *Geist* has a secure place in German language and literature, the same is not true of the word 'spirit' in our language. People today use the word and its cognates 'spiritual,' 'spirituality' with some vagueness and even embarrassment. The languages did not develop in the same way in this regard, and we open by highlighting the linguistic history, showing some of the sources of the term, and how the gap between English and

German widened over the centuries. This will allow us to reflect on whether the English word 'spirit' is even *capable* of bearing the weight of a philosophical concept. Bruno Snell's book *Die Entdeckung des Geistes* was translated into English, naturally, as *The Discovery of the Mind*. Golo Mann published a book called *Vom Geiste Amerikas*, but Henry Steele Commanger treated the same subject under the title *The American Mind*. How then and why would one ever use the term 'spirit' in English? A few hermeneutical observations will help.

The word 'spirit' and comparable words in other modern languages (*esprit, der Geist*, and the Danish *Aand*) have come down to us from ancient times through a complex history that played itself out differently in the languages in question. The most obvious result of the history is that 'spirit' plays a smaller, more restricted role in English than is the case with *esprit* in French and *Geist* in German. *Geist* has remained a constant in the German language for centuries, and is employed now, just as it was centuries ago, in common contrasts (*Geist und Körper* for 'mind and body'), conjunctions (*Geistesarbeit* for 'brain-work,' *Geisteswissenschaften* for 'the arts and humanities'), and modifications (*geistreich* for 'clever'). Some of the uses, of course, are decidedly religious: *geistige Lieder* are religious songs, *ein Geistlicher* is a clergyman. As with the German word, the French *esprit* has a wide range of everyday uses: it's a translation for 'mind'; *mots d'esprit* are witticisms. In French, however, the religious territory seems to be signified more frequently by the term *spirite* and its many modifications. English today does not employ 'spirit' in such profusion, especially not in everyday secular contexts. Though 'spirit,' 'spiritual,' 'spirituality' circulate today, few could supply a clear concept for them; what seems clear is that they signify something religious and yet non-dogmatic, non-sectarian. Briskly secular writers and hard-headed materialists will speak of spiritual values that are endangered in a commercial world, not feeling obliged to explain their terms any further. But when psychologists, philosophers, and scientists undertake to explore our cognitive life, consciousness, and so on, this term finds no place, though *Geist* and *esprit* are not under equivalent banishment in German and French science. Nowadays, however, this marginalization of the English word actually offers us an advantage, for it allows the term to be used for a much more specific and exact idea that comes to us from the Continental philosophers.

The underlying history can be understood when we realize that all the vernacular words entered modern languages as translations of inherited Latin, Hebrew, and Greek words. There is a particular translation-effect that arises when vernacular words are used to translate terms of holy scripture and liturgy, which I shall call reorienting translation. When the Bible was put into German, and when the Lutherans replaced the Latin Mass with the *Deutsche Messe*, the most crucial words of the tradition – *deus, spiritus, mundus*, and so on – were replaced by vernacular terms: *Gott, Geist, Welt*, and so on (obviously, a long history of vernacular preaching and counselling preceded these definitive substitutions). The etymology of these German terms is debatable, but in fact the native etymology is not of much consequence, because it was from the whole biblical and liturgical text that the German terms came to be reoriented. Whatever *Gott* and *Geist* had meant in older German, it was the biblical and liturgical text that determined them for the future, so that *Geist* was reoriented along the lines of *spiritus*, precisely as that term had been in use for centuries, bearing a Christian sense. Moreover, a similar effect had already occurred centuries before when the Latin Bible and the Latin liturgy had translated Greek, Aramaic, and Hebrew prototypes, becoming reoriented by them. However *deus* and *spiritus* had been used in ancient Latin, their meaning in medieval times was reoriented through biblical Greek and Hebrew prototypes. When the home language was reworked under the influence of the matter being translated, what most people understood by *deus* and *spiritus*, and later *Gott* and *Geist*, was what the Bible said about them. The effect was exactly the same in the emergence of the modern French and English words in the sixteenth century – though a series of later developments accounted for the differences we see today.

So: to begin with the Hebrew scripture. In renderings of the Hebrew Bible, 'spirit,' *spiritus*, and *Geist* are usually used to translate *ruach*. As *spiritus*, derived from *spiro*, 'to breathe,' signified from the beginning *breath* and *wind*, so the term *ruach* signified the *breath* that we emit (e.g., in Psalm 135:17 and elsewhere, where it is a token of life, for instance in Genesis 6:17) and the *wind* that blows (e.g., the east wind in Exodus 10:13).[5] The term is elaborated metaphorically to signify *vivacity* (see I Kings 10:5) and the *courage* that enables the fighter to fight (Joshua 5:1). Most characteristic of all is the idea that a spirit, *ruach*, sent down from God might descend upon a prophet or group of prophets, inspiring them to ecstasy, prophecy, and great deeds; it is an agitating, invigorating power that can be imagined by reference to a wind (see Numbers 11:17, I Samuel 10:6, I Chronicles 12:18). Here the *ruach* comes to be overlaid upon the human being who is already and in advance constituted as *flesh, basar,* and indeed flesh that is *living* or *ensouled* through the *nephesh* (though these are fluid and subtle semantical relations: in some texts, it is the divine *ruach* and the human *ruach* that first bring life, e.g., Psalm 104:29–30). But the key opposition in the whole discourse is between *ruach* and *basar*: what is strong and divine versus what is weak and human (Isaiah 40:6–7).

We turn to the Greek New Testament. Steeped from his youth in the traditions of the Pharisees, Paul knew the scriptures both in Hebrew and in Greek, and when he writes about *pneuma*, *psyche*, and so on, his connotations are those of the Hebrew Bible. I'll sketch his views briefly, referring only to Romans, following the guidance of Bultmann (my quotations will cite pages from his *Theology of the New Testament*).[6] Before he joined the Christian community, that community already possessed the beginnings of a theology, understanding that 'the bestowal of the Spirit [was] an eschatological gift' (p. 155), as in the narrative of Pentecost. But what was still left undefined in the early community was the manner in which the Spirit penetrated or filled an individual. (pp. 156–64).[7] That became one of Paul's themes. True to the scriptures, he operates with an opposition between spirit (*ruach* = *pneuma*) and flesh (*basar* = *sarx*). But this is overlaid upon an anthropological account that sketches out the human condition in a neutral form, a form that can become realized either in a spiritual existence or a fleshly one. For Paul, every human being is from the start a body (*soma*). When in Romans 12:1 he says, 'Present your bodies (*somata*) as a living sacrifice,' he means 'Present yourselves' (p. 194). This body, however, includes the soul (*nephesh* = *psyche*). 'He does not dualistically set body and soul in opposition to each other ... Rather, *psyche* in Paul means primarily the Old Testament *nephesh* ... – '"vitality" or "life" itself' (pp. 203–4). So the basic, neutral existence of the human being is as an ensouled body.

The fundamental theological contrast is that of the Hebrew scriptures, either *pneuma* or *sarx*, a duality that is *superimposed* upon our neutral existence as ensouled body, *soma* and *psyche*. *Sarx*, a translation of *basar*, signifies the human scene regarded in its weakness and infirmity, regarded in contrast with God (pp. 233–4). Spirit is an infusion coming from God, not, like the *psyche*, naturally inhering in the body. Paul, however, is not mainly focused on the miraculous outpourings such as at Pentecost, but on the possibility for our life to be spiritual, to 'walk according to the Spirit.' Spirit takes up residence within us, and comes to be the essential qualification of our life. When this succeeds, the life of the person, the whole person expressed as *soma* and *psyche*, is qualified as spiritual. This is expressed forcefully in Paul's vision of resurrection in I Corinthians 15:44, where the resurrected body is a spiritual body, *soma pneumatikon*. This text shows how deeply *soma* pertains to any human existence, and also how *the* soma-and-psyche *figure is criss-crossed by the double possibility that confronts every human existence:* sarx? or pneuma?

The Reformation in Germany not only preserved the biblical conno-tations of *Geist*, but emphasized them so strongly, under the influence of Luther and others, that *Geist* penetrated the entire German language and literature up through the time of Goethe, Schiller, and Hegel. Besides the Bible translation and the German liturgy, Luther wrote many hymns that called upon the Spirit, *Geist*, and in this way he and his successors in hymn-writing prepared the way for the mainstream tradition of lyric poetry in Germany. The famous *Ein feste Burg*, in the fourth stanza, calls upon the Lord God to fight on our behalf 'with weapons of the Spirit,' *mit seinem Geist und Gaben*. In *Gott sei gelobet* he prays, 'Let not your good Spirit forsake us, but that heav'nly minded he make us,' *Herr, dein Heilig Geist uns nimmerlaß, der uns geb zu halten rechte Maß*. The same word speaks of what is essential in ourselves and in God – this is also found repeatedly in the great hymn-writer Paul Ger-hardt. In 'If God himself be for me,' we hear in the fourth stanza, 'His Spirit dwells in my heart, and rules my mind,'[8] and in the seventh stanza, 'His Spirit speaks to my spirit, / with tender words of trust.'[9] These effects have often been lost in English translation. Salomo Franck's hymn 'Come Sweet Death' was selected by Bach for his can-tata no. 161, but the opening aria

> *Komm, du süße Todesstunde,*
> *Da mein Geist*
> *Hönig speist*
> *Aus des Löwen Munde*

is completely concealed by the English 'translation' offered by Teldec Recordings (Bach, *das Kantatawerk*, Vol. 38). Nothing remains of the spirit's tasting of honey from the mouth of the lion. In its place are mere words, 'Come sweet death / thou blessed healer, / welcome rest, per-fect peace, / quiet everlasting.'

There are many connections between this hymnody and the literary form that prevailed above all others in Germany, the mature lyric poem. We have the baroque, we have mystical writers like Jakob Boe-hme, we have the *Sturm und Drang*. But the maturation of this literature

is in the *Klassik* and the *Romantik* of the late eighteenth and early nineteenth centuries, manifested for instance in the poetry and drama of
Schiller and Goethe. Their lyric and dramatic works are abundant in
references to *Geist*. *Faust*, for example, speaks in the dedication of the
Geisterreich constituted by its *dramatis personae*; in the prelude, the 'Poet'
speaks of his own uncertain *Geist*; in the prologue in Heaven, the Lord
bids Mephistophcles to seduce the *Geist* of Faust, and numbers Mephis-
topheles himself among the *Geister* of negation; Faust in his study
shows himself conversant with *Geister*; employing the power of his
own *Geist*, he summons forth the *Geist* of the Earth; and so on. To read
their correspondence[10] is to grasp the depth of the idea of *Geist* in German thought as a whole, for the prose employed by both correspon-
dents shows the naturalness of the word. In the early stages of their
correspondence, Schiller speaks repeatedly of the impression made on
him by 'your *Geist*, ... which is what I must call the total impression of
your ideas on me' (23 August 1794). Goethe is the artist, whose 'creative
Geist can pull together the rich completeness of his ideas' (ibid.).
Schiller seeks to follow 'the progress of his *Geist*' (ibid.). In reply,
Goethe says that he has learned to value Schiller's eloquent earnest-
ness, and hopes soon to learn directly from him more of the 'progress of
his spirit' (*Gang Ihres Geistes*), especially in recent years (27 August
1794). For Schiller, Goethe's '*Geist* works intuitively to an extraordinary
degree, all the power of thought concentrated in the imagination' (31
August 1794). Schiller's recent ill health leaves him with a 'slumbering
Geist,' from which Goethe could perhaps arouse him (16 November
1794). Goethe's novel *Wilhelm Meister* shows 'what a great challenge
Goethe's *Geist* constantly sets for itself' (4 December 1794); he and von
Humboldt see in it 'the manly youthfulness, quiet power and creative
fullness of your *Geist*' (ibid.). The novel is 'a work of your *Geist*' (19 June
1795). In a less elevated vein, Goethe can speak of someone as 'an
annoying and superficial *Geist*' (19 July 1795).

   And this concept forms the centre of Hegel's whole philosophy, as
we may see by glancing at its manifestation in art. We see the necessary
link between the inspiration of the artist and the created work, the context that was familiar to Schiller and Goethe. Though the artist brings
forth a work, thereby establishing its independent being, this brings a
difference that is not a difference, it establishes an identity in difference;
and this is for Hegel the first characteristic of spirit. Giving itself outward expression is the central activity of spirit – to objectify itself, to
make itself manifest. In the poem, it has not become something *other*. It

remains the same, existing both in the subjective form (in the mind of the artist) and in the objective form (in the work). In contemplating itself, spirit is identical with itself even while being an object for itself. Spirit continues to return to itself as well, confirming its unity even in the difference.[11]

Hegel's philosophy of religion characterizes a second movement of spirit that supplements what we have already mentioned. We can grasp a common feature of art and religion if we turn the direction of thought upside down, as it were. We are no longer to think of the human being, the finite spirit, as an artist, but to analogize the human being to the work of art, and to conceive God now in the role of the artist, imbued with spirit for his own part. God is now the spirit that externalizes itself, and God does this in the medium of religion.[12]

The development of the idea of spirit in English speech and letters would naturally call for a lengthier treatment than I can provide here, but it is safe to say that 'spirit' never penetrated modern English literature and thought to a comparable degree. In my limited reading of Thomas Cranmer and the Anglican divines (and their Prayer Book), I find little trace of the thought that the Divine Spirit has an intimate tie to our human spirit, though I have found this idea prominently proclaimed by George Fox and the Quakers a century later,[13] evidence, I suspect, that the spirit doctrine so congenial to Lutherans was seen in England as tainted with dangerous enthusiasm. Even in Donne and Milton, there is little attention to the affinity of the divine and human spirit. The case of Shakespeare is different. Works like *Hamlet* and *Macbeth* are teeming with 'Spirits' of all kinds and descriptions: many of these are ghosts, sprites, and witches, sometimes spirits of the deceased (of Banquo, *Macbeth*, IV, i; of the dead King, *Hamlet*, I, i), sometimes supernatural agencies (*Macbeth*, I, v), sometimes natural fairies (*Macbeth*, III, v) like those of the comedies. But Shakespeare's characters are also capable of attributing people's thoughts and words to their 'spirits' (*Macbeth*, I, v) and observing people with a troubled spirit (*Hamlet*, III, ii). Shakespeare has eluded my conceptual net, but certainly the kind of theological idea I traced in the Bible and in the Lutherans is quite absent here. Shakespeare's spirits have a popular, medieval, and non-Christian heritage.

English philosophy of the seventeenth and eighteenth centuries presents a clearer picture. I have found only scornful and dismissive mentions of the term in Hobbes.[14] Locke, it seems, uses it in the manner that was common in French: like *esprit*, it is simply another word for our conscious faculties, a synonym of 'mind,' the word that occurs much more frequently in his *Essay Concerning Human Understanding*.[15] The force of his usage is to displace the term 'spirit' once and for all from philosophy and inaugurate a philosophy of *mind*. Berkeley also used 'mind' and 'spirit' as equivalents, whether in us or in God, but by the time of Hume there was no need any more for 'spirit.'

But that is not the end of the story. Romantic poetry revived the spirit in England, even to the extent of invoking the kinship between the finite spirit in ourselves and a vaster, greater, more mysterious spirit of the world or of God. It is especially to the deeper mind of Wordsworth that we owe this. The 'Lines Composed a Few Miles above Tintern Abbey' (1798) establish a framework that recurs in his later work:

> How oft, in spirit, have I turned to thee,
> O sylvan Wye! thou wanderer through the woods,
> How often has my spirit turned to thee! (55–7)

Then, as his meditation develops, we see the cosmic equivalent to the thinking poet:

> A motion and a spirit, that impels
> All thinking things, all objects of all thought,
> And rolls through all things. (100–2)

After this summary of the biblical sources, and noting the divergence of the German sources from the English sources, we might take note of the most salient points regarding spirit that will play a role in the remaining discussion.

(*a*) Spirit does not pertain to the neutral, or natural, condition of the human being, but is supervenient upon body and soul. In the tradition it is a divine dispensation.

(*b*) Therefore, spiritual life is a *possibility* for the existing self.

(*c*) It is an invigorating, turbulent power, untrammelled and uncontainable, bestowing power upon those who receive it.

(*d*) It is not confined to the single subject, but, through a self-outering, it exists outside the self as well, and very plainly in poems, music and other works.

The Existing Spirit

In his use of the term *Aand*, Kierkegaard continued in the philosophical wake of Schiller, Hegel, and other German thinkers, but we can also see

a very specific dependence on St Paul. It is in keeping with Kierkegaard's understanding of existence that it is neither an eternal truth
about the self that it is spirit, nor is it some species of natural fact. 'In
innocence, man is not qualified as spirit, but is psychically qualified in
immediate unity with his natural condition. The spirit in man is dream-
ing' (*Anxiety*, p. 41). To exist as spirit is for us a *possibility*, just as despair
and anxiety themselves are strictly speaking possibilities of existence
rather than psychological attributes of the subject *homo sapiens*. Thus he
repeatedly asserts (*Anxiety*, pp. 65–70; *Sickness*, pp. 42–7) that in 'pagan-
ism' (which means classical antiquity) the self did not exist as spirit.
This follows from Kierkegaard's historical thesis that it is only with
Christianity that the truth of human existence is discovered, existence
as spirit. If spirit is a domain of possibility, one particular possibility
within spirit is a devout existence, the possibility of a relationship to
God, a possible being with God, a capacity for God.

And there is a complexity of our constitution that forms an analogy
with St Paul. Kierkegaard emphasized the composite character of spirit.
Not just one of our faculties, it is a whole that comprehends all our
powers and endowments. The descriptions of spirit, in both books, are
guided by the co-presence of binary oppositions, which then become
supplemented. Let's look at the first one, from the earlier book:

> Man is a synthesis of the psychical and the physical; however, a synthesis
> is unthinkable if the two are not united in a third. This third is spirit ...
> Inasmuch as it is now present, it is in a sense a hostile power, for it con-
> stantly disturbs the relation between the soul and body. (*Anxiety*, p. 43)

This pattern is taken up in *Sickness* and given further extension (pp. 13–
14). The human being is spirit because it is a self; and a self is a relation.
That means, in the first place, that there are elements (relata) that stand
in relation to each other, and Kierkegaard first names three sets of
relata, three binary terms, that define a human being: the infinite and
the finite, the temporal and the eternal, freedom and necessity. He later
adds a fourth binary opposition, the one he had introduced first in *Anxiety*: the psychical and the physical. So spirit is not one element within
us, but is the regime in which one element may be related to another,
e.g., body to soul, or freedom to necessity. In each of these binary sets,
the two, related to one another, constitute, he says, a synthesis. But the
self also forms a total synthesis, meaning that all four relations become
related to each other in the self. In the text of *Sickness*, devoted to
despair, Kierkegaard will show how one form of despair is essentially

qualified by necessity – suffering a deficiency of freedom – while another is marked in the opposite way, a despair qualified by freedom and suffering from a deficiency of necessity. And so it is with each of the other terms in these binary relations. But next we must see that these relations are never merely inert relations, but, qualified by the spirit in which they abide, they are living and dynamic. What he calls despair has the closest possible affinity to the themes of conscience, fault, and guilt as we reviewed them in chapter 4, and so, for that matter, does the theme of anxiety.

Since Kierkegaard's principal theme in *Sickness* is despair, we shall follow the treatment in part 1, which could be called a phenomenology of despair, to see what light the phenomenon can cast on spirit.[16] The main point in both *Anxiety* and *Sickness* is that the self is not merely the presence of a relation, or the presence of a group of relations, inert and stable like the relation between your left hand and your right hand, or the inside of this building and the outside. Instead the synthesis is perpetually being brought into being: it is the kind of relation that cannot exist unless it relates itself to itself. 'The self is not the relation but is the relation's relating itself to itself' (*Sickness*, p. 13). Kierkegaard understands this self-relating of the relation as an event or an activity, and it is all-important to him to grasp the active self-relating as a further unitary factor in the constitution of the self: he calls it the positive third. In the inert spatial relationship of the outside of a building to the inside, the very relation itself might be reckoned as a third factor, but, according to Kierkegaard, it is merely 'negative,' meaning it lacks the being that characterizes each of those two spaces: it isn't another space. But where a relationship between two binaries must also perpetually relate itself to itself, the relation itself becomes a positive third – it has being just as surely as all the terms do. Such a relation is the self, and this accounts further for the qualification of the self as spirit. For the relation now is not merely defined by the constituent factors, the various binaries. Instead, as relating itself to itself, the self is itself in being *as* the relation, and, like a spinning top, maintains its balance by virtue of its activity. Spirit is entirely conceived as existing: its being is always the ability to be, and in no way a substance. Its self-balancing is more vital to it than are any of the binary factors; the relation relates itself to itself; the relationship among all these latter would fall apart, become misrelated, if the active self-relating of the self were to falter. The binaries that constitute the self set out the different possibilities of existence that are open to us, but it is the orientation of the positive third, the spirit itself, that decides the direction of our life. In these forms we find several possibilities for despair: the despair of freedom; the despair of necessity, etc. The self-relating of the self can take on the form, for instance, of willing to be oneself; it can also take on the form of not willing to be oneself (we come back to this decisive distinction later). Likewise, to revert to the earlier text, *Anxiety*, we discover that anxiety as well is one modality of the relation of the self to itself. 'How does spirit relate itself to itself and to its conditionality? It relates itself as anxiety' (pp. 43–4). These passions are the very form in which the relation is perpetually re-established. Thus the phenomenology of despair or anxiety is also a contribution to the ontological point, to understanding how the self is constituted through the active self-relations expressed by these passions.

We must be alert to the existential relation between being and becoming that shows up both in the phenomenon of despair and in the spirit itself that makes despair possible. Very near the start of *Sickness*, Kierkegaard asks about the origin of despair.

> [Despair is not] like a disease to which he succumbs, or like death, which is everyone's fate. No, no, despairing lies in the man himself ... And because the relation is spirit, is the self, upon it rests the responsibility for all despair at every moment of its existence. (p. 16)

Now if spirit is the essential origin, if it is the driving force of despair, we see that spirit itself is always becoming itself; it isn't stabilized like an object. 'In the life of the spirit there is no standing still (really no state either; everything is actuation)' (p. 94). Spirit is always the will to be spirit (p. 57); spirit is the perpetual becoming of spirit (p. 47). The special temporality of despair is the consequence of the character of spirit. This means that spirit is 'dialectical,' which in this context is interpreted as having its condition always critical, poised on the knife edge (p. 25).

The temporality of despair is not of the worldly sort. For one thing, if you have it, it follows that you have always had it (p. 24). Moreover, as the sickness unto death, despair does not come to an end in death.

> Thus to be sick *unto* death is to be unable to die, yet not as if there were hope of life; no, the hopelessness is that there is not even the ultimate hope, death. When death is the greatest danger, we hope for life; but when we learn to know the even greater danger, we hope for death. When the danger is so great that death becomes the hope, then despair is the hopelessness of not even being able to die ..., perpetually to be dying, to die and

yet not die, to die death. For to die signifies that it is all over, but to die death means to experience dying, and if this is experienced for one single moment, one thereby experiences it forever. (p. 18)

And how does despair prolong itself? Does it continue in the soul as a fever might continue in the body? No.

We say that someone catches a sickness, perhaps through carelessness. The sickness sets in and from then on is in force and is an *actuality* whose origin recedes more and more into the *past* ... [H]e brought it upon himself, but it cannot be said that he *is bringing* it upon himself. (p. 16)

But in the spiritual condition of despair, there is no continuing actuality of that sort. The entire condition is one of possibility. 'Every actual moment of despair is traceable to possibility; every moment he is in despair he *is bringing* it upon himself' (p. 17). No achieved state of despair follows upon the ability; despairing is always ability. The sickness *unto* death prolongs itself – it is precisely the sickness from which one does not die, the approach to death that is never ended by death. And so it is with non-despair.

Not to be in despair is not the same as not being lame, blind, etc ... Not to be in despair must signify the destroyed possibility of being able to be in despair; if a person is truly not to be in despair, he must at every moment destroy the possibility. This is generally not the case in the relation between actuality and possibility.

Moreover, there is a reflexive character of despair. What might seem at first to be despair over some piece of ill fortune will always reveal itself properly to be despair over oneself. Specifically, it is one's not willing to be oneself, though there does emerge a subtler variant, the despairing willing to be oneself, both of them forms of the sickness unto death.

The Phenomenology of Spirit: Intensity

The self-relating self that opts for one or another possibility (this or that kind of despair, for instance) does so in the midst of an extreme turbulence, a turbulence that is augmented precisely because existing as spirit was itself a matter of choice and possibility in the first place, rather than given by nature. The theme of the turbulence and volatility of spirit recalls the biblical view of *ruach*. And we have seen that Kierkegaard's views also recall those of St Paul on spirit, for a living activity is supervenient upon the elementary syntheses that are our first and elementary constitution: body and soul, the eternal and the temporal, and so on. The inner struggle among the polar constituents of the self determine much of the following analysis of despair, the polarity of finitude and infinitude, and that between possibility and necessity. In these dilemmas and passions we shall discover again the characteristics of existence that appeared along the way of our study: inferiority, failure, guilt, fault.

In these passions, the power of spirit itself appears – they are the evident phenomena for its (partial) unconcealment. Anxiety and despair plunge between possibility and necessity, finitude and infinity, in a perpetual motion that fuses or synthesizes those binary opposites. This perpetual motion is the very life of spirit. No binary opposite is left unaffected in the activity, and where all of them enter together into activity, the activity gains in intensity. Indeed, intensity is the very element of spirit. We understand it as the attraction of all the polar binaries to one another in a self-reflecting motion. It was well illustrated in *Anxiety*, where Kierkegaard defined anxiety as a 'sympathetic antipathy and an antipathetic sympathy' (p. 42).

The text of *Sickness* goes on, pp. 51–6, to outline some of the gradations in the consciousness of despair. These are all linked to gradations in the consciousness of self, which is to say, in the consciousness of oneself as spirit.

> If a person is to despair over himself, he must be aware of having a self ...
> furthermore there is a greater consciousness here of what despair is ...
> [W]hen the self despairs over its despair, his new despair comes from the self. (p. 62)

Next Kierkegaard traces the famous case of 'inclosing reserve,' pp. 63–6, of which one outcome is the 'restless spirit whose life certainly leaves its mark, a restless spirit who wants to forget.' (p. 66).[17]

At the opening of the book, Kierkegaard told us that there were two essential forms of despair, (*a*) in despair not to will to be oneself, and (*b*) despairingly willing to be oneself. All the varieties that we reviewed up to this point belong to group (*a*). At the end of part 1 Kierkegaard introduces the second form, under the heading 'Defiance,' a demonic despair, pp. 67–74, pure, undiluted spirit, the spirit of defiance. Specifically, this defiance is the cry that I am deeply faulty but intend to remain so, sick but unwilling to be cured. This is primarily a cry directed to God, although Kierkegaard certainly has interhuman instances of defiance in mind as well. What constitutes it is, first, the insistence on remaining unchanged; second, the consciousness of being faulty or in pain; and third, the consciousness of some other who is one's maker or who is in some way responsible for one. In defiance, it is as if God, our own poet, had made a slip of the pen, but the error took on a life of its own and refused to be corrected: 'I will stand as a witness against you, a witness that you are a second-rate author' (p. 74). In the next section, I shall argue that this posture of defiance coincides with ascetic autonomy, though I cannot follow Kierkegaard in branding it as the devil's despair.

The Problem of Grounding

It is evident from the opening account (pp. 13–14) that a God-relationship is central to the life of spirit, and the key to unravelling the phenomenon of despair. How does God figure in the anatomy of despair?

Spirit is the regime by which our constituent elements may all be related to one another. But this regime first needed to be established – somehow! It is never inertly given. With all the binary oppositions in the self, there is certainly the intention in the self to bring them into unity. That gathering or concretion promotes intensity, with all the binaries conjoined with one another within the activity of self-relating. And here the self raises for itself the question of its own grounding, including the grounding of these binaries. This question necessarily accompanies the intention of gathering the binaries together. The most profound aspect of anxiety and despair is that, in its self-relating, the spirit cannot evade the question of its own being, how it came to be, how it was originally established. 'Such a relation that relates itself to itself, a self, must either have established itself or have been established by another' (p. 13). In this deepest aspect, spirit's self-relating must relate itself further to what it defines as its ultimate grounding. In the quotation just made, Kierkegaard seems first of all to allow for two possible origins: established by God or by oneself. But on both pp. 13 and 14, it seems, he does not treat the alternatives as equal. He asserts (p. 13) that the 'human self is such a derived, established relation' – and this is generally taken by his readers to be opting for just one version of our origins, our derivation from God. Then the concluding sentence of section A, subsection a, reinforces this impression, referring to the over-coming of despair: 'in relating itself to itself and in willing to be itself, the self rests transparently in that power that established it' (p. 14). But if this is a reference to God, what happened to the *two* possible origins of the spiritual self? Having opened that door on p. 13, Kierkegaard seems to have closed it immediately. Now we must probe this very important question. The question we raise also touches on the relation-ship between part 1 (which earlier I called phenomenological, and which R.E. Roberts[18] calls psychological) and part 2, 'Despair Is Sin,' that operates within the discourse of Christian theology.

We can find texts that appear to contest the first interpretation. In the various types of despair, all of them have their own way of ignoring God, denying God, or being closed off to God. For example, one who is not conscious of existing as spirit 'never gained the impression that there is a God and that he exists before this God' (p. 27); in the despair of finitude, 'they have no self, no self for whose sake they could venture everything, no self before God' (p. 35); the despair of fatalism or neces-sity involves precisely the absence of God (pp. 38–9); unconscious despair involves ignorance of having a self and having God (p. 46). This is certainly the case with 'inclosing reserve' (pp. 63–6), and in a more complex way with the despair of defiance: an unwillingness to need God, a ruling out that God could offer a possibility of hope (pp. 70–1). Other texts that point in this same direction are found in part 2. He says that a self may take the criterion or measure for its life from worldly things and events, or it may take God as its criterion. In the second case, the self becomes magnified: these represent gradations in the being of the self. 'And what infinite reality the self gains by being conscious of existing before God, by becoming a human self whose criterion is God!' (p. 79). What does this imply? That just as spirit itself is a possibility for us (where a spiritless existence is also possible), so an existence as spirit brings two further subpossibilities, either to exist in a relationship with God or to exist without God.

In this way of reading the text, to have been established by God does not pertain to a neutral, metaphysical, or ontological profile of spirit. Rather, existing as spirit is a possibility for us that then harbours this further division, two possibilities for how it became established. The relationship with God is not an *a priori* fact about creatures, established by a metaphysical theology. Rather, this relationship is a possibility for the finite spirit, and so is the possibility of standing outside a relation-ship with God. I believe that Kierkegaard has said that where there is no belief in God, no consciousness of God, there is also no relationship with God.

In the following exposition, I want to say that autonomy is precisely the posture that wishes to establish that the finite spirit has established itself. This essential choice of its own being is open to spirit, a resolute autonomy of existence that opposes the second possibility of 'resting transparently in the power that established it' (p. 14). The divine grounding is never a mere fact. It is itself a volatile possibility that *requires* the very willing expressed by the finite, existing spirit. On this reading, it is Kierkegaard's own choice of a devout existence that becomes expressed in the concluding words of section A, subsection a, and in the entire part 2 of the text: the utterance of the Christian choice that was Kierkegaard's own. Kierkegaard, or Anti-Climacus, has already chosen not only to exist as spirit, but to exist as the devout spirit, for whom it is crucial to understand the self, the finite human spirit, as God's creature. Thus I claim that the commitment to a self-grounding – contrary to an acceptance of the divine grounding – coincides with the ascetic autonomy we described in chapter 4. It would seem that Kierkegaard's description here constitutes a Christian appraisal of ascetic autonomy, though he himself calls it 'stoicism,' intended in a very general way and not in the historical sense.

On the other hand, to posit God as the grounding for the self is the spiritual posture I am calling devotion.

God has entered the discussion because Kierkegaard wants to say that it is only the relationship with God that can free us from despair (see pp. 14, 15, 22, 30, 46, 131). This undergirds one of his central claims, that there is no 'immediate' state of non-despair, that the only existence without despair is that which has passed through despair and surmounted it. It follows that all ascetic autonomy, like defiance, does not wish to be freed from despair, or what in chapter 4 we called fault, blame, and guilt – it perseveres in them resolutely. Kierkegaard's further point is that this surmounting of despair is achieved through Christian faith. And so the concluding words of section A, subsection a, 'resting transparently in the power that established it' are germane, precisely because this is a reference to the self that is no longer in despair and wills to be itself.

How then does the two-fold possibility of the establishment of the spirit come into connection with the two basic forms of despair that he distinguishes on p. 14: either not to will to be oneself, or in despair to will to be oneself? This point can help us with the problem of grounding that we have treated. Kierkegaard says that the first form (not to will to be oneself) would have been the only possible form if the human self had established itself: the despairing will to be oneself would not be a possibility for an autonomous Promethean self that posited its own being. But on what basis does he argue this? Could not even a Promethean, e.g., a Fichtean, autonomous spirit will in despair to be itself? The answer is that wherever a self-positing self entered into despair (and all despair is ultimately a despair over oneself), this despair would be immediately converted into the will not to be oneself, which is the first form. The self-constituting self would not continue in its activity where despair over itself entered in. Kierkegaard now adds that the second form of despair, which wills in despair to be itself, implies a relation to one's Creator. This is the obverse of the previous point. Because all despair is despair over oneself, the will to be oneself has to be a heteronomous will if it is truly infected with despair. Nobody would charge an enemy sniper's nest in complete despair of victory unless he was acting under orders. Even less would the self persevere in being itself, quite in despair about itself, except in obedience. Next, Kierkegaard adds that this second species, willing in despair to be one-self, is the essential root and ground of *all* despair, meaning especially that the despairing will not to be oneself is somehow rooted here. How is this further point established? The context makes it evident that it will be on this basis, and not on anything metaphysical, that Kierkegaard establishes the human being's dependence on God.

God and the Self

Because it is the existing spirit that is under discussion, our theme is in principle the singular self, the individual 'I.' The dilemmas of despair affect our very ability to be a self. 'Every human being is primitively intended to be a self, destined to become himself' (p. 33). A later page even mentions, as Heidegger was to do, the purely formal capacity to be *a* self, along with the concrete difference of being *one*self, or *your*self: 'This form of despair is: in despair not to will to be oneself. Or even lower: in despair not to will to be a self. Or lowest of all: in despair to will to be someone else, to wish for a new self' (pp. 52–3).[19]

In this discussion, it is the spirit whose establishment we are considering. The two possibilities for grounding appeared to be exhaustive: either self-grounded or grounded in God. Kierkegaard does not consider a third possibility, such as being the outcome of a natural process (evolution, and sexual reproduction, for instance). To exclude biology and nature here is justified because the spiritual self that is to be established is the singular 'I.' Natural processes are indeed capable of accounting causally for some creature or other who may have been born at this time or that, and it could be that one of those creatures is you. But such explanations are universal in principle, not singular. They do not deal with the singular you. To see oneself as the outcome of a natural process is not a spiritual possibility; it expresses a form of life that is only intellectual. It can of course be combined with a spiritual possibility, for instance, taking radical responsibility for oneself, the posture we have been calling autonomy.

How to understand being grounded in God? It is not merely through our consciousness and reason that we stand in relation to God, but through our existence. Therefore, being grounded in God is expressed as the consciousness of owing something to God, of God's requiring something of you. But the deeper truth of this divine requirement is that it proceeds from the divine love. The unity of this demand with this love is the spiritual unity within God that establishes a spiritual affinity between God and the spiritually existing self. Here we can quote one of Kierkegaard's Christian discourses that is particularly eloquent about the Christian teaching on the divine initiative. In 'The Joy of It – that the Weaker Thou Dost Become, the Stronger Does God Become in Thee,'[20] we read:

> If God were only the Almighty, there would be no reciprocal relationship, inasmuch as for the Almighty the creation is nothing. But for love it is something ... But just for this reason love requires also something of man. It never occurs to omnipotence that a man is more than nothing – he is nothing for omnipotence. People are inclined to think that it is the almighty God that requires something of men, and so perhaps that it is the loving God that abates the requirement a little. Oh, sorry misunderstanding, which forgets that God's love must already exist in order that a man may in such wise be existent for God that there can be any question of requiring anything of him. If the Almighty were to require anything of thee, in that very instant thou art nothing. But the loving God who in incomprehensible love made thee to be something for him, lovingly requires something of thee. In human relationships it is the might of the mighty which requires something of thee, it is his love which remits. But it is not thus with the relationship with God. There is no earthly mighty man for whom thou art nothing, therefore it is his might which makes demands; but for God thou

art nothing, therefore it is his love which, as it made thee to be something, requires something of thee. (pp. 132–3).

This excellent passage indicates the fundamentals of the world opened up by spiritual communication and devout existence.

In part 2 of *Sickness*, Kierkegaard depicts the self standing before God and with the thought of God continually in mind (pp. 77–82). It submits to God in the sense that it adopts God as the criterion for the self. This is an application of the ontological point that the 'essence' of the self is its existence: here the existence of the self *with God* is adopted as your essence, which also means criterion. For Kierkegaard, this is a dramatic magnification of the self, and I would add of the being of the self, for the self is now intertwined with God: as Kierkegaard says, this is an augmented intensity of being (p. 80). In this relationship, it has to interpret its own despair as a falling-away from God, i.e., as sin. This gulf is a crucial feature of Kierkegaard's argument that must be borne in mind in all the subsequent treatment of forgiveness and justification. It constitutes the 'offence' that is proper to Christianity, (*a*) because the human estrangement is an offence against God, (*b*) because the divine overreaching of the gulf is an offence against the natural order of things, and (*c*) because the claim of Christ to be God offends both human reason and traditional religion.

Spiritually understood, sin is thoroughly dialectical. It is indeed the gulf between the self and God, but the gulf only appears when the self is annexed to God its criterion. For a spiritless and godless self, despair seems to be nothing more than a kind of malaise, not sin. But the drama of sin is expressed through God's forgiveness of sins. To despair over one's sin is to be oblivious of the divine forgiveness, which is an augmentation of sin that is especially evident in the autonomous self who wants both to sin boldly and then to take the consequences, who will say, 'I can never forgive myself' (pp. 109–12). Here we see the pathos: though 'I cannot forgive myself,' this reveals itself as a kind of complacency – perhaps both in the boldness of the offence and in the harshness of its self-condemnation. It closes itself off from God, for it refuses to consider that, while it cannot forgive itself, perhaps God could find it in his heart to extend forgiveness. This is precisely that despair that Kierkegaard said is the root of all despair, willing in despair to be oneself.

Such an autonomy develops naturally into a 'despair of the forgiveness of sins,' meaning a despair whether God could accomplish the forgiveness of sins (pp. 113–22). It is offended at this possibility. It becomes brazen in its address to God: 'No, you cannot do that!' Kierkegaard traces this rudeness to the history of Christendom, which violated Christianity by reducing the offence, the difference between God and the social world, culminating in the 'lowbrow' Feuerbach (and he was not alone) for whom God was nothing more than a European philistine writ large. It may not be initially evident how this tawdry history manifests 'despair of the forgiveness of sins.' The key to the connection is, of course, that the greatness and the power of God become manifest especially in the forgiveness of sins. 'God is separated from man by ... [a] chasmal qualitative abyss when he forgives sins' (p. 122), just what is denied and refused by the despair of the autonomous spirit.

There is another of Kierkegaard's discourses that deals precisely with the incomparable divine greatness that becomes manifest in the forgiveness of sins, one of the *Discourses at the Communion on Fridays* (1848) in the *Christian Discourses*, the one based on the text of I John 3:20: 'though our heart condemn us, God is greater than our heart.'[21] Kierkegaard begins by stressing the privacy and secrecy of the heart that inwardly condemns us: nobody else knows of it, and it may be indeed that nobody else condemns us at all – but still this torment continues silently within. But this heart that executes its judgments within can be after all too self-important. It may be appealing to the loftiest ideals or to social norms or even to the divine law, yet where does it derive its office and mandate? 'After all, it is essentially the same comfort we all have need of: God's greatness, that He is greater than our heart. *God's greatness lies in forgiving, in showing mercy, and in this greatness He is greater than the heart which condemns itself*' (p. 298). Thus, as the scripture continues, 'we may have boldness before him.' The key theme of this discourse is the greatness of God, and Kierkegaard stresses that the comparative phrase, 'greater than,' has an odd and instructive meaning here.

> The Apostle ... does not say that God is greater than the most loving man, but that He is greater than the heart which condemns itself. So then God and man resemble one another only inversely. It is not by the steps of direct resemblance – great, greater, greatest – thou dost attain the possibility of comparison, it is possible to attain it only conversely ... Deeply as the heart can abase itself, and yet never deeply enough to satisfy it, just in that measure is God's greatness infinitely exalted, or infinitely more exalted, in showing mercy. (p. 300)

Forgiveness and Justification

Kierkegaard's religion, and its deep historical sources, lead to a different appraisal of the phenomena of confession and forgiveness than we found in ascetic autonomy. There, it was not ruled out that one of us might confess to another, and hope for forgiveness, but this was not a central element in the autonomous life, and was never explicitly mentioned by Heidegger. And the further, deeper, ontological guilt could not even be brought to utterance in a confession, but was to be borne in authentic reticent resolution. There was no God to whom this could be confessed. But Kierkegaard, following in the line that led forward from St Paul, set a tremendous weight upon the status of sin, and the confession of sin to God, and the hope of divine forgiveness. 'Sin' is a specifically Christian concept, but we are not prevented from thinking of it as an interpretation of guilt or fault, thus bringing it together with the general terminology of moral existence.

Forgiveness is in principle an act prompted by confession, but in human interactions it is always related to some act or other; moreover, forgiveness is not only possible for one person to perform to another, it is commanded by religion. But the 'forgiveness of sins' means something more, and is more properly called the justification of the sinner. Justification of the sinner is not confined to a single sin – it is an alteration of the entire status of the person. It is applied to our life, our being, and this is what God alone can do. In the theology of Paul and his followers up to Schleiermacher[22] and Ritschl,[23] the human predicament was to be in bondage to sin so that we could not free ourselves. Only the imputation or infusion of God's own righteousness would suffice to vindicate us, the doctrine called 'justification by faith.' Though Kierkegaard at times protested against some interpretations of this doctrine made by Lutheran orthodoxy, he certainly did not reject the doctrine itself. The point of it was to go deeper than human forgiveness.

We may cite here the version St Paul gives in Romans. God's own righteousness or justice (*dikaiosynē*) has become revealed in a new way (1:17; 3:21–2; 5:1). Through Christ, God's righteousness has become our own: sinners are justified (*dikaioumenoi*) as a gift of God's grace (3:24) on account of the faith of Christ (3:22). This is expressed sometimes with an active verb: God justifies the believer (*dikaiounta* – 3:36), but more commonly with the passive: one is justified (*dikaiousthai*) by faith apart from works of law (3:28, and see 5:1). Paul also uses the noun *dikaiōsis* (4:25, 5:18) for this entire process, and there are many possible translations: justification, acquittal, vindication, rectification. Our question will be: Who or what is it that becomes 'justified'? What is the subject of *dikaiōsis*? Though 'forgiveness' is a common term in other parts of the Bible and in the Creeds, it is rare in Paul (one such text: 'in his divine forbearance [*anochē*], God had passed over [*paresis*] former sins' – 4:25). What becomes forgiven are sins, acts, deeds of unrighteousness; if we speak of the forgiveness of a sinner or wrongdoer, that still refers to those deeds – they will no longer be counted against him. But *dikaiōsis* does not have past deeds as its subject. It is applied to *us*, to ourselves; *we* become affected by it. Our being is altered.

A central issue that springs especially from the period of Luther and the Reformation is the relationship between justification and sanctification.[24] In his polemic against the penitential system of the medieval church, Luther insisted that the act of God, to justify the sinner, was entirely prior to any works of ours, so that our efforts to lead a holy life were irrelevant to our justification. The ability to lead a holy life is what theology calls sanctification. In Luther's dramatic imagery, the shield of an alien righteousness guards us against the attacks of the devil, our accuser, for no degree of human 'sanctification' could suffice in that battle. This doctrine offended the Catholics, and the Council of Trent insisted that sanctification was necessarily a part of justification. (Sometimes, regeneration was seen as a further element in human salvation, but we need not treat it separately here.) One element in the Reformation scheme is the forensic imagery in which the entire doctrine was couched. Though we have no righteousness of our own to claim, though our prosecutor, the devil, has all the evidence on his side, still God as judge has declared our acquittal. The reformers (more so Melanchthon than Luther) would call this sometimes the 'imputation' to us of that righteousness that was in Christ. This idea also attracted criticism from Catholics, who began to suspect that the Lutheran idea of justification was little better than a legal fiction, with God as it were pretending that we were righteous when there was nothing else that spoke for it.[25] The forensic 'imputation' expresses in the severest way the separation of justification from sanctification. Is there any other way to preserve the priority of justification? It seems that Luther himself, while speaking sometimes of 'imputation,'[26] was also ready to say on occasion that righteousness is 'instilled' in us or 'bestowed' on us,[27] placing more emphasis thereby on the reality of the righteousness that is in us.

I might propose that here it is the difference between the *self* ('I,' 'we,' 'you') and the *being* of the self that has come to the fore. Luther (like

Paul) was extremely vigilant about boasting. The claim that 'I am righteous' was always a betrayal, just like the corollary claim to be sanctified, to be leading a sinless life. Righteousness has no place in the direct consciousness of the Ego. Yet God's power is to work upon our lives through the works of Christ: they redeem or justify our lives, our being, our existence. This justification operates below the level of the watchful conscious Ego. It is for the watchful Ego simply to *trust* in the mercy and power of God, and, beyond that, to engage in the struggles of life with some hope of sanctification. That *trust*, however, is what Luther meant by faith, and so the foreground of the conscious Ego is taken up with the contemplation of Christ rather than with whatever works and deeds one might perform.

With this, we might also address a debate that has arisen since the days of Augustine, as to the *subjective* versus the *objective* character of justification. At its most subjective, in many branches of Protestantism, the doctrine expressed as 'justification by faith' was set against 'justification by works' as if it were a special act one could perform (instead of 'works') – just 'believing' – which sufficed for salvation. And this often became secularized, e.g., by Kant, as a moral faith that was the expression of a good will. Then faith was supposed to be a unique operation of the soul, with beneficial effects that could not come from mere knowing, or mere willing. This ultra-subjectivism was exposed to criticism by theologians who rightly deplored it as a kind of *Werkgerechtigkeit des Glaubens*, faith itself treated as a 'work' by which one might *earn* justification.[28] But the extreme opposite tendency, ultra-objectivism, viewed the justification coming from God as a kind of cosmic victory over the forces of evil, with grace then flowing in upon the Christian: such, it seems, was the view of Origen, apparently requiring virtually no activity on the part of that Christian.[29]

It is perhaps St Augustine whose thought can guide us best. One of his essays, 'The Spirit and the Letter,'[30] written in 412 during the Pelagian controversy, is a restatement of Paul's doctrine that can perhaps claim to synthesize the best in Luther's view with the best in the Catholic view. He makes much of the words of Philippians 2:13: 'For it is God who worketh in you both to will and to do, according to his good will.' In these pages,[31] Augustine shows that, in the process of justification, an involvement of our own will does not rule out the priority of God's sovereign action. 'Human righteousness itself, though not arising independently of man's will, is yet to be ascribed to the operation of God.'[32] Quoting Romans 3:21, Augustine proceeds:

> The righteousness of God [is] not that by which God is righteous, but that wherewith he clothes man, when he justifies the ungodly ... [They are] justified, then, not by the law, not by their own will, but 'freely by his grace': not that the justification is without our will, but the weakness of our will is [disclosed] by the law, so that grace may restore the will and the restored will may fulfill the law, established neither under the law nor in need of law.[33]

The statement appears to be faultless by Catholic standards, and perhaps close enough to Luther to earn his assent: he quotes this essay repeatedly in his commentary on Romans, though he and his Reformation colleagues wrestled repeatedly over Augustine's theology.

Augustine too must say that I am not by myself the agent in restoring or indeed regenerating my will, but only God (operating on my being, life, or existence – here Augustine would say 'soul'). The field of our cognitive life, surveyed by the intellect or understanding, coincides with the Ego or the self-conscious self, and a restored will can make different choices from this field than would the unregenerate will. Still, even those 'sanctified' choices would never be enough to merit justification. Justification does not merely disclose an antecedent righteousness, but implants it. Justification must have operated in advance by the divine power working upon the human soul or being. The divine act of justifying the sinner is both subjective and objective – not exercised principally on the conscious self, but not bypassing it either. What is most salient is that God does not justify (or forgive) merely particular acts and deeds, but the self as a whole.

A Spiritual Community

This chapter has treated the existing spirit and the possibility of its devotion to God. But the broader inquiry of this book always moved from the existence of the singular self to the community. Surely – one might say – spiritual life must also reveal itself ultimately as a spiritual community. There must be a community of devotion in which the singular self can lose itself in a greater 'We' that also prostrates itself before God. And a spiritual 'We' need not suspend the being or the freedom of the singular 'I.' In fact, there must be many evidences of a spiritual community quite apart from religious devotion, as in the communicative power of the arts, as in the ethical life of the community, and, in general, in all the phenomena that Hegel treated in his philosophy of the spirit.

Indeed, this idea is certainly implicit in the formal or abstract outline of the foregoing inquiry. More than that, it is an idea that expresses a profound human aspiration. But here, since we are at the conclusion of our inquiry, we need to ask a more modest question: What is actually implied by the foregoing inquiry regarding the possibility of a spiritual community? This is not the occasion to introduce utterly new perspectives into our inquiry, stemming from Hegel, or from Augustine and other theologians. Does our current study allow for the possibility that a spiritual community could be realized within the historical religions or the nations and movements that we know? We spoke of religious communities at the end of chapter 5 and of nations and movements at the end of chapter 6. Are they not spiritual too, as much as the existing individual?

Here we need to recall the character of our whole discussion. This is an inquiry that began from existence and never lost sight of that beginning. It recognized a tight link between existence and the question of our justification. It saw the latter as a possibility lying in existence, and likewise magnification as a possibility. Hence, for us, the present question is not whether the religious communities and the national communities are actual instances of spiritual community, but only whether a spiritual community is possible within them. And in this chapter too the treatment of the existing spirit began from the point that spiritual existence is a possibility; the discussion never transcended that status. Where this possibility is grasped, there remains always open the other possibility, of a non-spiritual existence. Indeed, so deeply is spirit marked by possibility that devotion itself is only one spiritual possibility, and we even accorded to ascetic autonomy some sort of spiritual status. As we said above, spiritual existence is always on the knife-edge.

The first difficulty that we encounter is that the spiritual community cannot be authentic if it overrides the very conditions of spiritual existence in the individual – existence as possibility. There is the danger of the 'Pericles' effect, in which the celebration of the community submerges the individuals altogether. In particular, the danger appears where the individual is thought to derive being and spirituality from the community. The strongest form of the idea of a spiritual community is that which makes it the condition of the possibility for the spirituality of individuals, where the heritage of religion and nationality is held to be the seedbed for individuals who find their possibilities bequeathed by tradition. Thus someone even as strongly individual as Socrates or

Luther or Kierkegaard would become possible only through the universal sustaining culture. Perhaps that is Hegel's view, shared with other communitarians, and this view would be opposed by our focus on existence.

There is, however, a milder view that we recognized in the figure of Socrates: that the care *for* the city or for the nation is the necessary complement to the care for the self. The spiritual community could consist in the shared devotion to the community.

A second difficulty arises from the manner in which we treated religions in chapter 5 and nations in chapter 6. Perhaps our view worked against the possibility of a spiritual community. It seemed that all communities seek to magnify themselves, and still today, they are all insistent on their own privilege and uniqueness. Thus the prospect of a *universal* spiritual community can be at best an article of hope. Could spirituality be confined then within one historical community? Is this the effect of the current situation? Yet if that were the case, these communities might well continue to manifest the communal version of self-righteousness. What then is the remedy for their conflict and militancy? Could the spiritual life of the nation or religion outreach these limits? A confrontation can arise between chauvinistic celebration of the finite tradition, and a prophetic challenge to the community. Perhaps this confrontation is at work in every religious tradition that is alive today, what was exemplified (in chapter 5 above) by the Hebrew prophets. Chapter 6 introduced the concept that might be an existential correlate of the Hegelian Spirit: civilization. Since all nations and religions might be, in principle, so many crystallizations of civilization, we must allow for the *possibility* of a universal communication coextensive with civilization.

8 Conclusion

Heidegger's Question Concerning the Meaning of Being

Our presentation has begun, in each case, from the existing self and then proceeded to the community – a procedure that is suitable for a discussion of the spirit as well. And we have in each case begun with magnification and then proceeded to justification, for the latter must in some way encompass the former. It is not merely the self, and the community, that are to become magnified and justified: in all cases, the analysis showed that it is our *being* that we seek to magnify and justify. The vulnerable self that seeks to magnify itself begins from some intimation of weakness or inferiority that attaches to its very existence. The self or the community that seeks magnification through nationalism or religious militancy begins from the sense of being threatened and brought down by external force. The singular self that wants to justify itself in moralism or self-righteousness is acting under the conviction of some fault that it will not bring to consciousness – the repressed conscience, the inability to be guilty. The city or the nation stands in need of justification through the citizen who is in touch with the deeper-lying principles of justice or civilization.

In all these circumstances, the central factor is that being itself (or existence) is marked by weakness and fault. Only because of this can our being be taken into our care, and only for that same reason can care itself constitute our being. The study of existence is well placed to highlight the many ways in which fault, lack, weakness, inferiority pertain to our being, whether in the singular self or in the community. The fault in being is not merely something subjective – though it is evident subjectively in existence, it does not arise merely in the sphere of existence or subjectivity. We are dealing here with a structure that pertains to being itself, whether that be realized in human existence or in any domain. Being itself is driven by *need*, *die Not*,[1] and reveals itself as utterly different from the principle of ancient philosophy, the self-sufficient foundation or *hypokeimenon* that came to be called substance. When an ontological inquiry guides itself strictly by a fundamental ontology of *Da-sein*, it must reveal the finitude of being. That is why such an inquiry is guided by a question concerning the meaning of being, *Sinn von Sein*. The *Sinn von Sein* is not given in any original endowment or intuition – it is to be *sought*. And the question of being (i.e., of the meaning of being) is not only an abstract inquiry concerned with materialism, atomism, idealism, essence, and so on. It is pursued, in its first movement, *within* the ontology of *Da-sein*. In that circumstance, the question concerning the meaning of being can take on the form of the question concerning the justification of existence.

Summary of the Argument

The successful celebrity who gains magnitude – we saw in chapter 3 – has a tendency to take this as a justification of his or her existence. But objectively, we saw, this cannot hold, nor can the contrary experience of being a failure rob existence of its justification. But it is true that achievement can justify our successes, and that the two together can be seen to justify our efforts and hopes. All this is a much lesser matter than a justification of existence.

Moral experience, when expressed in existence, certainly comes closer to a justification of the self and its being, as we saw in chapter 4. There is little sign here of magnifying, though magnifying does of course continue in the economic life that runs in tandem with our moral existence. In moral life as such, we saw that moralism, in expressing its condemnation, worked so as to *seem* to justify the self precisely in its opposition to that which it has condemned: if 'they' are greedy and selfish, 'we' must be kind and loving. Conscience is the great corrective to this inauthenticity, but it certainly does not produce any consciousness of my justification. If anything, it has the opposite effect. The ascetic autonomist, seeming to renounce justification, actually procures it by a roundabout route – though that justification proves to be actually a variety of magnitude.

Nothing is more familiar than the magnification of communities (typically through rhetoric). It is treated in chapter 5 because it affords a glimpse of our social being in connection with the self's existence. The rhetorical justification of the community proves to be instrumental to the magnification of the community.

A true justification of the community differs from that just as much as philosophy does from rhetoric (chapter 6). It proceeds with no magnifying at all, whether of the self or the community. Law, the Platonic Idea, and civilization show themselves as bestowing justification on a community.

Finally, Kierkegaard has shown us that a spiritual existence has the double possibility: an autonomous self-grounding or a devout relationship with God. It is in the latter case that it is able to hope for a divine justification of its being, whereby despair is surmounted. This gives us hope that the grinding oppositions of militant religions and nations – for they are the despair of humanity itself – may be overcome in a spiritual community.

Notes

1. Introduction

1 Martin Heidegger, *Sein und Zeit* (*SZ*) (Tübingen: Niemeyer, 1927); *Being and Time*, trans. Joan Stambaugh (Albany: SUNY Press, 1996). All page references here will be to the original German edition.

2 For instance, in A.J. Ayer, *The Problem of Knowledge* (London: Pelican, 1956); Nelson Goodman, *The Structure of Appearance* (Indianapolis: Bobbs-Merrill, 1966). In addition to phenomenological critiques of such views, see Donald Davidson's critique in, e.g., *Inquiries into Truth and Interpretation* (Oxford: Clarendon Press, 1984).

3 *Vom Wesen des Grundes*, in Heidegger, *Wegmarken* (Frankfurt: Klostermann, 1967); trans. W. McNeill, in Heidegger, *Pathmarks* (Cambridge: Cambridge University Press, 1998).

4 *Die Grundprobleme der Phänomenologie*, in Heidegger, *Gesamtausgabe* (*GA*), vol. 24 (Frankfurt: Klostermann, 1975). English translation by A. Hofstadter (Bloomington: Indiana University Press, 1988).

5 'Intentionality pre-supposes the Dasein's specific transcendence, but this transcendence cannot be explicated by means of the concept of intentionality' *BPP*, p. 175 [p. 249 of the German text].

6 'Transcendence first of all makes possible existence in the sense of comporting oneself to oneself as a being, to others as beings, and to beings in the sense of either the handy or the extant' (*BPP*, p. 323 [p. 460 of the German text]).

7 See the 'Letter on "Humanism,"' to be discussed in chapter 2.

8 Johanna Hodge, *Heidegger and Ethics* (London: Routledge, 1995); Frederick Olafson, *Heidegger and the Ground of Ethics* (Cambridge: Cambridge University Press, 1998); François Raffoul and David Pettigrew, eds., *Heidegger and Practical Philosophy* (Albany: SUNY Press, 2002).

9 Mark Okrent, *Heidegger's Pragmatism: Understanding, Being and the Critique of Metaphysics* (Ithaca: Cornell University Press, 1988); Babette Babich, ed., *Hermeneutic Philosophy of Science, Van Gogh's Eyes, and God: Essays in Honor of Patrick A. Heelan, S.J.* (Dordrecht: Kluwer, 2002); Joseph Kockelmans, *Ideas for a Hermeneutic Phenomenology of the Natural Sciences* (Dordrecht: Kluwer, 1993).

10 See 'Inferiority Feeling,' in *The Individual Psychology of Alfred Adler: A Systematic Presentation in Selections from his Writings*, ed. H.L. Ansbacher and R.R. Ansbacher (New York: Harper Torchbooks, 1956): pp. 114–19. See also *Alfred Adler's Individual Psychology: Superiority and Social Interest: A Collection of Later Writings*, ed. H.L. Ansbacher and R.R. Ansbacher, 2nd ed. (Evanston: Northwestern University Press, 1970).

11 John Rawls, *A Theory of Justice* (Cambridge, MA: Harvard University Press, 1971), 433, 440–6.

2. The Ability to Be

1 The best English-language orientations to it are Theodore Kisiel, *The Genesis of Being and Time* (Berkeley: University of California Press, 1993); and *Heidegger's Being and Time: Critical Essays*, ed. Richard Polt (Lanham: Rowman and Littlefield, 2005). More authoritative is Friedrich-Wilhelm von Herrmann, *Hermeneutische Phänomenologie des Daseins*, vols. 1 and 2 (Frankfurt: Klostermann, 1987, 2005).

2 I treated Heidegger's broader ontological investigations in another book, *Illustrations of Being: Drawing upon Heidegger and upon Metaphysics* (Amherst, NY: Humanity Books, 1997).

3 They can be sampled in Christopher Macann, ed., *Heidegger: Critical Assessments*, 4 vols. (London: Routledge, 1992); and in Miles Groth, *Translating Heidegger* (Amherst, NY: Humanity Books, 2004).

4 J.-P. Sartre's interpretation of Heidegger was in his *Being and Nothingness* (Paris: Gallimard, 1943).

5 See, e.g., William Barrett, *Irrational Man* (Garden City, NY: Doubleday Books, 1958).

6 For instance, Marjorie Grene, *Dreadful Freedom* (Chicago: University of Chicago Press, 1948).

7 *Brief über den 'Humanismus'* (HB) [1947], now in Heidegger, *Wegmarken* (Frankfurt: Klostermann, 1967), pp. 145–94; trans. F.A. Capuzzi, in Heidegger, *Pathmarks*, ed. W. McNeill (Cambridge: Cambridge University Press, 1998), pp. 239–76.

8 We now have many, many texts from the 1930s and 1940s that give us the

background of the 'Letter on "Humanism"'; one, particularly relevant for Heidegger's negative appraisal of existentialism, is *Die Metaphysik des deutschen Idealismus* (lectures, 1941), in Heidegger, *GA*, vol. 49, ed. G. Seubold (Frankfurt: Klostermann, 1991), pp.19–75.

9 D.F. Krell, in *Intimations of Mortality* (University Park: Pennsylvania State University Press, 1986), discusses and corrects some of the characteristic overstatements of Heidegger's 'turning,' *die Kehre*.

10 In J. Derrida, *Margins of Philosophy*, trans. A. Bass (Chicago: University of Chicago Press, 1982).

11 'Das Da-sein ist ein Seiendes, das nicht nur unter anderem Seienden vorkommt. Es ist vielmehr dadurch ontisch ausgezeichnet, daß es diesem Seienden in seinem Sein um dieses Sein selbst geht.'

12 'Das Sein selbst, zu dem das Da-sein sich so oder so verhalten kann und immer irgendwie verhält, nennen wir Existenz.'

13 'Das Da-sein versteht sich selbst immer aus seiner Existenz, einer Möglichkeit seiner selbst, es selbst oder nicht es selbst zu sein.'

14 S. Kierkegaard, *Concluding Unscientific Postscript to* 'Philosophical Fragments' [1846], 2 vols., ed. and trans. H.V. Hong and E.H. Hong (Princeton: Princeton University Press, 1992), vol. 1, p. 86. Everything in this book is attributed to 'Johannes Climacus,' a fictitious person.

15 Theodore Kisiel, in *The Genesis of Being and Time*, disputes this common interpretation of Heidegger, but the dispute is confined to the lectures and writings prior to *SZ*; he grants the Kierkegaardian, existential orientation of *SZ*.

16 Heidegger, *Nietzsche* (Pfullingen: Neske, 1961), Vol. 2, pp. 476–80; trans. J. Stambaugh in Heidegger, *The End of Philosophy* (New York: Harper and Row, 1973), pp. 68–74. See also Heidegger, *GA*, vol. 49.

17 *Ontologie (Hermeneutik der Faktizität)*, lectures from 1923, now in Heidegger, *GA*, vol. 63, ed. Käte Bröcker-Oltmanns (Frankfurt: Klostermann, 1988), pp. 5, 16–17, 30, 41f., 108, 111. English translation by John van Buren, *Ontology: The Hermeneutics of Facticity* (Bloomington: Indiana University Press, 1999). Kisiel does not comment on these passages.

18 Hans-Georg Gadamer, 'Existenzialismus und Existenzphilosophie' (1981), *Gesammelte Werke (GW)* vol. 3 (Tübingen: Mohr Siebeck, 1987), p. 176. This article is also available in Gadamer, *Heidegger's Ways*, trans. John Stanley (Albany: SUNY Press, 1994). Further documentation of Kierkegaard's impact on Heidegger appears in *GW*, vol. 3, pp. 314, 316, 398, 419.

19 'Zu dieser Seinsverfassung des Da-seins gehört aber dann, daß es in seinem Sein zu diesem Sein ein Seinsverhältnis hat.'

20 '[Zu dieser Seinsverfassung des Da-seins gehört aber dann, daß es in seinem

Sein zu diesem Sein ein Seinsverhältnis hat.] Und dies wiederum besagt: Da-sein versteht sich in irgendeiner Weise und Ausdrücklichkeit in seinem Sein.'

21 'Das Da-sein ist in der Weise, daß es je verstanden, bzw. nicht verstanden hat, so oder so zu sein. Als solches Verstehen 'weiß' es, *woran* es mit ihm selbst, das heißt seinem Seinkönnen ist.'

22 'Im Verstehen liegt existenzial die Seinsart des Da-seins als Sein-können.'

23 'Da-sein ist nicht ein Vorhandenes, das als Zugabe noch besitzt, etwas zu können, sondern es ist primär Möglichsein. Dasein ist je das, was es sein kann und wie es seine Möglichkeit ist.'

24 Translated from von Herrmann, *Hermeneutische Phänomenologie des Daseins*, vol. 1, p. 137.

25 See Daniel Dahlstrom, *Heidegger's Concept of Truth* (Cambridge: Cambridge University Press, 2001).

26 Martin Heidegger, *Die Frage nach dem Ding* (lectures 1935–6) (Tübingen: Niemeyer, 1962); *What Is a Thing?*, trans. W.H. Barton and V. Deutsch (Chicago: Regnery, 1967).

27 '*Da-sein* is never to be understood ontologically as a case and instance of a genus of beings as objectively present' (p. 42).

28 These formulations occur in important contexts later in the book, e.g., together with his treatment of Parmenides and Aristotle on p. 213, and on pp. 218–19.

29 Daniel Dennett, *Consciousness Explained* (Boston: Little, Brown, 1991), pp. 44–57.

30 I have dealt with the term *Da-sein* in the article 'The Constitution of Our Being,' *American Philosophical Quarterly* 36 (1999), 165–87; reprinted in *Heidegger's 'Being and Time': Critical Essays*, ed. Richard Polt (Lanham: Rowman and Littlefield, 2005), pp. 47–74.

31 The considerable discussion of formal indication in recent commentaries was initiated by Kisiel, *The Genesis of Heidegger's 'Being and Time,'* pp. 50–56, 160–70.

32 See Françoise Dastur, *Heidegger and the Question of Time*, trans. F. Raffoul and D. Pettigrew (New Jersey: Humanities Press, 1998); William Blattner, *Heidegger's Temporal Idealism* (New York: Cambridge University Press, 1999); Joseph Kockelmans, ed., *A Companion to Martin Heidegger's 'Being and Time'* (Washington, DC: University Press of America, 1986).

33 The positing of a 'present self,' problematically identified with a 'future self,' is widespread in recent English philosophy; see Derek Parfit, 'Later Selves and Moral Principles,' in *Philosophy and Personal Relations: An Anglo-French Study*, ed. A. Montefiore (Montreal: McGill-Queens University Press, 1973).

34 Derek Parfit, *Reasons and Persons* (Oxford: Clarendon Press, 1984).

35 'Das Sein des Daseins [ist] wesenhaft Seinkönnen und Freisein für seine eigensten Möglichkeiten.'

36 I borrow it from Sydney Shoemaker, 'Personal Identity: A Materialist's Account,' in *Personal Identity*, ed. S. Shoemaker and Richard Swinburne (Oxford: Blackwell, 1994), pp. 90–1. (Shoemaker does not by any means wish to exclude human beings from the class of continuants.)

37 Das "kann" heißt nicht "es ist möglich." Das "können" hat hier den Sinn von "etwas können." Das, was das Dasein "kann" ist sein eigenes Sein als Seinsverhältnis. Das Sein des Daseins ist als das Sich-in-seinem-Sein-zu-seinem-Sein-verhalten ein Können, dessen Gekonntes nicht etwas anderes ist als das Können, sondern dieses selbst als das Sein.' Friedrich-Wilhelm von Herrmann, *Hermeneutische Phänomenologie des Daseins*, Vol. 1, p. 113.

38 Von Herrmann, *Hermeneutische Phänomenologie des Daseins*, Vol. 2, p. 37.

39 *Being and Time*, trans. J. Macquarrie and E. Robinson, (New York: Harper and Row, 1962); *Being and Time*, trans. J. Stambaugh (Albany: SUNY Press, 1996).

40 'Visibility,' *PhaenEx: Journal of Existential and Phenomenological Theory and Culture* 1 (2006), www.phaenex.uwindsor.ca.

41 My references will cite the pages of the translation. This reinterpretation of *SZ* through *HB* is reflected in the authorial marginalia footnoted in the Stambaugh translation.

42 See the lectures mentioned above in Note 17.

43 Theodore Kisiel, 'The Demise of *Being and Time*: 1927–1930,' pp. 194, 196–7, 199, 206–7; and Dieter Thomä, '*Being and Time* in Retrospect: Heidegger's Self-Critique,' pp. 221–2; both in Richard Polt, ed. *Heidegger's 'Being and Time': Critical Essays* (Lanham: Rowman & Littlefield, 2005).

44 See Kierkegaard, *Fear and Trembling* and *Repetition*, ed. and trans. H.V. Hong and E. H. Hong (Princeton: Princeton University Press, 1983), p. 42 with Kierkegaard's footnote.

45 Ibid., pp. 286, 306–8.

46 Francis Suarez, *Disputationes metaphysicae* (Cologne: *editio princeps*, 1614), 31, sec. 4, n. 6. For this reference I am indebted to Heidegger, *Nietzsche*, vol. 2 (Pfullingen: Neske, 1961), p. 418; trans. J. Stambaugh in Heidegger, *The End of Philosophy* (New York: Harper and Row, 1973), pp. 16–17.

47 *Concluding Unscientific Postscript*, vol. 1, p. 351.

48 John Locke, *An Essay Concerning Human Understanding*, bk. 2, chap. 7, no. 7.

49 'When ideas are in our minds, we consider them as being actually there ... which is, that they exist': ibid.

50 *A Treatise of Human Nature*, bk. 1, pt. 2, sec. 6.

51 *Mind 14* (1905). In a series of articles (for example, 'Designation and Existence,' *Journal of Philosophy 36* [1939]) W.V. Quine added much more evidence
of how those existential statements take their place within the whole tissue
of discourse, being at times implied by other statements.

3. Magnifying the Self

1 See Robert B. Reich, *The Future of Success* (New York: Knopf, 2001).
2 Kenneth J. Arrow, 'Values and Collective Decision-Making,' in *Philosophy,
Politics and Society*, 3rd series, ed. P. Laslett and W.G. Runciman (Oxford:
Blackwell, 1967), pp. 215–32. See also Arrow, *Social Choice and Individual Values* (New York: Wiley, 1963).
3 Lee Iacocca with William Novack, *Iacocca: An Autobiography* (New York:
Bantam Books, 1984).
4 Jayson Blair, *Burning Down My Masters' House* (Beverly Hills: New Millen-
nium Press, 2004).
5 Laurence Olivier, *Confessions of an Actor: An Autobiography* (New York:
Simon and Schuster, 1982).
6 Guy Debord, *Society of the Spectacle* (Detroit: Black and Red=Radical America, 1970).
7 See Max Weber, *The Protestant Ethic and the Spirit of Capitalism*, trans. Talcott
Parsons (New York: Scribner's, 1958). (The original German texts date from
1904–5.)
8 Alain de Botton, *Status Anxiety* (London: Penguin, 2004), pp. 25–7, 32–5. The
reference to Hume's *Treatise of Human Nature* is on p. 27.
9 Stephen Glass, *The Fabulist* (New York: Simon and Schuster, 2003).
10 See Pamela Walker Laird, *Pull: Networking and Success since Benjamin Frank-
lin* (Cambridge, MA: Harvard University Press, 2005).
11 The philosopher W.V. Quine's autobiography, *The Time of My Life* (Cambridge, MA: MIT Press, 1985), is as much a success story as Iacocca's, and on
the dust cover he says, 'There is that which one wants to do for the glory of
having done it, and there is that which one wants to do for the joy of doing
it. One can want to be a scientist because he wants to see himself as a Dar-
win or an Einstein, and one can want to be a scientist because he is curious
about what makes things tick ... In normal cases the two kinds of motivation
are in time brought to terms ... In me the glory motive lingered.'
12 That he did write it himself is confirmed by the research of another of his
biographers. See Terry Coleman, *Olivier: The Authorized Biography* (London:
Bloomsbury, 2005), pp. 462–9. Coleman's biography confirms most of the

factual content of Olivier's own book, though sometimes revising the chronology.

4. Justifying the Self

1 Thus I do not intend a critique of Kant's moral theory such as we find, e.g., in Bernard Williams's *Ethics and the Limits of Philosophy* (Cambridge, MA: Harvard University Press, 1985).

2 The work is now available in Mary Gregor's translation in the Cambridge edition of the *Works of Immanuel Kant*. Page references are to the Prussian Academy edition of Kant's *Works*, vol. 6, and appear in the margins of the translation.

3 See the Introduction to the *Metaphysics of Morals*, Vol. 6, 211–8, and the Introduction to the *Doctrine of Virtue*, Vol. 6, 379–413.

4 The text is more complex: *Da-sein ist Seiendes das je ich selbst bin* (p. 114). It could read '*Da-sein* is that being which, in each case, I myself am' or '*Da-sein* is, in each case, what I myself am.'

5 'Es könnte sein, daß das Wer des alltäglichen Da-seins gerade *nicht* je ich selbst bin' (p. 115).

6 Translating 'wer *ist es, der in der Alltäglichkeit das Da-sein ist?*' – (top of p. 114). The Stambaugh translation reads as if the words *das Da-sein* were in the genitive: *des Da-seins.*

7 The question does *not* mean 'What agent or persona undertakes to be *Da-sein* in everyday life?' even though such a question would be expressed by another correct translation of the German wording, moving the word 'is': 'Who is it that is *Da-sein* in everyday life?' The second translation supposes that, in everyday life, something or other comes to be *Da-sein*; it postulates some unknown agency *behind Da-sein*. But the actual point here is that, in everyday life, *Da-sein* is making itself manifest *as* this or that.

8 There are various translations: the 'They,' the 'One,' Everyman, 'people.' All are imperfect because of lacking the idiomatic force of the German indefinite pronoun, as in *man sagt* or *man meint*, 'one says' or 'one does think ...'

9 'Das Da-sein versteht sich selbst immer aus seiner Existenz, einer Möglichkeit seiner selbst, es selbst oder nicht es selbst zu sein' (*SZ*, p. 12).

10 This was translated by Douglas Steere and published, in a revised edition, by Harper and Brothers, New York, in 1948. The current translation by H. Hong and E. Hong, Princeton University Press, is entitled *Upbuilding Discourses in Various Spirits: Part One, An Occasional Discourse* – no doubt closer

to the Danish, but never has an author burdened a work with a less appealing title.

11　Charlotte Brontë, *Jane Eyre*, ed. Michael Mason (London: Penguin Books, 1996).

12　Anthony Trollope, *The Last Chronicle of Barset* (London: Thomas Nelson and Sons, n.d.).

13　Sinclair Lewis, *Main Street* (New York: International Collectors' Library, 1948).

14　The longest series of such quotations is in his *Religion within the Limits of Reason Alone*, bk. 4, pt. 1, 'The Christian Religion as a Natural Religion,' trans. by T.M. Greene and H.M. Hudson (New York: Harper Torchbooks, 1960), pp. 147–51.

15　*Critique of Practical Reason*, Prussian Academy edition of Kant's *Works*, vol. 5, 113–14.

16　*Leviathan*, Part 1, chapter 6. Spinoza concurs: *indignatio* is 'hatred towards someone who has maltreated another,' *Ethics*, pt. 3; see 'Definitions of the Emotions,' no. 20.

17　J.R. Miller, *Shingwauk's Vision: A History of Native Residential Schools* (Toronto: University of Toronto Press, 1996), pp. 184–5. Parenthetical citations in the following few paragraphs are to this work.

18　See Roland Chrisjohn, Sherri Young, and Michael Maraun, *The Circle Game: Shadows and Substance in the Indian Residential School Experience in Canada* (Penticton, BC: Theytus Books, 1997).

19　In another Trollope novel, *The Warden*, a London newspaper, the *Jupiter*, waxes indignant over the stipend paid to an elderly clergyman who supervises a hostel for the poor. A more outrageous case of journalistic indignation appears in Tom Wolfe's *The Bonfire of the Vanities*, where *The City Light*, funded and staffed by socialites, poses as the advocate for ghetto youths.

20　Trollope's *Jupiter* was certainly seized with righteous indignation, perhaps to the point of self-righteousness, but there is no reason to call it hypocritical. Wolfe's *City Light*, however, added hypocrisy to self-righteousness.

21　I am indebted here to Reinhold Niebuhr's *The Nature and Destiny of Man* (New York: Scribner's, 1941), especially vol. 1, chap. 7, which contains an acute analysis of self-righteousness.

22　*Grounding for the Metaphysics of Morals*, from the Prussian Academy edition of Kant's *Works*, vol. 4, p. 407, trans. James W. Ellington.

23　See the excellent study by Rebecca Kukla, 'The Ontology and Temporality of Conscience,' *Continental Philosophy Review 35* (2002), 1–34.

24　See *Phaedrus* 242b–c.

25 Emmanuel Lévinas, *Totality and Infinity*, trans. Alphonso Lingis (The Hague: Nijhoff, 1969), sec. 3, 'The Face and Sensibility.'

26 The question has been raised whether Heidegger omits the case of a psychopath, understood as someone who lacks a conscience. The omission is characteristic – in his treatment of language and speech Heidegger never treats the psychological problem of aphasia; where he discusses hearing, he omits to treat deafness. And so on. His response, I think, would be to claim that the 'psychopath' is someone who does not *heed* the call of conscience. He might argue that the psychopath did not even 'hear' it, or did not understand it, though there was a call.

27 'Der eigene geworfene Grund zu sein, ist das Seinkönnen, darum es der Sorge geht' (p. 284).

28 J.-P. Sartre, *L'Être et le néant* (Paris: Gallimard, 1943), quatrième partie, chapitre premier, III, *'Liberté et responsabilité'* (pp. 638–42): 'Ainsi, en un certain sens, je *choisis* d'être né.' (p. 641).

29 See *Phänomenologische Interpretationen zu Aristoteles: Einführung in die Phänomenologische Forschung* (Freiburg lectures, Winter Semester 1921–2), ed. W. Bröcker and K. Bröcker-Oltmans in Heidegger, *GA*, vol. 61 (Frankfurt: Klostermann, 1985), pp. 2, 131–55.

30 'Das Da-sein ist von ihm selbst als eigentlichem Selbstseinkönnen zunächst immer schon abgefallen und an die "Welt" verfallen' (p. 175).

31 'Uneigentlichkeit ... [ist] gerade ein ausgezeichnetes In-der-Welt-sein ... Das Nicht-es-selbst-sein fungiert als *positive* Möglichkeit des Seienden, das wesenhaft besorgend in einer Welt aufgeht. Dieses *Nicht-sein* muss als die nächste Seinsart des Da-seins begriffen werden, in der es sich zumeist hält' (p. 176).

32 The essential atheism of Heidegger in the *SZ* period was made clear to me by Sean McGrath, *The Early Heidegger and Medieval Philosophy* (Washington, DC: Catholic University of America Press, 2006).

33 *Der Begriff der Zeit*, trans. William McNeill, bilingual edition (Oxford: Blackwell, 1992): 'Wenn der Zugang zu Gott der Glaube ist und das Sich-einlassen mit der Ewigkeit nichts anders ist als dieser Glaube, dann wird die Philosophie die Ewigkeit nie haben' (p. 1).

34 'Phenomenology and Theology,' trans. James G. Hart and John C. Maraldo, in Heidegger, *Pathmarks*, ed. William McNeill (Cambridge: Cambridge University Press, 1998), p. 53.

35 *Einführung in die Metaphysik* (Tübingen: Niemeyer, 1953), pp. 5–6; *Introduction to Metaphysics*, trans. Gregory Fried and Richard Polt (New Haven: Yale University Press, 2000), pp. 7–8.

36 Theodor Adorno, *Jargon der Eigentlichkeit* (Frankfurt: Suhrkamp, 1964), pp. 82–134.

37 Galen Strawson, 'A Fallacy of Our Age,' *Times Literary Supplement* (15 October 2004), pp. 13–15; also in G. Strawson, ed., *The Self?* (Oxford: Blackwell, 2005).

38 Derek Parfit, *Reasons and Persons* (Oxford: Clarendon Press, 1984).

39 Richard Dawkins, *The God Delusion* (Boston: Houghton Mifflin, 2006).

5. Magnifying the Community

1 On communitarianism, see Charles Taylor, *Multiculturalism: Examining the Politics of Recognition* (Princeton: Princeton University Press, 1994), and Michael Sandel, *Liberalism and the Limits of Justice*, 2nd ed. (Cambridge: Cambridge University Press, 1998). On liberalism, see Ronald Dworkin, *Taking Rights Seriously* (Cambridge, MA: Harvard University Press, 1977), and Will Kymlicka, *Liberalism, Community and Culture* (New York: Oxford University Press, 1989).

2 Herman Philipse, *Heidegger's Philosophy of Being: A Critical Interpretation* (Princeton: Princeton University Press, 1998). See, e.g., pp. 26–7, 346ff.

3 Hubert Dreyfus, *Being in the World* (Cambridge, MA: MIT Press, 1991), in chap. 4, taxes Heidegger with this error, although he adds that Heidegger is confused over this point, mixing up the ontologically inevitable *Mit-sein* with the kind of social conformism that is by no means inevitable.

4 A typical statement of this critique is Louis Mackey, 'The Loss of the World in Kierkegaard's Ethics,' in *Kierkegaard: A Collection of Critical Essays*, ed. J. Thompson (New York: Doubleday, 1972), pp. 266–88. While Martin Buber, philosopher of dialogue, also criticizes Kierkegaard for turning away from society, his remarks are far more nuanced and dialectical, combining endorsement and critique; see his 'The Question to the Single One,' *Between Man and Man*, trans. R.G. Smith (New York: Macmillan, 1948).

5 It is lacunas of this sort that David Carr had in mind in his critical article 'Die fehlende Sozialphilosophie Heideggers,' in *Zur philosophischen Aktualität Heideggers, 1, Philosophie und Politik*, ed. D. Papenfuss and O. Pöggeler (Frankfurt: Klostermann, 1991), pp. 234–46.

6 Emmanuel Lévinas, *Totality and Infinity*, trans. Alphonso Lingis (The Hague: Nijhoff, 1969).

7 '[Mit] Geschick ... bezeichnen wir das Geschehen der Gemeinschaft, des Volkes. Das Geschick setzt sich nicht aus einzelnen Schicksalen zusammen.' (p. 384).

8 *History of the Peloponnesian War*, trans. Rex Warner (Middlesex: Penguin, 1954). The chapter divisions are due to the translator, and I supplement them with reference to the section numbers given in each book in the Greek text (Oxford: Oxford Classical Texts, 1900).

9 It is part of a text called *Structures of Power* that first appeared in *Wirtschaft und Gesellschaft* (1922), though written prior to 1914. English translation in *From Max Weber: Essays in Sociology*, ed. H.H. Gerth and C.W. Mills (New York: Oxford, 1946), pp. 171–9. A good philosophical attempt to apply Weber is David Copp, 'Do Nations Have the Right of Self-determination?' in *Philosophers Look at Canadian Confederation*, ed. S. French (Montreal: Canadian Philosophical Association, 1979), pp. 71–95.

10 Richard Reeves, *President Kennedy: Profile of Power* (New York: Simon & Schuster, 1993), p. 108.

11 *Khrushchev Remembers, with an Introduction, Commentary and Notes by Edward Crankshaw*, trans. and ed. Strobe Talbot (Boston: Little, Brown, 1970), p. 513.

12 See, e.g., *Hegel's Phenomenology of Spirit* (lectures of 1930–1), trans. P. Emad and K. Maly (Bloomington: Indiana University Press, 1988).

13 See H.-G. Gadamer, *On Education, Poetry and History*, ed. D. Misgeld and G. Nicholson (Albany: SUNY Press, 1991), pp. 9–10.

14 *Die Selbstbehauptung der deutschen Universität*, now published by Klostermann of Frankfurt, 1983. It is here that he uses the composite term *Volksgemeinschaft*, for instance in the twenty-third paragraph.

15 See my article 'The Politics of Heidegger's Rectoral Address,' *Man and World* 20 (1987), 171–87.

16 Bernhard Radloff, *Heidegger and the Question of National Socialism: Disclosure and Gestalt*, New Studies in Phenomenology and Hermeneutics, ed. Kenneth Maly (Toronto: University of Toronto Press, 2007).

17 *Einführung in die Metaphysik* (Tübingen: Niemeyer, 1953); *Introduction to Metaphysics*, trans. Gregory Fried and Richard Polt (New Haven: Yale University Press, 2000).

18 *Einführung*, p. 28; *Introduction*, p. 40.

19 See any church history, e.g. J.H. Nichols, *History of Christianity 1650–1950* (New York: Ronald Press: 1965), pp. 404–9.

6. Justifying the Community

1 A parallel text, *Apology* 30b, speaks of care for the soul, *psychēs*, evidently intended in the same sense by Plato.

2 Such is the reading offered by C.D.C. Reeve, *Socrates in the 'Apology'* (Indi-

anapolis: Hackett, 1989), p. 159. But these are the external paraphernalia that Socrates does *not* busy himself about, with his concentration upon *autēs tēs poleōs* and the self or soul itself.

3 'Der Spruch des Anaximander,' *Holzwege* (Frankfurt: Klostermann, 1950). English translation by Julian Young in *Off the Beaten Track*, ed. J. Young and Kenneth Haynes (Cambridge: Cambridge University Press, 2002). I'll cite the page number of the German text first, then, after a stroke, the English page number. Many of the thoughts of this essay recur in the famous late text that echoes back upon *SZ*: *Time and Being* (*Zeit und Sein*) in *Zur Sache des Denkens* (Tübingen: Niemeyer, 1969).

4 '[G]riechisch ist die Frühe des Geschickes, als welches das Sein selbst sich im Seienden lichtet und ein Wesen des Menschen in seinen Anspruch nimmt, das als geschickliches darin seinen Geschichtsgang hat, wie es im Sein gewahrt und wie es aus ihm entlassen, aber gleichwohl nie von ihm getrennt wird' (310/253).

5 'Jedesmal, wenn das Sein in seinem Geschick an sich hält, ereignet sich jäh und unversehens Welt. Jede Epoche der Weltgeschichte ist eine Epoche der Irre' (311/254).

6 On Parmenides see 'Moira (Parmenides, Fragment VIII, 34–41),' and on Heraclitus see 'Logos (Heraklit, Fragment 50),' both in *Vorträge und Aufsätze* (Pfullingen: Neske, 1954); translations in *Early Greek Thinking*, by D.F. Krell and F.A. Capuzzi (New York: Harper and Row, 1975).

7 Let us print here the minimal text of Anaximander along with the translation published in *Off the Beaten Track: kata to chreōn: didonai gar auta dikēn kai tisin allēlois tēs adikias*; 'along the line of usage; for they let order and reck belong to one another in the surmouning of disorder' (p. 280).

8 Jeffrey Barash's book *Martin Heidegger and the Problem of Historical Meaning* (Dordrecht: Nijhoff, 1988) succeeds in showing in part 1 how the *SZ* doctrine of *Geschichtlichkeit* was rooted in German debates almost a century old. And he shows in part 2 how the thoughts in Heidegger's later period about *Seinsgeschichte* are not *just* a break from *SZ* but a continuation of it on a wider scale.

9 A brief summary drawn from an ode from Sophocles' *Antigone*, lovingly translated by Heidegger in *Einführung in die Metaphysik*, pp. 112–13; *Introduction to Metaphysics*, pp. 156–58.

10 Werner Jaeger, *Paideia: The Ideals of Greek Culture*, trans. G. Highet (New York: Oxford University Press, 1965), vol. 1, p. 142.

11 James Doull, 'The Philosophical Basis of Constitutional Discussion in Canada,' in *Philosophy and Freedom: The Legacy of James Doull*, ed. D.G. Peddle and N.G. Robertson (Toronto: University of Toronto Press, 2003), pp. 392–465.

7. A Spiritual Existence

1 [N]ur als ästhetisches Phänomen ist das Dasein und die Welt ewig gerecht-fertigt.' *Die Geburt der Tragödie* [1871], #5; *The Birth of Tragedy,* trans. W. Kaufmann (New York: Vintage, 1967), p. 52. The remark is repeated in #24 and in Nietzsche's self-critical Introduction, (Kaufmann, p. 22).

2 Jürgen Habermas, 'Communicative Freedom and Negative Theology,' in *Kierkegaard in Post/Modernity,* ed. M.J. Matustik and M. Westphal (Bloomington: Indiana University Press, 1995), especially pp. 190–1. See also, in the same volume, Patricia Huntington, 'Heidegger's Reading of Kierkegaard Revisited: From Ontological Abstraction to Ethical Concretion,' pp. 43–65. See also Habermas, *The Future of Human Nature* (Cambridge: Polity, 2003), pp. 5–15.

3 *The Concept of Anxiety,* trans. Reiner Tomte (Princeton: Princeton University Press, 1978).

4 *The Sickness Unto Death,* ed. and trans. H.V. Hong and E.H. Hong (Princeton: Princeton University Press, 1980). It is attributed by Kierkegaard to the pseudonym 'Anti-Climacus.'

5 My discussion has drawn upon Edmond Jacob, *Theology of the Old Testament,* trans. from the French by A. Heathcote and P. Allcock (New York: Harper, 1958), especially part 2, chap. 3; to the best of my knowledge, this work expresses a consensus among biblical scholars.

6 Rudolf Bultmann, *Theology of the New Testament,* vol. 1, trans. from the German by K. Grobel (New York: Scribner's, 1951). I draw mainly upon sects. 14, 17, 18, 22, and 38.

7 Following Bultmann's translator, I spell 'Spirit' with a capital 'S' some of the time and with a lowercase 's' some of the time, depending on whether the divine Spirit seems to be the subject. This is also the practice in Nestle's Greek New Testament and in most translations of it (in Romans 8:16 both occur in one sentence). But the matter is very insecure and dubious, and the difference would not have been signified in the early texts.

8 'Sein Geist wohnt mir im Herzen,/ regiert mir meinen Sinn.'

9 'Sein Geist spricht meinem Geiste/ manch süßes Trostwort zu.'

10 *Der Briefwechsel zwischen Schiller and Goethe,* ed. E. Steiger (Frankfurt: Insel Verlag, 1966).

11 *Hegel's Aesthetics: Lectures on Fine Art,* trans. T.M. Knox, vol. 1 (Oxford: Clarendon Press, 1975), pp. 39, 72–3.

12 *Lectures on the Philosophy of Religion: One-Volume Edition; The Lectures of 1827,* ed. and trans. Peter Hodgson et al. (Berkeley: University of California Press, 1988), p. 104.

13 Henry van Etten, *George Fox and the Quakers* (New York: Harper Torchbooks, 1959), pp. 24–7, 29–30.

14 *Leviathan*, pt. 1, chaps. 8 and 9.

15 *Essay Concerning Human Understanding*, bk. 2, chap. 21, sec. 5, and chap. 23, sec. 5, treat 'mind' and 'spirit' as synonyms.

16 The relation between part 1 and part 2 of the book has been treated helpfully by Robert E. Roberts, 'The Grammar of Sin and the Conceptual Unity of *The Sickness Unto Death*,' in *International Kierkegaard Commentary: The Sickness Unto Death*, ed. R.L. Perkins (Macon, GA: Mercer University Press, 1987), pp. 135–60.

17 That the text we have been covering offers many advantages over Heidegger's account of selfhood in *SZ* is well established by Dan Magurshak, 'Despair and Everydayness: Kierkegaard's Corrective Contribution to Heidegger's Notion of Fallen Everydayness,' in *International Kierkegaard Commentary: The Sickness Unto Death*, pp. 209–37.

18 Roberts, 'The Grammar of Sin,' pp. 135–60.

19 The theme of individual selfhood was prominent right from the beginning of the book: 'to venture wholly to become oneself, an individual human being' (p. 5).

20 *Christian Discourses*, trans. W. Lowrie (Princeton: Princeton University Press, 1940), pp. 129–38.

21 Ibid., pp. 297–303.

22 Friedrich Schleiermacher, *The Christian Faith*, trans. H.R. Mackintosh and J.S. Stewart (Edinburgh: T. & T. Clark, 1936), pp. 496–505.

23 Albrecht Ritschl, *The Christian Doctrine of Justification and Reconciliation: The Positive Development*, trans. H.R. Mackintosh and A.B. Macaulay (Edinburgh: T. & T. Clark, 1900).

24 See the volume *Justification: What's at Stake in the Current Debates?*, ed. Mark Husbands and Daniel J. Treier (Downers Grove, Il: InterVarsity Press, 2004).

25 Mark Seifrid, 'Luther, Melanchthon and Paul on the Question of Imputation,' in *Justification*, ed. Husbands and Treier.

26 *Commentary on Galatians* (1531), in *Martin Luther: Selections from his Writings*, ed. John Dillenberger (New York: Doubleday, 1962), p. 101, 112, and passim.

27 'Two Kinds of Righteousness' (1519), in *Martin Luther*, ed. Dillenberger, pp. 86–8 and passim.

28 See, e.g., Schleiermacher, *The Christian Faith*, English translation, p. 504.

29 My reference is taken from Paul Tillich, *Systematic Theology*, vol. 2 (Chicago: University of Chicago Press, 1957), p. 171.

30 *Augustine: Later Works*, ed. John Burnaby (Philadelphia: Westminster Press, 1955).

31 Ibid., pp. 196–205.
32 Ibid., p. 199.
33 Ibid., p. 205.

8. Conclusion

1 This is stressed especially in Heidegger's posthumously published work from the late 1930s, *Beiträge zur Philosophie (Vom Ereignis)*, in Heidegger, *GA*, vol. 65, ed. F.-W. Von Herrmann (Frankfurt: Klostermann, 1994). Translation by P. Emad and K. Maly, *Contributions to Philosophy (From Enowning)* (Bloomington: Indiana University Press, 1999). The difficult text is considerably elucidated by Richard Polt, *The Emergency of Being: On Heidegger's 'Contributions to Philosophy'* (Ithaca: Cornell University Press, 2006); and by Kenneth Maly, *Heidegger's Possibility: Language, Emergence – Saying Be-ing* (Toronto: University of Toronto Press, 2008).

Index

ability to be, 7–8, 24–8, 41–4; as the character of human being, 39–44, 48–9; contrast with modal possibility, 39–40; contrast with potentiality, 40–1
ability to hear/see, 43–4
Abraham, 138–9
achievement, 67–73
Adler, Alfred, 14–5, 61
Anaximander, 131–3
anxiety, 102–3; and conscience, 97–9; and authenticity, 104–5
application, 12–13, 47–9
Arrow, Kenneth, 52
Augustine, St, 165–7
authenticity, 42, 98–103; and autonomy, 105–10; and atheism, 107–10; inauthenticity 80–92
autonomy: in Sartre, 99; ascetic, 104–10; versus devotion, 141–2, 156–62

being: as ability to be, 39–44; being-with, 21, 112–15; as existence and community, 7–8; question of meaning of, 19–20, 169–70
Blair, Jayson, 62–7
Brontë, Charlotte, 85

Bultmann, Rudolf, 146–7

Canada, 139–40
care, 3–8; and conscience, 96–7; about existence, 12–18; as fusion of existence, facticity, and ruination, 24–8; for self and *polis*, 126–30; about success, 50–61
Christianity, 160–6; versus 'Christendom,' 162
civilization, 133–40
community 111–15; magnified, 116–24; justified, 125–40; spiritual community, 166–8
concern. *See* care
confession, 100–1, 163

Da-sein: the word, 19–20; phenomenological explanation of, 28–35; and self, 34–5, 74
Dawkins, Richard, 108–10
death, 42; being-towards-death, 103
de Botton, Alain, 53, 61
Dennett, Daniel, 33–4
Descartes, René, 47
Doull, James, 139–40

ecstasis, 35–9, 56
existence, 20–4, 82–3; and life, 5–6;
　　and being, 8; and facticity, 24–8;
　　and ecstasis, 35–9, 45–6; critical
　　concept of, 47

facticity, 25–6, 44–5
failure, 62–7
forgiveness, 100–1, 159–66
formalism, 34–5, 47–9, 84; formal
　　indication, 34

Gadamer, Hans-Georg, 24
God, 156–66; absence of, 100, 104,
　　107–10
Goethe, Johann Wolfgang, 148
guilt, in Heidegger, 98–102

Habermas, Jürgen, 142
Hebrew Scriptures, 145–6
Hegel, Georg Wilhelm Friedrich, 46,
　　142–3, 148–9, 166–8
Heidegger, Martin: Being and Time, 7–
　　12, 19–47; on care, 3, 24–8; on com-
　　munity and history, 112–15, 130–
　　40; on conscience, 95–104; on exist-
　　ence, 6–8, 20–4; Letter on 'Human-
　　ism,' 44–5; on phenomenology, 8–
　　12, 28–35; on the pre-Socratics,
　　131–3; Rectoral Address, 121–2
hermeneutics, 53–4, 144–50
Hesiod, 136–8
Hobbes, Thomas, 88, 149
Hume, David, 47, 61, 150

Iacocca, Lee, 54–61, 67–9
indignation, 88–9

justification, 78–9; justification by
　　faith, 163–6; justifying our being,

59–60, 100–5, 109–10, 126–30; a
　　kind of care, 15–7

Kant, Immanuel: ethics, 75–8, 98; and
　　moralism, 83–4, 86–8, 90–1; and
　　selfhood, 105; and faith, 165
Kennedy, John F., 120–1
Kierkegaard, Søren, on existence, 22–
　　4, 45–6; on spirit, anxiety, and
　　despair, 142–3, 150–9; Purity of
　　Heart Is to Will One Thing, 83, 91–2;
　　on God and forgiveness, 159–62
Kruschchev, Nikita, 120–1

Lévinas, Emmanuel, 97, 113
Lewis, Sinclair, 86
life, as zōē, bios, and existence, 4–8
Locke, John, 47, 149–50
Luther, Martin, 147, 164–6

magnifying: a kind of care, 13–15;
　　magnifying our being, 59–60, 73–4;
　　magnifying the community, 116–
　　22; magnifying the self, 52–3, 59–60
Miller, J.R., 88–9
moralism, 75–6, 84–8
morality, 75–8, 83–4

nation, 118–22, 133–40
nationalism, 120–22
New Testament, 146–7
New York Times, 62–5
Nietzsche, Friedrich, 122, 132, 142

Olivier, Laurence, 71–3

Parfit, Derek, 36–8, 106–7
Paul, St, 146–7, 151, 163–4
Pericles, 116–18
phenomenology, 8–12, 28–35

polis: in Thucydides, 116–18; in Plato's *Apology*, 126–30

Quebec, 118, 139–40

Rawls, John, 16–17
Reich, Robert, 50–1
religion: militant, 123–4; fundamentalism, 123; devotion, 141–68
remorse, 92–5; as incorporating shame, 94–5
Ritschl, Albrecht, 163
ruination, *das Verfallen*, 103; an element in care, *die Sorge*, 26
Russell, Bertrand, 47

Sartre, Jean-Paul, 19–20, 99–100
Schelling, Friedrich Wilhelm Joseph, 46
Schiller, Friedrich, 148
Schleiermacher, Friedrich, 163
Shakespeare, William, 149
self/selfhood, 34–5, 36–7; ability to be a self, 43, 80–3; dissolution of self, 105–7
self-righteousness, 89–92
Socrates, 96, 126–30
Solon, 137–8
Sorge, die. See care
spirit: vocabulary, 143–50; the existing spirit, 150–9
Strawson, Galen, 106
Suarez, Francis, 46
success, 50–3; pragmatic, professional, and mega-success, 54–61

theology, 79, 142–3, 156–62
Trollope, Anthony, 85–6
truth *qua* disclosure, 30–3

von Herrmann, Friedrich-Wilhelm, 29, 40

Weber, Max, 59–60, 118–19
Wordsworth, William, 150

New Studies in Phenomenology and Hermeneutics

General Editor: Kenneth Maly

Gail Stenstad, *Transformations: Thinking after Heidegger*

Parvis Emad, *On the Way to Heidegger's Contributions to Philosophy*

Bernhard Radloff, *Heidegger and the Question of National Socialism: Disclosure and Gestalt*

Kenneth Maly, *Heidegger's Possibility: Language, Emergence – Saying Be-ing*

Robert Mugerauer, *Heidegger and Homecoming: The Leitmotif in the Later Writings*

Graeme Nicholson, *Justifying Our Existence: An Essay in Applied Phenomenology*

Ladelle McWhorter and Gail Stenstad, eds., *Heidegger and the Earth: Essays in Environmental Philosophy,* second, expanded edition